RISING TO THE TOP

GLOBAL WOMEN ENGINEERING LEADERS SHARE THEIR JOURNEYS TO PROFESSIONAL SUCCESS

-

INTERNATIONAL FEDERATION OF ENGINEERING EDUCATION SOCIETIES
&
GLOBAL ENGINEERING DEANS COUNCIL

Copyright © 2019 by IFEES Inc.

All rights reserved. No part of this book may be reproduced or used in any manner without written permission of the copyright owner except for the use of quotations in a book review.

First edition: October 2019

Published by the International Federation of Engineering Education Societies and Global Engineering Deans Council
www.IFEES.net | www.GEDCouncil.org

ISBN Paperback 978-0-359-91449-4
ISBN Hardcover 978-0-359-95581-7
ISBN eBook 978-0-359-95358-5

Jacket design by 5mediadesign.com
Cover illustrations Shutterstock.com
Edited by Bonnie Munday
Interior design set by Kayla Hellal

A SPECIAL THANK YOU TO THE COORDINATING COMMMITTEE

Soma Chakrabarti
Stephanie Farrell
Hans Jürgen Hoyer
Khairiyah Mohd Yusof
Bonnie Munday
Prathiba Nagabhushan
Şirin Tekinay

ABOUT IFEES

The International Federation of Engineering Education Societies connects engineering education societies around the world to leverage the collective strengths of its members and community to improve engineering education worldwide. IFEES' network works to enhance global engineering education through collaboration between educational, corporate and other organizations interested in engineering education. Learn more at IFEES.net.

ABOUT THE GEDC

The Global Engineering Deans Council serves as a global network of engineering deans, industry affiliates, former deans, and other leaders in the field, leveraging the collective strengths of its members for the advancement of engineering education and research. GEDC Regular Members include deans, rectors, or principals of engineering colleges and faculties. The GEDC's goal is to provide a space for leaders of engineering institutions to connect and share the successes and challenges of providing world class engineering education programs in an increasingly interconnected and fast-paced world community. Learn more at GEDCouncil.org.

TABLE OF CONTENTS

ARÇELIK INTRODUCTION..VIII
    Oğuzhan Öztürk

COORDINATING COMMITTEE INTRODUCTION..............IX
    Soma Chakrabarti, Khairiyah Mohd-Yusof, and Şirin Tekinay

JOURNEY 1.. 1
    Minds of the future, by Tania Bueno (Brazil)

JOURNEY 2.. 11
    The road to happiness: perceptions of a woman in engineering education, by Bibiana Arango Alzate (Australia)

JOURNEY 3.. 23
    The trials and triumphs of being a woman engineer, by Dawn Bonfield (United Kingdom)

JOURNEY 4.. 35
    Youthful deans no longer an oxymoron, by Jesennia del Pilar Cárdenas Cobo (Ecuador)

JOURNEY 5.. 43
    For the love of math, and innovation, by Jenna Carpenter (United States of America)

JOURNEY 6.. 57
    The accidental engineer, by Soma Chakrabarti (United Kingdom)

JOURNEY 7.. 63
    Engineering change for good, by Elizabeth Croft (Australia)

JOURNEY 8 77
At the crossroads to the future, by Catherine (Kitty) Jay Didion (United States of America)

JOURNEY 9 93
Learning and loving STEM, by Brenda Discher (United States of America)

JOURNEY 10 107
Real success is in touching humans and adding value for humanity, by Tuncay Döğeroğlu (Turkey)

JOURNEY 11 121
Reflections on making the most of opportunities, by Jane Goodyer (Canada)

JOURNEY 12 133
The difference that parents can make, by Maria João Viamonte (Portugal)

JOURNEY 13 139
A letter to Sophie, by Gudrun Kammasch (Germany)

JOURNEY 14 153
Can a woman engineer a better world?, by Marlene Kanga (Australia)

JOURNEY 15 167
Women in academic leadership, from an Indian perspectivem by Sushma S. Kulkarni (India)

JOURNEY 16 183
Problem-based learning and me, by Archana Mantri (India)

JOURNEY 17 193
    Women in engineering, from the Malawi perspective, by Theresa Mkandawire (Malawi)

JOURNEY 18 201
    It's about making a difference, by Khairiyah Mohd Yusof (Malaysia)

JOURNEY 19 217
    Engineering: It's a way of life, by Naadiya Moosajee (South Africa)

JOURNEY 20 229
    Suddenly, the impossible!, by Lueny Morell (United States of America & China)

JOURNEY 21 239
    Incredible opportunities on an unlikely path, by Tagwa Ahmed Musa (Sudan)

JOURNEY 22 255
    From outside-in: Ponderings of an educator, by Prathiba Nagabhushan (India)

JOURNEY 23 267
    Daughter, mother, wife: My life as an engineer, by Adriana Cecilia Páez Pino (Colombia)

JOURNEY 24 277
    Making history, and leading women into the future, by Sarah A. Rajala (United States of America)

JOURNEY 25 291
    Things are not always as they seem, by Julie M. Ross (United States of America)

JOURNEY 26 303
    What motivates a woman to study engineering?, by Martha Rubiano Granada (Colombia)

JOURNEY 27..313
   Knocking down stereotypes, by Karin Saavedra (Chile)

JOURNEY 28..319
   Feeling grateful, by Ariela Sofer (United States of America)

JOURNEY 29..335
   "Natural unusualness", by Şirin Tekinay (Turkey)

JOURNEY 30..347
   From commitment to impact, by Cristina Trois (South Africa)

JOURNEY 31..363
   A career of inclusion, by Renetta Tull (United States of America)

JOURNEY 32..385
   Taking HEED: My journey in humanitarian engineering experiences and design, by Christina White (United States of America)

AFTERWORD...399
   Hans Jürgen Hoyer

A SPECIAL THANK YOU TO ARÇELIK,
WHOSE GENEROUS SUPPORT HAS
HELPED MAKE THIS BOOK POSSIBLE

Arçelik

www.arcelikglobal.com

INTRODUCTION
PRINT BOOK SPONSOR

OĞUZHAN ÖZTÜRK
Chief Technology Officer
Arçelik

Over the last three decades, I have had the honor of taking on key roles in Arçelik's transformation from a local manufacturer into a global player in the home appliances industry. I have observed a few outstanding female engineers take on crucial roles in Arçelik's expansion, especially in developing countries, with exceptional cognitive competence and an innovative approach. Diversity and inclusion are crucial for countries and companies that aspire to have global reach. Gender balance should be a priority for engineering communities in academia and business. Disruptive innovations in research and technology that improve quality of life, such as work on sustainability issues or development of artificial intelligence software, require engineers to have excellent technical skills, as well as superior social and digital talents, in order to work in collaborative project teams. I am extremely excited about this compilation of inspiring stories shared by women leaders in engineering and academia. At Arçelik, we strive to create similar success stories for the female engineers working in our 17-site global manufacturing network and international R&D centers.

INTRODUCTION
COORDINATING COMMITTEE MEMBERS

SOMA CHAKRABARTI
KHAIRIYAH MOHD YUSOF
ŞIRIN TEKINAY

You are holding in your hands a collection of journeys taken by different women from all the different continents, women from backgrounds and environments that differ in more ways than can be counted, including culturally, educationally, ethnically, and generationally. What weaves the collection together is that the authors are engineering leaders, mostly from academia, and several from industry, who have "made it" or are role models.

At least, that was the initial idea: to have women engineering leaders from around the world contribute to this project by sharing their personal journeys. We ended up with not just that, but much more.

It started with candid conversations initiated by Prof. Hans-Jürgen Hoyer, Secretary General of the International Federation of Engineering Education Societies (IFEES) and Executive Secretary of the Global Engineering Deans Council (GEDC). He had become inspired after reading a piece written by Tagwa Musa, of Sudan, about her journey in academia (a piece he had requested). This led to those candid conversations with women engineering leaders, including ourselves, about the possibility of doing this project, and it came to fruition when he sent out invitations to contribute to this book. Prof. Hoyer has been the thrust behind this exciting project that depicts colorful life journeys of women engineering leaders spanning the world.

We needed little, if any, motivation to share the stories of paths trodden. Diversity is critical—especially gender diversity in engineering in different cultural contexts—and it is what the world needs now. We need all the innovations, all the solutions, all the designs, all the creativity of all the people of our planet to achieve the vision of ensuring "continuation of life on the planet, making our world more sustainable, secure, healthy, and joyful." We are thrilled to be a part of and to present this compilation of authentic stories generously shared by exceptional colleagues who are all hoping to inspire others in every corner of the world. The stories open windows into the lives of women in various cultures and backgrounds, providing a wider world view towards understanding what it takes to study and work in engineering in distinct settings. It seems we have all gone against the grain, swam upstream, and jumped over hurdles, at least in parts of our journeys.

However, this isn't all that binds the book together. It is simply beautiful to find that the contributions end on a positive, encouraging, hopeful—even cheerful—note. Perseverance and grace run as common threads through this book, as part of implicit or explicit advice to be taken away, despite numerous challenges faced. Various cultural contexts depict resilience among all the authors, who smashed the stereotype of the "weaker" gender while contributing to the engineering world in their own unique ways. Through the different sections, fight after fight, success after success, there is an air of modesty, unpretentious humility. Despite all obstacles, there is no resentment, no animosity; rather, simply gratefulness.

These journeys were not taken alone. Indeed, the leaders had to overcome often imposed and seemingly insurmountable difficulties. However, as Sushma Kulkarni noted, with the right mentoring, self-aspiration, and confidence, women educators can definitely occupy top leadership positions. But the positions often bring challenges; as Tagwa Ahmed Musa writes, a woman in such a position will typically be exposed to many tests. Some will describe her as an iron woman, while others refuse to accept her leadership role and assume that she is too weak and soft to be a leader. Often, family members, parents, and especially fathers played important roles in the authors' early lives. Adriana Cecilia Páez Pino, Soma Chakrabarti, Tânia Cristina D'Agostini Bueno, Dawn Bonfield, Jenna Carpenter, Archana Mantri, Theresa Mkandawire, Khairiyah Mohd Yusof, and Naadiya Moosajee write how a little encouragement from their fathers in their childhoods made all the difference, helping them grow and flourish in engineering.

Often these leaders appreciated the roles of inspiring mentors throughout their journeys toward the top. Thus, many have taken on the role of mentor to young girls and women who want to be, or are, engineers. Renata Tull, Jesennia del Pilar Cárdenas Cobo, Şirin Tekinay, Brenda Discher, Lueny Morell, and Marlene Kanga vividly describe how their mentors contributed to their journeys and why they mentor others to help them continue their own.

None of the authors see themselves as being at the end of their journeys, or at the top of the mountain. There is still endless work ahead.

In fact, it turns out, we view our journeys as a continuum: even though most of us were the originators—the first, the pioneer, or the outlier—we prefer to think of our life's labor as a flag to put into the hands of upcoming generations of women and men who will enjoy a more inclusive, diverse world in peace.

As leaders of three engineering associations, we have been privileged to see the changes over the years in the lives of women engineers, especially in developing nations. Over these years, we have tried our best to mentor, encourage, and help young women to become top engineers. Hopefully, these narratives will touch and open the hearts of young women towards engineering as a calling, a way they can contribute to making the world a better place. We have enjoyed reading the journeys of our fellow authors, each one being unique yet somehow connected in intangible ways. We hope you will find this book as enjoyable as we do, and that you will share these valuable stories with your friends, colleagues, and especially the younger women following in your footsteps.

JOURNEY 1

MINDS OF THE FUTURE

TÂNIA CRISTINA D'AGOSTINI BUENO

*Chief Technology Officer
MR Predictions S.A.;
President
i3G Institute;
First Vice President & Treasurer
International Federation of Engineering Education Societies*

BRAZIL

During my childhood in Brazil, I was surrounded by the pioneering spirit of my parents. My father was well-educated; a lawyer and a journalist, he knew several languages in addition to Portuguese (English, French, German, and some Italian). My mother was a philosopher and a teacher. When I was a baby, they left Erechim, a well-established city founded by Italians and Germans in the interior of Rio Grande do Sul, and moved to the state of Paraná in the southern part of Brazil on the Paraguay border. They wanted to be pioneers of a new city called Santa Helena next to what was to become a lake created by the

Itaipú Binacional hydroelectric company.

But the lack of good schools and violence in this border city in the 1970s, during the period of military rule, forced my parents to make a difficult decision: they would have to send me and my siblings away so that we could get a good education.

I was nine years old when I went to live with my grandmother in the city of Cascavel, more than 100 kilometers away from Santa Helena; my brother was seven and my sister was six. I had a good education, and took music and dance at the Marist school in Cascavel. I received a medal for being the best math student. I was studious and introspective. During my teenage years, when I'd return home to visit my parents during holiday periods, my only amusements were the two libraries: one in the College

ABOUT THE AUTHOR

Tania Cristina D'Agostini Bueno is First Vice President & Treasurer 2017-2019 of IFEES. She is Director of Technology for MR Predictions S.A., President of the Institute for Electronic Government and Intelligence and Systems - i3G, and Founding Member. Tania received a nomination to "Who's Who in Science and Engineering 2008-2009" and "Who's Who in the World 2007." She completed her PhD and Master's degree in Production Engineering from Federal University of Santa Catarina in 2005 and 1999. In 2008, she did a specialization in Software Engineering with UML, in Senai/CTAI, Florianopolis/SC. She coordinated many projects, some of them international: Ontolegis, Ontojuris, TECLIN (UNESCO Chair), and MGov2. Tania has published 93 papers in conference proceedings, has written nine book chapters and has published two books. She participated in the development of 10 software products (five are patented and two are in the registration process), two processes or techniques, and 31 other items of production technique. She has participated in 18 research projects and coordinated six of them.

of Sisters and the other in the College of the City. Reading biographies has always been inspiring and challenging for me. Starting at age 8, I read several interesting biographies, such as Thomas Alva Edison, Mother Teresa of Calcutta, Golda Meir, Madonna, Marcia Haydee, and many others. I finished the Jules Verne collection when I was 12 years old—and it was at that moment that I fell in love with science.

I dreamed a lot about adventures. When the Itaipú hydroelectric dam was finally completed in 1984, I put my books aside for a while and, together with my brother, set out for exploration. We built rafts and camped around the area. I had a lot of freedom and I did the same things my brother did, but still danced ballet, and remained a good student. I dated, too. Basically, I had a life like most of the high-middle class teenagers who lived in the interior of the country in the 1980s.

Following tradition, after finishing high school I moved to the state capital, Curitiba, to enter university and join a big dance studio. But when I was 22, I made a really difficult but important professional decision: I left classical ballet to dedicate myself to studying law at Pontifical Catholic University of Paraná.

As a lawyer I really wanted to change things for the better. By now I was married, and in 1984 my husband, Hugo, and I delved into the area of legal computing. Then, we were invited to participate in a new area of production engineering at the Federal University of Santa Catarina

(UFSC): Applied Intelligence. It was a magical moment, and it came at a time when I was extremely dissatisfied with the legal system in Brazil, after a terrible court case.

Unlike the dreadful feeling I had when I made the decision to leave ballet, switching from the law profession to engineering was delightful. Production engineering at UFSC was already a multidisciplinary and diverse environment, and I studied with several professionals: engineers, mathematicians, computer scientists, economists, pedagogues, biologists, librarians and, of course, lawyers. The internet was just starting in Brazil, and was spreading around the world. In the applied intelligence area of the production engineering graduate program, from 1996 to 2005, I did my master's and my PhD. It really was a special time: our daughters, Oriana, Milena and Lara, were born in this period. The production engineering graduate program was opening doors to students from several different areas, and Florianópolis is now a city that's recognized nationally and internationally as being a leader in software development, thanks to UFSC.

I found programming languages to be procedural, like logic in law. Prolog was easy, yet Matlab was very difficult. I became a systems builder, a software engineer; that's what I am, and that's what I love. I associate language with mathematics, and emotion with organization. In fact, that's what my thesis was about: Mind engineering. Everything went so well that we created a research institute called i3G, with 18 members along with some fellow students. (Today we have 94 members, and I'm still the president and a researcher at this institution. I later founded a company, WBSA.)

Artificial intelligence (AI) is something incredible that I was introduced to at the beginning of my postgraduate studies. The science fiction I had only ever seen in movies and read about in books was a reality I could actually play with. I immersed myself deeply in the academic activities and research projects, and soon we were publishing internationally—and getting praised for it ("amazing work" were the words of one reviewer). Our work gained visibility, and newspapers and television programs invited us to speak about the AI being developed. Our laboratory became a point of pride for the university.

I have always been an entrepreneur; the law profession demands this mind-set in front of the labor market. When we created the i3G Institute, I became a leader and an entrepreneur. The goal was not just research or creating a product; we genuinely cared about the customer, the market, and the team. What surprised me most about this process was that when the researchers I coordinated became employees, it changed everything, and not for the better. It seems that when you take away the autonomy people felt they had as researchers, they no longer feel they are doing positive work; they became employees.

When we started WBSA, a company that designed and developed innovative software for the Brazilian government's police intelligence, I found that being in business was a unique, challenging experience as a woman, mother, and researcher. Being entrepreneurial is more challenging for women than it is for men; there are very few women and the environment is predatorial. I survived, and my family survived (and eventually the company grew and was incorporated by another company). But I felt alone.

So I've concluded that the world of academia is a good space for women: it's a place that is kind, where people protect others, and where individual and team growth is stimulated. I love that. Because in business there is little room for women; the environment is too competitive, too destructive. As a boss I have always tried to offer and stimulate equal treatment for all who work with me, but I have always noticed the differences. Gender differences are understood through conversations and exchanges of ideas. Where and when I am coordinating, no one needs to fit in or adapt. One must strive to understand that there are differences and they need to coexist, and this can create a very creative work environment. I fight for this intensely.

Throughout all of this, my family has filled my soul and given me support to face the most difficult challenges in this environment. As a mother I have often felt I was failing to devote enough time to my daughters, so I struggled to get into their world. Because my husband and I have been workmates, we had to learn to respect each other's space to continue working together, which we do even today. Society places demands on a woman's role in her marriage that I have not always been able to meet. Fortunately, I have an understanding and supportive husband.

✻ ✻ ✻

As a leader, I offer and encourage equal treatment among all those who work with me, but I have always noticed the different challenges women face. I am very understanding and sympathetic towards working mothers, since I am one myself. As my expertise has been validated by my academic institution, issues of respect and belief in the ideas I develop were rarely challenged. I have always been busy training new workers, associates, and directors, establishing a common and shared language of our knowledge and goals.

Here are some reflections I have about women in engineering:

How it feels to be a female engineer/engineering educator. I was educated to lead, so I naturally seek a role in coordinating, even if that is not initially the goal. I believe the workplace environments of computer engineering, IT, and knowledge management are more welcoming to female leadership than most engineering areas, although the "nerd" archetype is still male. In my experience, female leadership was very well accepted because we were in such an autonomous environment. You have to be very sensible to organize a team to work on highly individualistic projects. With my approach, I've always had great results and a unified and synchronized team. My knowledge helped me have my space respected, both in the academic and the professional areas. The only place I have felt unwelcome is in the business sphere.

How to encourage women to be engineers/engineering educators. Women receive a different education, especially here in Latin America, regarding leadership. We have been taught to await orders, not to issue them. But that is slowly changing. This difference has helped me observe and utilize different approaches when dealing with men and women, especially when it comes to demanding deadlines. Women need to be incentivized to create new challenges, and not take orders without questioning. Building a creative and non-hierarchical environment is a challenge even without the gender factor.

The changing role of women engineers. We are living in an era of big changes in the workplace and in jobs. It's not just women's roles that are changing; there is still so much we need to do to achieve gender equality in the workplace. But the most important thing is that we know, no matter our gender, that we will all have to be prepared for the next industrial revolution. The overarching role of technology reformulates all jobs and careers. Software engineers are currently the most sought-after professionals in developed and developing countries. That says so much when we think about how we should position ourselves and what we must change to remain up to date and competitive.

How IFEES can get the best out of women engineers. Women are becoming the majority in social careers like law, pedagogy, social services, and the like. But in the engineering careers, we are still the minority, not just in Latin America but in the world at large. Personally, I didn't choose to major in engineering; I chose to be a lawyer. I thought it would be more challenging. Women have few role models to follow; rarely are our aunts or our mothers engineers. The few of us who stand in the spotlight do so at an enormous personal cost, challenging the status quo and sometimes our own families. These are challenges we face alone, and often without someone to look up to. Even when we major as engineers, the opportunities are few and many give up on it as a career. This is why TED Talks are so important for girls. Awards and recognition are, too. We need to look at what happens in social media, too, at who their role models are; today, there is so much emphasis on beauty, and how many followers and likes someone has. Being an "influencer" has become a career and it's girls who are incentivized to pursue it. Studying hard doesn't appear to compensate in this frenetic, superficial world we currently live in. I think IFEES can have an important place in helping incentivize a new generation of engineers.

What I dream of for women engineers. I imagine our children dominating technology from as early as kindergarten. We should study engineering from elementary school, building models and robots. Lego could be part of our most basic instruction, along with reading and writing.

The things that matter to women engineers in industry and academia. Money, status, job satisfaction, positive change in the workplace, recognition—it all matters, but I believe each of us has different motivations to exert our professions. Satisfaction is entirely dependent on our personal values, the ones we learned from our families, and the ones we picked up along the way. Initially, what motivated me in engineering was the access to amazing tools, such as AI. Today, what drives me is knowing I can help reshape the world for the better.

How women help women. I've personally encouraged fellow women colleagues, especially when it comes to scientific publishing. I've worked in different countries in Latin America and have found amazing women in different places, working in engineering and engineering education. Our exchanges of information and research have been intensive; there has been a tremendous amount of knowledge exchange.

Why engineering is the best job. I believe we will have a better world when intelligent systems are able to assist humans in every area. These areas include improving performance, avoiding mistakes, assisting in the creative process, and performing small and large tasks independently, while always seeking to make humans happier and fulfilled. That is what I am working on: building knowledge through AI so that we can better comprehend people's wishes. Yes, it's a big goal—but engineers are up to the task.

JOURNEY 2

THE ROAD TO HAPPINESS: PERCEPTIONS OF A WOMAN IN ENGINEERING EDUCATION

BIBIANA ARANGO ALZATE

Sessional Lecturer
International College of Management, Sydney

AUSTRALIA

I was born in Medellin, Colombia, in the mid 1970s. When I was six years old, my family decided to go to live in Caucasia, a small riverside town about 300 kilometers away. Despite Caucasia being simpler and slower-paced compared to the big cities, those were the best years of my childhood: there was always a sense of freedom thanks to many outdoor activities, an abundance of fresh fruits and friendly people. Then, three years later, we moved back to Medellin. This was because my parents felt that the most important thing for my two sisters and me was our education, and there were more opportunities to be successful and go to university than in a small town.

We were not exactly a wealthy family—both my parents were schoolteachers—so if we wanted to go to university, we would need to be granted positions at one of the public universities in Medellin. For my older sister that was quite simple: she was always a really good student, and she got in at her first attempt. My situation was different; I wasn't as good a student, and it was only on my third attempt that I was offered a place in 1992 at the two public universities in Medellin at the time.

I decided to study forestry engineering. My decision was based on a lovely time that I spent with an Auntie when I was in my early teens. My sister and I had gone to live with my mother's aunt in Medellin for a time, and she had two daughters and a son. One of the daughters was studying forestry engineering, and I remember accompanying her and her boyfriend, who was studying in the same field, on some of their work in the forest. They were both passionate about the path they'd chosen, and

ABOUT THE AUTHOR

Bibiana Arango Alzate has an undergraduate degree in Forestry Engineering from the National University of Colombia and a PhD in Forest Resources from the University of Sao Paulo (Brazil). From 2008 to 2018, she was a lecturer in postgraduate and undergraduate in Medellin, Colombia. Bibiana began her professional career as Academic Coordinator of Specialization in Innovation Management and the Master's degree in Technology Management. In 2012, Bibiana led the development of Colombia's first PhD program in Technology and Innovation Management (TIM). She has also been a consultant in the creation of the Master's degree program at the University de Santiago de Chile, where she was invited to be a visiting professor in 2015. In addition, Bibiana has authored and coauthored multiple articles and books, and has presented at a number of events in the area of technology and innovation management.

it was infectious: I remember thinking at the time that this is what I, too, would like to study one day. I loved being out in the forest, in open spaces.

It was great to be studying at one of the best universities in the city, and I had an amazing time. Everything was new to me: new friends, new subjects, new lifestyle, and the best part was the practices I did in the forest. Everything was wild, and it was an adventure every time—there was no place to take a shower, and no toilets. Once, we had to wait for a snake, a venomous pit viper, to come out of our food bag before we could eat! At the time it was not funny, but looking back now it's a great story, and overall the field experiences were some of the greatest I ever had while I was a student.

Unfortunately, it was during that time that I started to experience what it's like to be a career woman in a masculine environment. I don't remember exactly how many women started in my class, but for sure we were outnumbered. There were bad experiences—never with my colleagues, but with some of the male teachers. For example, they would tell me to go to their office to obtain the results of my assessments instead of giving me the results in the classroom like they did for everyone else. They would look at me in inappropriate ways and make unwelcome comments. I did not understand these kinds of things very well at the time, but now that I work in an academic environment, I can understand how naïve we are as students. Sadly, this kind of behavior still exists, and those teachers who like to intimidate students and make them feel miserable and unsafe are a blight on our profession.

That was how I came to understand what sexual harassment and bullying were all about. In one specific course, when I refused to visit any teacher's office when invited, I became the first student in years to fail the course. Naturally, I was not happy. I was even angrier when I failed the course for the second time, under the same teacher. When I was doing the course for the third time—my last opportunity—I had to confront him. I said to him, "I know you will fail me again, which means I will be expelled from the university. So, it doesn't matter whether I present you with a new report or not; therefore, I'm not going to do another one. You can do whatever you want." I then walked out of his office. When I got my final marks, I had passed the course.

Despite these things, I really enjoyed my time at university. And it wasn't just me and my elder sister getting a post-secondary education at that time: my father and mother had also been accepted for university studies, and were doing so remotely. Now that my sister and I had grown up, they were in a better financial position, and were able to further their own education. Their passion to study was a huge example to us; it must have been very difficult for them to work, study, and look after three girls at the same time. My father is actually still studying—law, his third or fourth career—and he is 67 years old.

When I finished my degree in forestry engineering, I knew that one day I would have a family of my own, and I figured the best way to secure a good future was to study for my master's degree in forestry engineering in Brazil. Brazil had one of the best schools in the world for this, Universidade de Sao Paulo—Escola Superior de Agricultura "Luiz de Queiroz" (ESALQ/USP), in Piracicaba, a city in southeastern Brazil. I still remember the incredible feeling I had when I received notification on my birthday in December 1999 that I had been granted a position on the course. It was the best birthday present.

But my start there began with a misunderstanding. I arrived in Piracicaba—it was a long way from home, around a six-hour flight—thinking that I had been granted a scholarship, which would allow me to be able to afford to live there. But I had been wrong, and my living expenses would not be covered. Because my family was not wealthy and were not able to support my studies in Brazil, I decided to not say anything to them about the situation and to do my best to resolve it. So, the first thing I did was visit the university welfare department—and I was so lucky: the friendliest people helped me, offering me a place to live in the postgraduate student residence.

I will be forever grateful for that opportunity, even when I realized that I would be living with six other women in a two-bedroom house with very basic facilities, and that it was a 45-minute walk to the university. I slept on the floor on a foam mattress next to my luggage for more than six months. But I wouldn't trade that time for anything, and I have some fond memories. One of the best memories was a game I played with my roommates. Our TV was an old black and white. We'd try to guess the color of the clothes being worn by the people on TV, and then go check who was right by looking out our window into our neighbors' home, as they had a color TV.

After resolving the issue of where to live, I just needed to figure out how I was going to pay for food and the basic things I needed to live. At the time, my elder sister was doing her master's in Sao Paulo with my brother-in-law—both were on scholarships—so they kindly supported me financially for almost one year until I was granted a scholarship. That support was really important for me, but the most important thing is that thanks to their emotional support I became one of the best students in my program. This, in turn, provided me with the opportunity to do my doctoral studies: The department granted me a position on the Direct Doctoral program, which meant I would finish with a PhD in a total of five years (at that time, it was two years for a master's degree and a further four for a doctorate). The decision of whether to take that on was a huge one for me; I had been in Brazil for two years, and would now have to stay for another three years. On the other hand, it was a golden opportunity: the normal process was to apply for the doctoral program and then wait to be accepted, whereas I had been granted a position because of my academic results. I decided to accept this new challenge.

I am so glad I did. During those five years, I had marvelous experiences in a different culture; I met beautiful local people who became my friends and with whom I still keep in touch. One of the challenges was the language. I did not speak Portuguese then, and all the courses, tests, and reports were in Portuguese. However, I did my best, and by the end I reached quite a good level; I wrote my thesis in Portuguese without needing any style corrections. I admit, I was really proud of myself, as it was one of my goals when I started to study. I also had really enjoyed playing water polo during my engineering studies, so when I arrived in Brazil one of the things that helped me to keep my mental health was to swim in the university's pool. This led to occasionally training the male water-polo team!

But not all of my experiences were so positive. Some local men (never my postgraduate colleagues or teachers) questioned what kind of woman left her home to study so far away. I was really shocked; to them I was not a "decent" woman, yet in fact it had been the biggest challenge of my life so far to leave my country, my home, my friends, and my comfort zone in order to achieve something that could offer me better work opportunities.

I had almost finished my doctoral studies when I learned that my mother was very ill; she had cancer. I got permission to leave school and went home to look after her for six weeks. Two days after returning to Brazil to present my doctoral thesis—"Characterization of wood from clone trees of Eucalyptus grandis, E. Saligna and E. grandis x urophylla"—I received the terrible news from my father: my mother had died. I talked to my tutor and was granted permission to delay the presentation. That flight back to Colombia was the worst and longest of my life. I was devastated.

Before my mother became ill, the presentation of my thesis was going to be the most important day for me. But when I returned to Brazil from Medellin after a couple of weeks at home, doing that presentation was now just one more thing that I had to finish. And for the next two years, I was lost. Suddenly my life did not make any sense. When you are in that state, it is not possible to get positive things out of life—after all, a boat without a course does not get anywhere. So, I decided to go back to Colombia and try to get some professional help. Fortunately, I found a marvelous psychologist who was able to bring me back to life, but not with medicine. He taught me how to discover the essence of myself, and the universe of opportunities I still had in my life even without my mother. I think the most important thing he taught me was how to be myself and how to be empowered in my life...to live with more awareness, conscious of everyday things and of my actions.

So, I recovered. And ever since then, I make sure I think about my goals, what I want to achieve, what makes me happy and how to build a better future, regardless of what's going on around me. That change in my attitude has brought me job opportunities. At the beginning it was not easy, because now that I was ready to confront life, my own country was not ready to receive doctors. Apparently, I was the second person (and I believe the first woman) in the country with a doctorate in that specific area; I never checked if that was true, because to be honest, that wasn't very important to me. The important thing is that when I applied for a position at one of the multinational companies in the area, their answer was, "Sorry. What can we do with a doctor in our company?" At that point I started to understand how unprepared my country was for people with doctorates. Forestry engineering was not, and I think it still is not, the most popular area of engineering, and that meant there were few places where I could apply.

I applied for a number of professorial positions at different public universities within the area of my doctoral studies and travelled to places across Colombia to take tests. For example, I would have to prepare five different subjects for a presentation in front of a group of teachers; they then chose the subject I was to present at the last moment. It was really stressful, but I was strong enough to cope. And then there were the emails I received, saying absurd things like, "Thank you, but you do not have two years of experience as a teacher"—which I had already made clear in my resume. I remember being really disappointed with my country, because basically I had worked hard for five years and I wanted to offer something that for me was important, but unfortunately, I couldn't make any progress. So, I decided to change my area, but not without first sending a letter to the President of Colombia telling him how disappointed I was with my experience, and how it would also affect future generations.

The area I moved into was one that I had taken some courses in: basic concepts of management. I had been absolutely fascinated with the area and thought at the time how useful it could be to study them deeply as an engineer. I didn't consider it a career option at the time, but then I decided to go for it. After all, one of the biggest learnings from my doctoral studies was that I could learn whatever I wanted. And that's how I found myself applying for a job in Brazil in the forestry area while at the same time applying for a job in Colombia in management—and, surprise: I was granted both opportunities! I decided to stay in my country.

My work experience has been full of emotions, challenges, and adventures and, most importantly, it's been full of learning. I began to learn about, and then work in, technology and innovation management. While forestry is a beautiful and different world—I love my trees—with this new subject, I discovered a different world, a dynamic world that opened a lot of opportunities for me, the most important of which was to become an engineering educator. For me, that has been the best "life gift" I have received as a professional and I will always be grateful for it. I never imagined I would be a teacher, even though my grandmother and both my parents were teachers; I suppose it's in my genes.

Ever since that time, my passion has been to teach, and to learn how to engage the new generations (who, in my opinion, are absolutely different from us—yet we keep teaching them in the same way). As a teacher I have experienced a number of emotions: fear every time I am in a new class; sometimes frustration; but most often I have a sense of satisfaction that I find hard to describe.

I have held a number of different roles (including head of a postgraduate program, academic advisor, and professor) and I have learned so much in each. The academic environment is really dynamic, as we interact with a lot of people at multiple levels within different institutions. Has everything been easy? Certainly not. I had experiences of sexual harassment, both verbal and non-verbal. I also experienced persecution at work, bullying because of my background, and on occasions my dignity has been compromised. I discovered how difficult life can become in male-dominated environments when you are a smart professional, have people skills, and are single and attractive. This is especially true in a country where improper behavior from men is socially acceptable, and sadly, if you have the courage to mention it, it will probably be the last complaint you make in that workplace. One piece of advice I would offer is simple, but quite sad: don't smile too much, because you may be perceived as sending the wrong message—i.e., "It's your fault."

Another experience I had, which I came to realize is quite common, is how difficult it can be to work with other women. The opposite should Abe true. We should support each other, but unfortunately some women feel uncomfortable working with other women, and that can really complicate your work.

The good news is that, thanks to all those experiences, both positive and negative, today I am a stronger person. I have learned that the most important thing is to always stay true to yourself, to keep your values no matter what happens, and fight for just causes, especially when they involve you. I never give up and I never show how something has affected me. To this day, I do things from my heart and am conscious about my decisions and their consequences. I know that if I do that, everything will be okay. The important thing, in my opinion, is to never become one of those people who believes that to be successful you have to do whatever it takes, hurting others on the way to your own success.

I am now living one of my dreams: to learn about and understand another culture (I'm based in Australia). This presents both opportunities and challenges. Most of all, it means I have the privilege to continue doing what I love to do: teach. It keeps a smile on my face, which is part of my philosophy on having a happy life: Always be grateful, always have dreams, receive what you deserve—and never be afraid to be happy.

JOURNEY 3

THE TRIALS AND TRIUMPHS OF BEING A WOMAN ENGINEER

DAWN BONFIELD

Visiting Professor of Inclusive Engineering
Aston University;
Director
Towards Vision

UNITED KINGDOM

I describe myself in different ways depending on where I am and who I am with. Mostly, I think of myself as an engineer, despite no longer working in what would be seen as a traditional engineering role. But more and more these days, I see myself as an advocate, campaigner, change agent and, well, an engineer with a difference. That's because I work part time in the education sector as a Visiting Professor, and part time for myself on projects and passions that I choose. The short version of my career is this: I trained as a materials scientist, and for the first part of my career I worked in the aerospace and automotive sector. Then, after I had a family, my career became something more difficult to describe—but possibly much more interesting. Let me tell you all about it.

I grew up in Burscough, a small village in the northwest of England where my father was an engineer working for the glass manufacturer Pilkingtons, and my mother was an occupational therapist. I guess you could say that my brother and I were somewhat juxtaposed when he followed my mother into the nursing profession, and I followed my father into engineering. Whereas my brother struggled with his mathematics O level (the UK qualification for 16 year olds), I went on to take three mathematics A levels (the qualification for 18 year olds), so we were definitely wired differently. Being the only girl in a small "Triple Maths" group in a large comprehensive school in the early 1980s, and taking physics and chemistry as well, I found that most of my time was spent in male company. This is mostly how things have been ever since.

Looking back now, I didn't ever notice this as anything unusual. I feel in some ways that without any other women to reflect your own femininity,

ABOUT THE AUTHOR

Dawn Bonfield, MBE, is a Materials Engineer by background, and is now Royal Academy of Engineering Visiting Professor of Inclusive Engineering at Aston University in the UK. She is Founder and Director of Towards Vision, a company that aims to work toward a vision of diversity and inclusion in engineering. She is Past President and former Chief Executive of the Women's Engineering Society (WES), and was founder of International Women in Engineering Day, which is celebrated on June 23 annually. She established and still runs the Magnificent Women project, celebrating our historical women in engineering. Dawn is a STEM Ambassador and a Year of Engineering Ambassador. She regularly promotes engineering, materials, and inclusion in schools.

you lose sight of it yourself. I think it would have been more noticeable (to me, at least) had there been another woman to compare myself with, even if subconsciously. But since there wasn't, I suppose I just got used to this situation and normalized it so that it became unremarkable. For this reason, I didn't notice any barriers to my entry to a scientific degree (at Bath University) as this was certainly the path of least resistance, given my situation of having "engineering capital" (i.e., a family member who worked in engineering) and a set of school qualifications that effectively led to only one outcome: a STEM career. I am well aware from my later work in engineering outreach, however, that such an easy route into engineering is not one that many females can claim, and that is something I now try to address in my outreach work and as an advocate for diversity in engineering.

My university experience was fabulous. I worked hard—I had always been conscientious—but also spent a long time playing sport, continuing my lifelong netball, volleyball, and squash interests, even playing volleyball for the Welsh national team. It was at university that I met my future husband. Peter, who is originally from Hertfordshire where we now live, was also a materials scientist in the year above me. He would become my biggest source of support throughout my career. (In fact, without that support, my current career would certainly have been impossible.) I gained a First Class degree at university, the only one on my course to do so.

My first job was in France for the automobile company Citroen at Velizy, a suburb to the southwest of Paris. There, I worked on a research project to find a thermal barrier coating for the piston head. It was a great job and a fabulous experience to live in Paris in my early 20s and learn about life in a foreign country and even learn a foreign language. Although it wasn't always easy being on my own in a strange place, frequent visits by my future husband Peter kept me going, and I enjoyed the many challenges and experiences of life in Paris.

Returning to the UK at the end of my contract, I found a graduate job for British Aerospace in Bristol, in the southwest of England, where its research centre was based. The only woman in the intake that year, I worked in the area of thermoplastic composite materials and was in charge of the manufacturing facility, which comprised hot press and autoclave equipment.

I felt perfectly at home in this environment, despite it being male dominated. Yet this is where I had my first encounter with unwanted attention. I remember one day finding that my lab had been adorned with pink ribbons, and when I walked to the canteen that day, there was a sign hanging in the window of the lab of the technician who had done it. The sign had my name on it with hearts surrounding it. No doubt it was intended as an affectionate gesture, but I was embarrassed, and after that, I always walked to the canteen by another route.

While working at British Aerospace I married Peter, and although it didn't seem odd at the time, it was probably pretty unusual that my "hen" party consisted of only one woman—a school friend who happened to be working in Bristol—and 20+ men. I am sure that if somebody had suggested I join a women's employee network at that time as a means of support (had it even been possible to form one, given there were so few women employees), I don't think I would have thought this necessary at all. Yet this is exactly the type of thing I went on to advocate in my later roles as a champion of diversity and inclusion in the workplace.

Many women, including today's young female engineers, tend to see women-only support networks as unnecessary and even perverse. I didn't have the option of joining one when I was young, but I imagine I would have felt that way then. It's not until we get older and begin to see the injustices in the workplace, the micro-inequalities, and the lack of progression, that we deem these interventions to be necessary. Indeed, part of my work these days is on "identity" in engineering, because I feel that as women, we instinctively suppress our individual and our social identities in order to progress our professional identity as engineers. I certainly didn't recognize my female identity at all at the time, and even today I feel that I have to hide my professional identity in order to fit in with my female social group of friends. This is a situation that we must change if we want to create a future that is fair and accessible, and considered as normal for women as it is for men.

Back to my story. Once married, I followed my husband's career by transferring to the branch of British Aerospace where missiles were made— later called MBDA— based in Stevenage in Hertfordshire. My husband was starting his career at the time at the Building Research Establishment, having finished his PhD at Bath University. My role changed from work on carbon fibre composites to metal and ceramic matrix composites, and from there to systems engineering, where I worked on a change process called Business Process Re-engineering. I felt that my career was progressing well, and I had been singled out from a number of my contemporaries for certain roles. I was becoming more visible and more senior.

Things were good at work, and in 1995 I had my first child. After the statutory maternity break of six months, I returned to work full time. Eighteen months later I had my second child, but when I went back to work part-time, I noticed that instead of being given the level of work I had enjoyed before the children, I was put onto "back-water" projects—ones that didn't seem like projects at all but just ways of keeping me busy. I felt like I had been downgraded to a second-tier employee who was not only off the fast track, but deprived of meaningful work. This was soul destroying, and the source of much misery for many years to come.

Dissatisfaction crept in, and I started to have nightmares. They endured for years, even after I had left work; I'd dream that I was shirking my job, and feared that one day I would get found out for taking money without doing anything to earn it!

I continued to be unhappy at work. The worst of it was when I was the subject of a harassment case that ended in the perpetrator being sacked. Here's what happened: one of my colleagues of a similar age decided that he disliked me, and displayed very threatening behavior, especially at night when the open-plan office was practically empty of people. After he punched the metal filing cabinet next to my desk, I became so afraid of him that I positioned a mirror on my desk so that I could see if he was approaching me from behind. Finally, following a number of other incidents, I reported his behavior, which led to his dismissal. But it had really disturbed me, and I never forgot the feeling of being scared; even now, 25 years later, I still remember certain incidents as clearly as if they had happened yesterday.

Two years later I had our third child—after which I never returned to the world of engineering in the same sense. This was effectively the end of my true engineering career, which is a sad thing to admit. With three children under age four, it was neither affordable nor practical to continue to work as an engineer, so I took five years off to bring up the children. I concentrated on local issues and enjoyed a different set of challenges. I became chair of our local play group, chair of our village Scout Committee, and I took a job as a councillor to postnatal women with the National Childbirth Trust. I also worked as a childminder, which was a useful experience in terms of learning the regulations, inspections, and procedures that are involved in becoming self-employed.

In this period, I gained many skills and experiences that would not have come my way had I stayed in my engineering role, and in subsequent years I have done a lot of campaigning for the value to any business of women who take career breaks, trying to find ways of using these skills to our advantage in engineering. It saddens me that many women drop off the professional register at this point in their lives, just when they are starting to gain valuable skills that are much needed in management. Luckily for me, my father saw the value in retaining my professional registration (chartership) and he paid my fees; had it been left to me I most certainly would have let them drop. I felt like my engineering career was over, and couldn't imagine ever going back to it, but in fact, my second engineering career was about to begin.

Once all of my children were in school, I started to miss my previous life as an engineer, and to miss the inherent interest I had for materials science. I started volunteering for my professional institution so that I could attend conferences free of charge. Working from home, I became an invaluable resource for the conference team, and started to get more and more work, to such an extent that I couldn't possibly offset the work I was doing voluntarily with the free conferences I was able to attend! At this point I became an employee and took on the role of Conference Coordinator for a series of one-day "hot topic" conferences that I was in charge of curating. This was a good use of my professional knowledge, my organizational talents, and my outgoing nature, and I enjoyed the freedom of choosing conference themes that interested me, and pulling together a programme that gave a top level overview of a particular topic for members of the institution. Having had a taste of being my own boss while on maternity leave, however, I started to miss the level of creativity

I had grown used to, and found that I wanted to move on.

I approached another professional engineering institution close to my home in Hertfordshire—the home of the Institution of Engineering and Technology (IET)—to see whether they had any volunteer work I could get involved in. Instead, they put me in touch with another organization they hosted called the Women's Engineering Society (WES), which was undergoing some difficulties at the time. I started to volunteer at WES and quickly realized that a lot needed doing, and before long I was working there on a full-time basis as a volunteer, starting in 2011. This continued for some years, and I must thank my husband at this point for supporting me to do this voluntary work, which took such a lot of my time. WES is a charity that has a fabulous history going back to its formation in 1919 at the end of the World War I, and there was so much to do to promote women in engineering—a topic that was becoming much more mainstream as companies realized that they were facing a growing skills shortage.

Some of the work I am most proud of took place during this time. I became WES President in 2014, and then its Chief Executive Officer in 2016—a paid role, at last! Although I had no experience of being a charity CEO, I believe that my many experiences of chairing charities during my career break, and my experience of setting up my own childminding business, were all important in enabling me to take on this role. One of the best things was being able to carry out this role according to my own values and skills, and not having to follow in the footsteps of others. Encouraging women to lead in their own way is crucial for increasing inclusion in the workplace, and ensuring that we reap the rewards of this diversity of thought and style. This goes back to my earlier comments on valuing identity.

While at WES I founded what is now called International Women in Engineering Day (INWED), a UNESCO sponsored awareness day that takes place on June 23rd annually. Although it was extremely hard work in those first few years to gain momentum for the day, it has become a hugely influential and impactful event on the calendar, and is now celebrated around the world. I remain very proud of this achievement, and indeed this was the basis for my receiving a number of awards, including a special national honor: an MBE (Member of the British Empire) Award, which I received in 2016.

WES continued to grow and to become more professional, and when I eventually left the organization we employed eight part-time staff and had numerous sponsors. Our fortunes had turned, and we were again the influential organization we had been in the past. But in my role, I was feeling constrained, and felt I wasn't able to take the organization in the direction I wanted. I felt it was time for another change. This brings me to the final chapter of this story, and to the work I do currently.

I started to realize after many years of campaigning for more gender equality in engineering that we needed a different focus. We needed to focus on more diversity of all under-represented groups; a more inclusive culture; and the removal of barriers at every step of the way. I established a company called Towards Vision—meaning, working towards a vision of diversity and inclusion in engineering. I now work on a variety of projects of my own, some of which are still heavily linked to promoting women and girls in engineering, and others that look more at engineering education and, increasingly, on embedding the Sustainable Development Goals in Engineering.

I now have a fabulously diverse, multi-faceted, and very rewarding suite of roles, all facing in the same direction: promoting diversity and inclusion in engineering. I lead a project called Magnificent Women, which celebrates women in engineering history and delivers outreach work in schools, as well as other initiatives. I am part of the setup of a new wave of Technical Education in the UK through a set of qualifications called T levels. I represent the UK on the World Federation of Engineering Organizations (WFEO) on the Women in Engineering committee. And I work as a Royal Academy of Engineering Visiting Professor at the University of Aston, where I promote a discipline that I call Inclusive Engineering. This is based on changing engineering mind-sets to become more inclusive of the needs of the entire population, and to ensure that bias and discrimination are not built into our products, systems, and services. It involves considering ethics, our global responsibilities, the appropriateness of the technology, and the Sustainable Development Goals. I feel that, at last, I am back in a true engineering role.

I have come to a point in my career where I have the freedom, the vision, the network, and the influence to make the changes I feel are important. And, crucially, I feel that the unusual trajectory I have followed has served to strengthen my creativity, depth of vision, and confidence to deliver according to my own priorities. I love my current role, although one thing that is lacking is financial reward. I continue to survive, however, thanks to my husband's support, and I remind myself that success is not all about financial gain, but about impact, effectiveness, and ultimately happiness.

I encourage many young women to pursue engineering careers, as I know that this sector has the power to ensure a sustainable future for the world. My advice is always to be yourself, and make sure you act on your own values and differences. That way, we will begin to see the true benefits of diversity, and we will each be more included, valued, and rewarded in the engineering sector. I hope that you, too, are able to follow your own trajectory to success, however unique that trajectory may be. Enjoy the journey!

# JOURNEY 4

YOUTHFUL DEANS: NO LONGER AN OXYMORON

JESENNIA DEL PILAR CÁRDENAS COBO

Dean
School of Engineering Sciences
Universidad Estatal de Milagro

ECUADOR

I am fulfilled by the position I find myself in today. But reaching this stage has not been easy.

I was born in the 1980s in San Francisco de Milagro, a small town in the province of Guayas, Ecuador, but grew up in an even smaller town: Marcelino Maridueña. My father worked at the sugar mill, which was, and still is, the main source of employment in Marcelino Maridueña, one on which many people depend.

I loved school. My mother says that from the time I was started walking, I wanted to attend school. Indeed, I was only 10 years of age when I finished elementary school at the all-girls private school called Juan De Dios Martínez Mera. (Most kids were 12 when they finished.) I repeated the school's name with pride every time I was asked, because I just felt so good studying at a place where there were only teachers and compañeras, all women. I guess that's why I felt no biases at that age, and why I was so successful academically. Bullying must have existed at that time, but if the other girls were talking about me—because I was very thin, because of the braided hairstyle that my mother did for me, or because of the multicolored clothes I wore when she learned how to sew—I did not have enough time to pay attention to it. I was so active that my interest was more focused on other things, such as being able to stand on stage every Monday and recite poems to the flag, a tradition at the school to help us develop our oratory skills. I do remember a certain competitiveness among the girls, but I overcame it simply by not fearing it.

ABOUT THE AUTHOR

Jesennia Cárdenas Cobo is a Professor and Dean of the Faculty of Science and Engineering at the State University of Milagro. She is a Systems Analyst with a Bachelor's degree in Information Systems from the Escuela Superior Politécnica del Litoral (ESPOL), a diploma in Higher Education from the Competencias-Universidad Técnica de Ambato, and a Master's degree in Business Administration from the Universidad Tecnológica Empresarial de Guayaquil. She is also a PhD candidate in Software Engineering at the University of Seville in Spain. Cárdenas Cobo has more than 16 years of professional experience in the area of higher education. She worked at the State University of Milagro as Vice-Rector for Academic and Research (2014-2017), Dean of the Faculty of Engineering (2012-2014 and 2016-present), Director of the Systems Career (2005-2012), and has been a research professor since 2003. She was also head of software development projects for various organizations including the Provincial Council of Guayas, the European Union, the Municipality of Simón Bolívar, and others. Her research focuses on software lines, artificial intelligence applied to engineering education, and quality assurance of higher education.

My next academic stage was the best time of my life. It brought me two novelties. The first was leaving my family home at age 10 and going to live with my grandparents in the city where I was born, Milagro, to be close to my new secondary school. And the second was that my new school had teachers who were dedicated to specific subjects, and it was co-ed; for the first time, there were also boys in my classes. It was a difficult change and it took me a while to adapt, but I think I did it well. The two great memories from that first year were that everyone was friendly, and I was warmly welcomed. The oratory—reciting poems and making speeches—continued, and I studied hard to achieve good grades.

Even though my mother was not living with me during that time, she was very protective, almost overprotective, of me. Milagro can be a dangerous environment for young girls; there is street crime and harassment. Plus, the behavior of girls is often questioned. But even though I was not permitted to go to many of the social events that are common for young people, I was able to adapt and, deep down, I did not mind.

In my last year of high school, I wondered what I could do to help my parents to pay for my studies. Every weekend, I checked the newspaper with my grandpa, and that's where I found the opportunity of my life: One of the best polytechnic universities in the country was promoting computer careers, and I had the opportunity to take the entrance exam while I was still in high school. I got a scholarship, and this helped my family financially. Thus started my first university adventure. I graduated from high school at only 16 years old, and, accompanied by my mother, began my studies at ESPOL, the Polytechnic School of the Litoral in the province's capital city, Guayaquil.

It was very difficult. All the subjects required great effort, and almost two hours of travel every day from my home to Guayaquil. I left at five in the morning and returned at midnight. Even on weekends, I spent all day at the university. The library was like my own room, and in the same way ESPOL's computer lab became my second home. I had chosen an incredible path, but one in which a computer is essential. But, ironically, I could not even afford to buy one until I finished my studies and began to work.

Studying computers allowed me to see everything as a system. Learning to program was hard, I admit, but once I got over the challenge, it opened my mind (bringing to mind the title of the book Open Minds by my friend Hans Hoyer). I learned to make decisions and solve problems, both in my family life and in the companies for which I started to develop software. After finishing university, I started my own software development company, and this is how I met many people—and where I learned to listen. Listening is a very special skill that every software developer needs in order to be able to adapt the systems to the needs of their clients effectively and efficiently.

A new opportunity unexpectedly opened up for me when, one weekend, my mother and aunt showed me the local newspaper. The university in my city, the State University of Milagro, was looking for professors for a degree in systems engineering. Most of my company's work was in Guayaquil, where I had to go regularly to visit my clients and continue to develop new systems. But, accustomed as I was to this kind of travel, I saw with some disbelief the possibility that was opening to me—a job close to home—even though I did not have experience teaching (besides having been a laboratory assistant). I was selected for a teaching job, part time. The 15 hours of class per week allowed me to be able to continue to work with my software company.

The days were really long because, just after returning from Guayaquil, I started my classes at 4 p.m. I recall that I was so young at the time—only 20—that outside the classroom on the first day, a student asked me if I was his new classmate. "No," I replied, "I'm your new programming teacher." I still remember the surprised face of that student when he saw me enter the classroom and introduce myself to him and all his classmates.

Two years later, I got married and I started a family. It was a vital part of my life that, as a woman, I would repeat. But I had to close my software development company because when I became pregnant with my first baby, the director of the engineering department, Dr. Fabricio Guevara, was promoted to a better position—and he in turn offered me a great opportunity: the position of Career Director. He told me, "If you accept the challenge, you must work full time." That meant dedicating myself to the administration of an academic unit, which required selecting professors, planning and monitoring the teaching activities. I accepted the challenge. The rector at that time doubted that I could manage so much responsibility. But I showed that even though having a baby while working was difficult, it was never an impediment. (I took just 15 days off;

my mother helped care for my baby.)

Breaking the glass ceiling in a masculinized engineering faculty, where most of the teachers and students were men, was not simple. But everything has its time. In 2012, I was offered the position of dean, at first temporarily, and then, three months later, definitively. I was 33. Then began my journey at the front of the ship with all its crew. In this way, the faculty became like a family, where everyone worked hard together to meet the quality standards of the Ecuadorian government's regulatory body for universities.

At this point, I would like to make a special acknowledgment to the dean with whom I started working, the engineer Efraín Sánchez, who always placed his trust in me to develop my career in academic management. Both he and my friend Hans Hoyer, GEDC Secretary, show that, despite the difficulties that women in the workplace usually face—we are always questioned about our abilities—there are also those who champion us.

I often tell the anecdote of how I met Hans, and how he became a professional mentor to me. In 2012 when I attended my first GEDC conference, entitled "Paradigms of the Deans," some attendees questioned how someone as young as me could be a dean. One colleague stated, "To be a dean, you need experience that only years can give." I could not keep quiet, and I answered: "Actually, to be a dean you need to meet certain requirements: have a master's degree, published articles and five years of experience as a tenured teacher. And I have them." Other colleagues congratulated me. Hans then invited me to participate at the next GEDC conference in Chicago. But that's another story.

Universities are living institutions. This is not only because of the coming and going of students every year, but also because of the changes that take place in management. In 2014, I assumed the challenge of being Academic and Research Vice-Rector. I would no longer run a single faculty; now the challenge was the whole university of around 300 professors and their different ways of thinking. I was again questioned for being a woman, and "young" (I was 35). The rector and I formed a team, and together we increased the level of research, added more incumbent teachers, approved a new academic offering and, most importantly, generated a friendly work environment.

Being the dean of the faculty of engineering is still a context that presents other difficulties, such as the constant changes in government policies that govern the academy in my country. Processes we are required to implement are continuously modified; in fact, the changes are so frequent that they do not even allow us to evaluate a process once it is implemented. Some say that the changes are good. Regardless, it seems we have been able to keep afloat while surfing the waves of uncertainty. I'm often told, "You are the only one who protests," and that constant pressure is sometimes demotivating. But still, my answer to that is, "Maybe instead I'm the only one who analyzes."

Management within an academic organization requires a great effort, especially in a political context like the one Ecuador is currently experiencing. Political instability, changes in educational policies and regulations, the environment of constant political campaigning even in "peacetime," the demand to lead by example on a team of men… it all adds up to excessive weight for everyone on my team. My slogan? Keep working, and defend my principles to the end. My goals of sustaining the academy and serving the university community are the tools I use to get through every day.

Sometimes, I wonder if it's worth it. If it is worth the effort that requires us to combine professional development and family life. To arrive home late, feel bad because you forgot to pick up your children (my kids are ages nine and 12) from school, be almost too tired to help them with their homework, to get their uniforms ready each morning, to organize the chaos that all kids create, and to organize even myself. When all of this upsets me, I tell myself strongly: "I do it for my children, and because I like it." I know my children admire my strength and they like the fact that I work, so I want to continue to be a positive role model for them as a woman and a mother. Not only that, I love what I do, and relish the opportunity to serve others. When I remind myself of all of those things, my restlessness disappears.

I would like to conclude with a mantra I regularly repeat. It's a mantra about opportunity, since that has been a key theme in this story and throughout my academic career: "Opportunity is the taxi that takes you to your next destination. When you see it, do not hesitate to take it, because it may not come back again."

JOURNEY 5

FOR THE LOVE OF MATH, AND INNOVATION

JENNA CARPENTER

Founding Dean & Professor
School of Engineering
Campbell University

UNITED STATES OF AMERICA

As a child and teen growing up in the 1960s and 1970s, I loved to read and did so ferociously. I also loved history, and still do (it's one reason that I love to travel). I was a big fan of the arts, taking painting lessons, along with 11 years of piano, seven years of flute, and one year of organ. I enjoyed, and still enjoy, crafts and handwork like cross-stitch; in fact, needlepoint is my newest hobby.

But my love of math won out over all those things. As a young child, I spent a lot of time playing with blocks (which I now know are "pre-math" skills), and later in junior high and high school, I went on to take the hardest and most advanced math courses—as well as the most advanced science, English and history classes—offered at my school, along with journalism and band.

Unfortunately, my small, rural high school did not offer calculus and, aside from my high school geometry teacher (along with my junior high math teachers), the math classes I took from sixth grade on were less than engaging. It was probably my enthusiastic and brilliant 10th grade geometry teacher who inspired me and helped me decide that I could do math with the best of them. Despite the stereotypes in the US that say things like "girls can't do math," I never believed that those applied to me. Why? Well, research suggests that being strong-willed is a plus for both boys and girls when it comes to success in math (that fits me!). But it also says that for girls, your father's opinion of whether or not you can do math

ABOUT THE AUTHOR

Dr. Jenna Carpenter is Founding Dean of Engineering at Campbell University. Her research focuses on innovative STEM curricula and success of women in STEM, with $4.3 million in federal funding and 130 publications/ presentations. Dr. Carpenter has a TEDx talk and has interviewed/written for publications such as The Chronicle of Higher Education, U.S. News & World Report, American Way, ASEE's Prism and MAA's Focus. Dreambox Learning named Carpenter one of 10 "Women in STEM Who Rock." Dr. Carpenter served seven years as Steering Committee Chair for the NAE Grand Challenge Scholars Program. She is on the Executive Committee of the Global Engineering Deans Council and the US Engineering Deans Council, an ABET Program Evaluator and Fellow of the American Society for Engineering Education (ASEE). She is a past ASEE Vice President; past WEPAN President; and past Mathematical Association of America (MAA) First Vice President. She chairs the ASEE Long Range Planning Committee, ASEE Constitution and Bylaws Committee, MAA Council on the Profession, and co-chairs the mathematical societies Joint Committee on Women. She received the 2019 ASEE Sharon Keillor Award for Women in Engineering Education, WEPAN's 2018 Founders Award, and the 2013 Distinguished Service Award.

matters. I was blessed with a dad who thought that I could (and that it was appropriate for me to) do all kinds of things, including math and science.

I finished my last year of high school as class valedictorian and thought I'd like to go on to become a high school math teacher. My high school counselors told me that I was too smart to teach (why would a smart person not teach, I wondered?). They pushed me toward engineering when I started applying to college. Like many high school students, I wasn't really sure what engineering was, but based on the information I could find—these were pre-internet days—it didn't look particularly interesting to me. That was mainly because of the stereotypical ways in which engineering was described. If I had known the broad range of opportunities that a career in engineering offers, I would have been far more enthusiastic about it. Industrial engineering and biomedical engineering attracted my attention the most. I ended up selecting biomedical engineering as my major because, like many girls, I could see how it would lead to a career helping people.

My Depression-era parents were not wealthy. They worked hard to provide me with opportunities, so I really wanted to do well at university. Starting out as a biomedical engineering major in the fall of 1980, I felt unprepared because I had gone to a small public high school, while many of the other students had gone to private schools or high schools in larger cities where they were able to take calculus. Plus, I had only a poor grasp of algebra and trig; indeed, there were topics in those subjects that I didn't learn until I taught the courses myself as an assistant professor of mathematics (I later completed a BS, MS and PhD in mathematics).

While the doors to women in engineering were technically unlocked by the time I started college, they weren't necessarily open or welcoming for anybody, male or female. Why? Back then, the "weed-out" philosophy still very much reigned in engineering higher education circles. The feeling was that an engineering major was suitable for only the best and brightest; an exclusive club, so to speak, and the majority of students were not smart enough to join. Certainly engineering was not viewed as a major that should attract the masses. Therefore, the unspoken goal of faculty was to run off as many engineering majors as possible, under this premise that most students could not make it in engineering.

Being a woman in engineering was in many ways a strike against you. No one was welcoming or helpful. No one seemed to care if you succeeded or not. Meanwhile, the faculty in the math department were nice to me. They actually knew my name and noticed my abilities. When they offered me a full-tuition scholarship to major in mathematics in the spring of my freshman year, I left engineering, in part because I knew the money would help pay for my education and in part because it was a welcoming environment. I dove head-first into mathematics, thinking that I could get a master's degree and teach mathematics at college. After all, teaching math was what I had really wanted to do all along.

When it came time to apply to graduate school, I was married, and since my husband had already graduated with a BS in civil engineering and was employed in Baton Rouge, my only choice for graduate school was Louisiana State University in Baton Rouge (the next closest graduate program in mathematics was about an hour away). I initially applied for the master's program in mathematics, but the math department contacted me and asked me to apply for a prestigious new LSU Alumni Federation Graduate Fellowship. To do so, however, I would have to apply to the PhD program. So I switched my application, received one of the fellowships, and the rest is history.

I have thought about how very different my career trajectory and life would have been if I had stopped with a master's degree. I really didn't know anyone with a PhD, so it wasn't even on my radar. I have always been grateful that I did go for a PhD, even though it was a pretty stressful experience (it was incredibly difficult; while there were several women in the program, the vast majority of students were male). I did run into some occasional bias against women from graduate faculty, but by and large we were treated about the same as our male counterparts. (I did pick a PhD advisor who had a number of women PhD students, in part because he was welcoming and supportive.) My PhD has certainly provided me with a world of opportunities I would not have otherwise had.

❋ ❋ ❋

When I started looking for a tenure-track faculty position in mathematics after graduation with my PhD, I applied to a number of universities and received several on-campus interviews and offers. Oddly, being a woman was really a non-issue. I ended up going back to my undergraduate alma mater, Louisiana Tech University. For one thing, they offered me more money than I asked for, plus I knew that they had a nice balance of teaching and scholarship. While I could do the research, my heart was still in teaching. Again, it was a fortuitous move, one that would provide me with unique career opportunities to do things I hadn't even dreamed of at the time.

My mother once told me that she could have done better if she had been able to foresee the opportunities that might come her way. Having been one of the first decade of students to graduate from the new country high school in July 1941, she had no way of knowing how World War II would change the world and provide opportunities for her far from the small family farm where she grew up. She never elaborated on what opportunities she missed, but I, too, have thought that I could have moved up earlier in my career if I had ever thought that being a dean was a possibility.

So what were those opportunities that were beyond my imagination when I joined Louisiana Tech? Around the same time I received tenure (six years after I joined the faculty), Louisiana Tech embarked on an innovative administrative restructuring and the subsequent creation of a remarkable new undergraduate curriculum in engineering. The College of Engineering merged with the School of Science (which included the mathematics department) to form the new College of Engineering and Science. It had no departments, only programs (like majors). Administrators included "academic directors" (who were really super-department heads responsible for two to four programs each), along with "program chairs" from the major discipline. I was asked to serve in an administrative role (first as a program chair of mathematics, then as an academic director for engineering) in this new administrative structure. I was also part of a team of six faculty who created, implemented, and taught the new undergraduate engineering curriculum. Being on the ground floor of these new beginnings would end up totally changing my career and providing me with opportunities that were unique not just at my university, but in the entire nation.

  I was the inaugural program chair for mathematics. After a two-year stint in that role, I was promoted to academic director for the next 10 years. The new leaders in this unique administrative structure were selected for their leadership skills and openness to innovation versus their disciplinary expertise. That meant that people ended up being administratively responsible for programs that differed from their own technical areas of expertise. I was responsible for all seven of the engineering programs, computer science, and both engineering technology programs at one time or another, rotating specific program responsibilities every two to four years (which remains the common pattern there). Such an unusual career path allowed me to learn about all of the programs and gain expertise with ABET engineering, computer science, and engineering technology accreditation, as well as engineering education and diversity issues in engineering.

These local leadership positions soon translated into national leadership opportunities with the Women in Engineering Proactive Network (WEPAN), where I spent almost a decade on the board of directors, including a term as president. I became active in the American Society for Engineering Education (ASEE), serving on its board as vice president for Professional Interest Councils, among many other roles, carrying out multiple duties to this day: chair of the Constitution and Bylaws Committee, chair of the Long-Range Planning Committee, and delegate to the Committee on Diversity, Equity and Inclusion. After going through ABET accreditation four times as an academic director (and later with another 10 programs as associate dean), I became an ABET program evaluator. It was a logical next step to capitalize on all the work I had done and everything I had learned. And after a decade in the role of academic director, I wanted to move up to associate dean.

My dean's workload had grown to the point that he was not able to do many things that needed doing. He needed an executive associate dean. My broad experience made me the ideal person to step into that role, so I spent the next six years as associate dean for Administration and

Strategic Initiatives for the College of Engineering and Science. It included some routine administrative duties along with the opportunity to lead many interesting new initiatives, from starting a National Academy of Engineering (NAE) Grand Challenge Scholars Program (GCSP)—the fifth such program in the US (which led to my chairing the national NAE GCSP Steering Committee for seven years)—to serving as principal investigator for a National Science Foundation ADVANCE grant for six years. This provided me with more national leadership opportunities focused on the success of women faculty (and students) in STEM fields. With another reorganization, I moved into the role of associate dean of undergraduate studies for two years before "retiring" from Louisiana Tech after 26 years.

Why did I decide to retire from Louisiana Tech? It was time to take advantage of another once-in-a-lifetime opportunity.

❊ ❊ ❊

Campbell University in rural North Carolina extended me an offer in 2015 to become their founding dean of engineering. It was an offer I could not refuse. Stated another way, I retired from Louisiana Tech and agreed to move 1,000 miles from my family to build an engineering school from scratch. My family did not come with me; my son was in graduate school in Texas, and my husband stayed in Ruston to be near our daughter, who has epilepsy and was an undergraduate at Louisiana Tech at the time. I will note that people have responded overwhelmingly negatively with regard to our decision to do this (even though it is none of their business!). If I had been a man, people would not have thought so much about it. It's one of the most overt experiences of gender bias I have ever experienced in my career.

Campbell is in the "Research Triangle" region of North Carolina, which can best be described as the Silicon Valley of engineering. The university had spent 18 months studying the proposal to build an engineering school, so they were committed, financially and otherwise, to do what it takes to build a quality program. They were looking for an innovative leader. My accreditation and national leadership experience were viewed as a plus. Campbell is an entrepreneurial institution and one that has hired a strong and diverse cohort of leaders in my time here. I have enjoyed the broad latitude to create a program that would actually do what industry feedback, engineering education research (including research on diversity and reaching under-represented students), and all the national reports (like the NAE's "The Engineer of 2020" and "Educating the Engineer of 2020") say we should be doing. These include things like attracting a more diverse cohort of students (including women, underrepresented students, first-generation college students, veterans, athletes, students from low socio-economic backgrounds, etc.). This opportunity was the perfect way to capitalize on my years of unique experience and my passion for educating students.

In the last four years, we've been able to build an innovative, project-based, hands-on curriculum at Campbell with strong professional development training, service opportunities, and student professional organizations. Our students have wowed employers as interns at major companies. We have assembled an outstanding faculty. Currently 70 percent of our faculty in engineering at Campbell are women and all of our administrators are women, likely among the highest percentage of women engineering faculty at any institution in the US. We have hired outstanding staff (about half of them are women engineers) and built innovative class labs, like those we had in the NSF-funded first-year program at Louisiana Tech, which we imported here. They combine small lecture spaces with lab facilities to support our innovative approach to hands-on learning from freshmen through senior year. And we will graduate our first class in May 2020. We will literally and figuratively be graduating the "Engineers of 2020," with the types of skill sets and engineering educational approach called for by the National Academy of Engineering in its report of the same name.

It has been a tremendous amount of work, akin to a start-up business. A friend told me that building a school from scratch would be like starting a business, and they were right. It has required me to develop and use broad skill sets, from marketing to recruiting to facilities design, but it has been a blast! The opportunity to put my almost three decades of higher education experience to use to build a program that is as close to ideal as possible was definitely one of those unique and unforeseen opportunities my mom told me about. Looking back, my unusual academic career path has meant I was as prepared for the challenge of building an engineering school as anyone could be.

With our first class set to graduate in 2020, what's next? We hope to expand our program and facilities to add more concentrations, perhaps an interdisciplinary graduate program and a new building. I personally relish interesting work like I have found at Campbell that provides me with opportunities to learn and grow. In my opinion, engineering dean is about the best gig in higher education.

But higher education is facing a trio of pressures at the national level. For one thing, years of population declines have finally hit higher education, with dwindling numbers of high school graduates and therefore college freshman. This is one of the reasons that it is imperative that we crack the code on how to attract more women and other underrepresented groups to engineering. It's no longer just the right thing to do; it's our only hope of producing enough engineers to meet workforce demands. Secondly, public sentiment toward higher education has grown increasingly negative in the last few years (which I personally think is crazy; a good education will pay you dividends for the rest of your life, and it's your best insurance against poverty). This sentiment is fueled in part by increasing student debt and its lifelong consequences, which are clearly coming home to roost. Lastly, since the economic downturn in 2008, state and even federal support of higher education has declined. Universities grappling with declining enrollments are consequently facing declining tuition revenue. Together, these are at least in part responsible for increases in tuition, combined with the higher expectations of today's freshmen regarding available services and amenities, along with the assumption that today's post-secondary institutions must provide a wide array of services and accommodations that were unheard of even 10 to 20 years ago—all of which cost money. Considering this trio of pressures, I am afraid that the future of the US higher education system, widely regarded as one of the best in the world, is in peril, particularly when today's job boom goes bust, which it surely will.

But I am also hopeful. Hopeful that enrollment pressures will usher in changes in higher education that will finally succeed in diversifying our undergraduate population in engineering to attract more women and underrepresented students. That more innovative hands-on, project-based approaches to engineering education, which also emphasize communication, teaming, and other broad skill sets, will produce engineers motivated and prepared to tackle the grand challenges facing our world in the 21st century. And that this, in turn, will help the public realize the value of a university education. I'm hopeful that good jobs in engineering will help young people pay off student debts quickly (I often see engineering graduates be able to do so). And I'm hopeful that we as university faculty and staff will be able to continue to innovate so that we can successfully navigate the challenges of providing a world-class education at a competitive price—an education that can transform the lives of the next generation of women and provide them with a myriad of opportunities to make a difference in the world.

JOURNEY 6

THE ACCIDENTAL ENGINEER

SOMA CHAKRABARTI

President
International Association for Continuing Engineering Education
ANSYS Granta Education Division

UNITED KINGDOM

Growing up in India in the 1960s and 1970s was not easy. I was privileged to be born into a Calcutta family in which education was deeply valued and girls were just as welcome as boys were. Yet the thought of becoming an engineer never occurred to me when I was growing up.

My father was a university professor and my mother, though she had a master's degree, stayed at home. She and my aunt—my father's sister, who lived with us—encouraged me to play with dolls, and my younger brother, Ananda, to play with a Meccano set (model construction systems kids use to build bridges and other infrastructure). If I ever wanted to use the Meccano set, I was quickly whisked away by the ladies to play with a doll's house. The only person who supported and encouraged my interest in "boys' toys" was my father. One day he brought home a chemistry set for me, and it was one of the most interesting things I'd ever had to play with. Then appeared a small box of Lego for my brother, who reluctantly let me play with it at times. Ironically, it turned out that I was better than him at building many things with both the Lego and the Meccano set.

I was good in mathematics and science, so studying in the science stream at high school made sense. To be honest, I was horrible in art, history or similar subjects, and I used to get my brother, who was a natural at these things, to do my art and drawings homework. We had a deal: I did his math homework and he drew all the landscapes and figures for me. While my parents were unaware of this bartering activity, they knew that being in the science and math stream would be my only option.

Becoming an engineer was a pure accident because no one encouraged

ABOUT THE AUTHOR

Dr. Soma Chakrabarti has been President of the International Association for Continuing Engineering Education since 2016 and has more than 25 years of experience in leadership, administration, teaching, and research in both academia and industry. She leads the Resources Team of the Granta Design Education Division at ANSYS, Inc., in Cambridge, United Kingdom. Previously, she was an Assistant Dean at the University of Wisconsin-Madison Continuing Studies, Director of Continuing Studies at the University of Delaware, and Director of the Center for Engineering and Interdisciplinary Professional Education at the University of Kansas Continuing Education. Her work focuses on engineering education, the future of learning, and the lifelong learning of engineers, technologists, and scientists. She is known for developing international partnerships with all major aircraft manufacturers and aviation safety organizations.

me to do so despite my affinity towards the boys' toys. After high school, I applied for and was offered admission to an engineering school, but I was forced to study chemistry because, rather unfortunately, I scored highest in chemistry in the final exam. Bethune College was an all-girls college where the teachers lectured a lot without offering much experiential learning. I found physics and math minor classes more interesting, but I was often absent from the chemistry classes, instead going to the movies for matinee shows. Obviously, my exam results weren't so impressive, and I was called into the department head's office. She was Dr. Debi Chakrabarty, a doctorate in chemistry from Oxford University, and she happened to have been my father's classmate when they were doing their master's degrees. Instead of scolding me, she thoroughly investigated my strengths and weaknesses, my desires and reluctances, and gave her verdict: that I should think about changing to engineering. I would first have to finish my BSc in chemistry at the University of Calcutta and then, with her help and that of another friend of my father, I was able to convince my parents that I should get a Bachelor of Technology degree.

I still remember my first day at the department of chemical technology at the University of Calcutta. Two young men told us females in the class that we were wasting the seats; they should have gone to men, who were much more deserving. "Why?" I asked. One of the men said, "Because you won't do well in exams, and you will eventually just sit at home and cook." It was the 1980s. I was stunned; it's not like we were the first-ever female engineering students. Yet this actually happened to us.

I proved these nay-sayers wrong and came top in my class that year (and all the subsequent years, too). In fact, all the women students scored higher than the men. We knew we had to do well, and that we would be working after we graduated, so we worked hard, very hard. Even during the internships, we had to prove that we could work and thrive in factories.

I went on to do my master's degree and now I wanted to continue with doctoral studies at the Indian Institute of Technology in Delhi. But doing so would have a big impact on my personal life: it would mean I wouldn't be able to marry the man who had proposed to me. That's because his family was not in favor of me doing graduate studies and then pursuing a career. So I chose to break the relationship. It wasn't easy. I left my home city and moved to a place where I knew few people.

Not only did I survive, it was one of the best things I did in my life. Had I not taken that decision, I would never have gained the courage to venture into a new world and experience studying at a premier institution in India. From time to time, I have used this experience to gather the courage to defy an imposed situation and choose my own destiny. It is interesting how our childhood often shapes our lives. Yet, we also have the power to reshape it later.

In the 1990s, I married a faculty member of the University of Kansas in Lawrence and immigrated to the United States. That transition wasn't a smooth one. In the 1990s, there weren't many women in engineering departments and even the students sometimes preferred male professors. As a colored immigrant woman with a different accent, I was not always made to feel welcome by my male colleagues. I learned to ignore this behavior and work as best as I could. In those five to six years of teaching, I met budding women engineers in my classes. These girls came from various backgrounds, but all were extremely motivated to complete their degrees and compete for jobs with everyone else. Over and over I saw them scoring high grades, a testament to their hard work, determination, and ability. I would have continued in teaching and research, but life took me in another direction.

Nowhere in my wildest dreams did I imagine that I would run a business. So, I was the one who was most surprised when I was asked to open BioComp Systems, Inc., an engineering research and development business in Lawrence, to seek, obtain, and lead small-business innovation research grants. I enjoyed it thoroughly, despite hearing speculation that I was given grants because I was a woman. I learned to work with and lead people, and to manage the business to get work done. I learned to negotiate with attorneys and to market products. I learned that engineering needs business to make things happen. Funny as it may sound, many people had thought of me as being a soft-spoken, "nice" woman who could never be strong and bold enough to get things done. But I have proven them wrong every time.

I loved the business side of the grant management and R&D operation. So, when an opportunity came, I joined the University of Kansas continuing education department and led its education programs for eight years until I moved to the University of Delaware and then the University of Wisconsin-Madison.

As I work at the ANSYS Granta Education Division in Cambridge, UK, leading the materials engineering educational resources team, I often reflect on my experiences in the engineering business world. I'm pleased to see that women engineers are making a real difference at the helm of many well-known organizations. Each one of us has a story and a life we left behind to achieve what we wanted to. Maybe some of them were also told they were wasting seats at the engineering schools; maybe some of them had parents who let them play with boys' toys as they grew up. And maybe some of them had teachers who told them that they would shine as engineering leaders.

My former supervisor at the University of Kansas continuing education department, Fred Pawlicki, then its executive director, encouraged me to go everywhere in the world to represent the university and to be who I was. He told me that women engineers can be the most disciplined and emotionally intelligent leaders in the workplace.

So, the thought I want to leave with our future engineering leaders—educators and technology professionals alike—is that their future is indeed bright.

And, in case, you are wondering: my brother Ananda, with whom I'm very close to this day, became a renowned art historian and liberal arts professor in Toronto, Canada. We are both proud to have broken the norms.

JOURNEY 7

ENGINEERING CHANGE FOR GOOD

ELIZABETH CROFT

Dean
*Faculty of Engineering
Monash University*

AUSTRALIA

Being the dean of engineering at Monash University is a wonderful honor and a great responsibility. Since beginning in January 2018, I have also at times felt the weight of serving as the first female dean of engineering at a university named after celebrated World War I hero and prominent Australian engineer Sir John Monash. I do, however, appreciate the openness to change that my appointment signals. I've worked hard to gain the trust and respect of my academic, technical, and professional staff—and I've learned in most of the engineering organizations I've been involved with that trust and respect are not given easily. So, because it's been hard-earned, it's much more satisfying. Let me describe my journey, and then offer some insights that could help you, too.

Although both my parents were doctors, I was always more interested in the workings of the physically-constructed world. While I was a child growing up in Canada in the 1960s, my grandfather, a cattle farmer, taught me to take things apart and fix them. When I was a teenager, I decided to become a mechanical engineer after a family friend, who was a professor of mechanical engineering, showed me the plans of a Boeing 767. I was fascinated to learn that jet aeroplanes began with drawings on a page, and that math and physics could be used to calculate the creation

ABOUT THE AUTHOR

Professor Elizabeth A. Croft (B.A.Sc UBC '88, M.A.Sc Waterloo '92, PhD Toronto '95) is the Dean of Engineering at Monash University. She is also Professor, Mechanical and Aerospace Engineering; and Professor, Electrical and Computer Systems Engineering. From 2013-2017 she was Associate Dean for the Faculty of Applied Science at the University of British Columbia (UBC), where she was Director of the Collaborative Advanced Robotics and Intelligent Systems (CARIS) Laboratory. Her internationally recognized research in industrial robotics and human-robot interaction advances the design of intelligent controllers and interaction methods that underpin how people and autonomous, collaborative systems can work together in a safe, predictable, and helpful manner. Applications range from manufacturing to healthcare and assistive technology. Professor Croft is a champion for diversity and inclusion in engineering and has led research and institutional projects resulting in sharp increases in the participation of women in science and engineering. She held the NSERC Chair for Women in Science and Engineering (BC/Yukon) from 2010 to 2015 and the Marshall Bauder Professorship in Engineering Economics, Business and Management Training from 2015 to 2017. Her recognitions include the Peter Wall Early Career Scholar award, an NSERC Accelerator award, WXN's top 100 most powerful women in Canada, and the RA McLachlan Award—the peak career award for professional engineering in BC. She is a Fellow of Engineers Australia, the Canadian Academy of Engineers, Engineers Canada, and the American Society of Mechanical Engineers.

of real, moving things.

After finishing university, I began work in my first role as a mechanical engineer. I was the only female engineer working in a company in Vancouver that undertook motor vehicle accident investigations, and I was trying my best to fit in with all "the guys." I worked alongside them in junkyards and during site visits, wearing my standard uniform of jeans, a T-shirt, and runners, looking very much like a guy, except with a ponytail. I enjoyed working with them; they were like my brothers.

Then something happened in 1989 that remains painful even to this day: at École Polytechnique in Montreal, 14 women were killed in a mass shooting. Nine female mechanical engineering students were shot in their classroom; six of them died. The gunman sent the 50 male students out of the classroom first before shooting the women, whom he targeted solely for being women who'd chosen to study engineering.

When news of the massacre broke, the whole country was horrified. But as a Canadian woman in engineering, one of a very small number at the time, this event was particularly painful. These women were just like me, only a couple of years behind me in their studies. Suddenly, I didn't feel like one of the guys anymore. Previously, I'd been happy to dress and act like a male to fit in. But after the massacre, I realized, "No, I'm female. I need to be accepted for who I am."

In the days following, I felt quite alone. Since I worked in an open plan office, I took myself off to a separate space where I could sit quietly, work on engineering reports and quietly mourn these women without anyone seeing me. After a while, the director of the company came to find me. He sat beside me and said, "I just want you to know that everyone in the company values you, and shares the loss you feel." It was a very generous and healing gesture that still touches me today. In that moment, he helped me realize that the way forward requires women and men to work together to address exclusion and intolerance. Still, there is much work to be done.

Looking back, I can see that many of my Canadian female engineering colleagues of the time were also changed by what happened at École Polytechnique. We banded together, started "women in engineering" groups, and worked hard to make change in our schools and workplaces that was systemic and sustainable. As horrific as the shooting was, it became our strengthening scar.

Culture change in engineering remains a work in progress, and women are conscious that backlash against gender and diversity initiatives could strike at any time. Sometimes, it feels like we're walking in high heels, trying to avoid the landmines. Still, I believe that engineering is a wonderful career choice for both women and men, and I hope that the perspectives I have gained from my career will be helpful for those who follow.

THE ONLY NURSING MOM: CREATING CHANGE FROM THE START

I was eight months pregnant with my first child when I attended an interview at the University of British Columbia (UBC) in Vancouver for my first academic job and, despite many surprised and worried looks, they hired me. I became one of only five women academics in the entire faculty, one of only two women academics in the mechanical engineering department, and certainly the only nursing mother with a baby. It was a new experience for everyone, and I soon realized that in order to be part of the community, I immediately had to advocate for family-friendly policies. So, department meetings were changed from 6 p.m. on Mondays to lunchtime on Thursdays, and caregivers were then allowed to come along to department retreats. These types of changes were also appreciated and supported by my male colleagues with young families themselves. There's power in being a nursing mom.

Still, when I later told my department head I was pregnant with my second baby, he looked genuinely horrified and shocked. His first reaction: "Oh no! What do we do?" I almost felt sorry for him. With the help of the department manager, I was able to work out a leave schedule that covered my classes and minimized disruption. My experiences as a pregnant academic later fed into the improved parenting-related policies at UBC, including documented policies on the reduction of teaching duties and support to maintain research activities during leave.

After I returned from maternity leave, my mom encouraged me to keep nursing until my baby was at least nine months old. "But I'm working!" I said to her. "Well, you can pump," she replied. So I did, because my mom was a doctor with expertise in newborn development, and of course I wanted to do the right thing.

Expressed breast milk is "liquid gold"; every ounce pumped counts. Pumping is tough and can be painful, and takes a long time. I'd bring the little Gerber baby bottles to work, lock my office door and pump away, challenging myself to see how many ounces I could produce each time. Then, I'd put the lid on the bottle and take that hard-earned milk to the tea room to put in the fridge, ready to take home at the end of the day.

One day, I found a senior academic—let's call him Joe—standing in the tea room holding his coffee cup, just as I was carrying in a bottle. "Ah, Elizabeth!" he exclaimed. "You're the one bringing in the milk!" Over the past few weeks, I'd noticed that something wasn't quite right with the amount of milk I could see in the bottles I had left in the fridge. I'd been looking at them thinking, *I could swear I made more ounces than that....*

In that moment, my suspicions were confirmed. I realized that my senior male colleague had been pouring my breast milk out of a baby bottle straight into his coffee! Stunned, all I could think was that a lot of that hard work I'd put into pumping milk had been wasted.

I said, "Joe, do you realize...that's my milk?"

"Yes," he said, taken aback. "But, of course, you don't mind sharing it?"

Left with no other option, I was forced to spell it out.

"No Joe," I said, slowly. "You don't understand. I *made* that milk!"

Finally, he got it. Joe suddenly realized exactly what he'd been drinking. He turned mottled green-grey in shock and scuttled straight out of the tea room. He couldn't look me in the eye for weeks.

Joe's mistake was a remarkable illustration of the changing environment we were in. For him, a baby bottle, and the idea that it might contain breast milk, was a foreign concept. For me, the idea that someone would not recognize a baby bottle was equally foreign. Despite our newly-made "connection," how likely was Joe to understand any of the other challenges I was facing as a woman in engineering? And how could I explain them to him? When dealing with far more challenging and difficult situations, I find it's always very helpful to share this story with other women. And, yes, many years later, it still makes me laugh, every time I talk about it.

"OPPORTUNITIES FOR SERVICE": MEN MUST SHARE THE LOAD

Being a young academic and one of the very few women in engineering, I had plenty of "opportunities for service" on top of my research and teaching commitments. Every time they needed a woman on a committee, I'd be on it. Anytime there was outreach needed, it was me doing it. Anytime there was a crying female student, it was my job to help her. In short, anytime there was a "girl thing," it was left to me.

It was committee after committee after committee, and sometimes it just wasn't appropriate. I remember serving on the search committee for a new head of mining engineering. I was a brand new academic at the time, having only just arrived. What the heck was I doing there? I had no context of what we were looking for at all.

Until the numbers improve, the extra service load on women academics remains problematic, particularly when it comes to university committee work, when a certain percentage of female representation is often mandated. Messages are mixed and young women academics often feel they're in a no-win situation; they're advised to be careful about doing too much service work and to remain focused on research and teaching, while simultaneously being asked to serve on a disproportionate number of committees. I am happy to see more male colleagues stepping forward to take on service work, particularly in the area of diversity and inclusion. We're always better together.

THE EVIDENCE IS CLEAR: GENDER DIVERSITY WORKS

It's the unspoken nature of the sexism in engineering that often makes it hard to perceive and identify. When you're dealing with inappropriate "pin-up" posters on walls or academics having meetings in strip bars, those types of behaviors are visible and can be directly called out. However, the covert sexism, the implicit bias, and the assumptions aren't as visible. They're the ton of feathers women are often buried under.

In 2015, I coauthored a book, *WWEST's Gender Diversity in STEM: A Briefing on Women in Science and Engineering*, in which we brought together both the case and straightforward action plans for organizational gender diversity. The book also explored the covert nature of microaggressions, unconscious bias, and stereotype threat. We compiled the research that supports best practices—and found a correlation between organizations with high gender diversity in leadership, and several measures of organizational success.

For example, if a group includes more women, the collective intelligence rises. If a board includes more women directors, the business improves its ability to navigate complex strategic issues, and reduces internal conflict and negative corporate social practices. Fortune 500 companies with the most women on their board of directors were found to outperform companies with the fewest female board members. As an academic, researcher, and engineer, I believe it's important that the case for gender diversity, and the inclusion of those who think and experience the world differently, is clearly underpinned by scholarly research.

IT TAKES GENUINE COMMITMENT: SUPPORTING WOMEN FOR THE LONG HAUL

Many academics believe in the concept of meritocracy: that outcomes in an academic system are based only on merit. And this is patently not true, because life is not fair. If you're born into privilege, you're lucky, and have a higher likelihood of attaining academic success, all other factors held equal. Someone else who works just as hard, is just as smart and "meritorious" but doesn't enjoy the same socio-economic advantages has to work much harder for the same results.

I have found that the lucky ones had a great supervisor they got along well with, or perhaps knew somebody who could recommend them to someone important. They fit into the culture easily, they talked to the right person at the right time—someone who saw them as their younger self and was inspired to help them along the way. The lucky ones were sponsored, invited to give a big talk, or to work at a great lab.

Because of that, I always look for people who don't fit the norm. They're the ones who achieved their successes fingernail by fingernail. They haven't had all the breaks, they didn't have the right connections, and they've had to struggle. They didn't necessarily have the right supervisor, or enjoy the best opportunities. Yet they can be the ones with the biggest potential, those who just need the right support to reach it.

When you support someone from a disadvantaged group, you must commit for the long haul; otherwise, you're setting them up to fail. Too often, our academic and business systems implement diversity policies in an attempt to be seen to be doing the right thing, but without the resourcing or long-term planning required. In these cases, women can be pushed forward, and then quickly experience the rug being pulled out from underneath them. People watch them fail, then say, "See? She can't do it." If you're going to support women, you have to really support them, with genuine commitment and mentorship over the long term. I continue to see this as a challenge in all academic systems.

ADDRESSING THE CHALLENGES: KNOW YOUR VALUES AND SET STRATEGIC GOALS

I moved from Canada to Australia to take up my role as dean, and I appreciate that I've been given the benefits and privilege of working at two excellent universities across two free, first-world countries with stated commitments to fairness and equality. The positives are far-reaching. I'm in a position where I'm empowered to create and advocate for real change for students, staff, industry, and the engineering profession. The opportunities for engineers to contribute change-making discoveries and innovations towards the UN Sustainable Development Goals inspire our research and education.

As we commit to addressing these global challenges, we've also set another goal for our faculty, an ambitious one: to reach a 50:50 gender balance in our enrollments within five years. It's a challenging stretch-goal, and we'll work collectively to achieve it. In addition, we are working on finding new pathways to include diverse students from wider local and international backgrounds. Solutions for the planet must come from the people of the planet—and diversity and inclusion must be a core part of our strategy.

The inclusion of women in engineering has seen steady progress over my career, but challenges remain. Women in senior roles are still few, with a growing number of junior women seeking support to manage the same walls and biases we thought were addressed years ago. In some quarters, the barriers have become more insidious—the pin-up posters are gone, but the attitudes and comments remain. Many women still experience exclusion, harassment, and systemic bias within organizational structures that were historically designed by men, for men. Women who are promoted still fight the insinuation that they were promoted because they're women, and not because they earned it. This bias is exacerbated for people who are also members of visible minority groups.

But I can attest to the fact that there are many silver linings. Over my career, I learned a great deal from those many extra "opportunities for service" I was given, and from undertaking projects that were the right thing to do, rather than the strategic thing to do. The way you do your work is as important as the work itself.

When people ask me for advice, I always start with the need to be positive. Then, I follow with the need to believe in yourself, because if you don't, it's pretty hard for anyone else to get on board with you. Having friends with similar careers and challenges as a common sounding board seems obvious, but it's essential when things don't quite fit together. There's nothing like shared experience to help reframe situations. It's always good to ask for help; the worst someone will say is, "No." And it's good to ask for advice. Once you receive the advice, you can decide for yourself if you want to take it, because not all advice is good advice.

Regardless of gender, class or status, it's also best to be gracious during the tough times, and to keep a sense of humor. Kindness, compassion, seeing the best in people, having an open mind and heart, and having a desire to learn will always help you to create the right career opportunities. Setting strategic goals, seeking wise counsel, attracting the best minds, valuing excellence, and monitoring progress is crucial to any project.

Most of all, know your own values, make time for other people—and time to look after yourself. Smile with confidence, stand up for others, and pick your battles. Go well.

JOURNEY 8

AT THE CROSSROADS TO THE FUTURE

CATHERINE (KITTY) JAY DIDION

Executive Director
Women in Engineering ProActive Network, Inc

UNITED STATES OF AMERICA

In a recent moment of reflection, it became clear to me that my journey has been one of intersections and crossroads—both literally and metaphorically. Many of these were "STOP," "DANGER," or "DO NOT ENTER" signs, which I usually ignored, often resulting in great adventure, acquisition of a few bruises, and much success personally and professionally.

My parents are such an intersection. My father, Raymond Jay, was born on a dairy farm in northern Wisconsin where his father taught physics and coached football. My dad and his twin sister were born in the middle of a blizzard; the local doctor improvised to use the farm's oven as an incubator, keeping my dad and his twin sister warm in shoe boxes in the oven. He was never given a middle name as the assumption was that he would not survive. His relatives had fought in the American Revolution and the family stories included many amusing tales of my great grandmother traveling by covered wagon out west as well.

My four siblings and I were city kids, and my father would cajole us about our lackluster approach to our daily chores with stories of how far he walked to school and how many cows he milked. ("Can we milk cows too?" we'd joke. "Where is the closest one?" This kind of talk usually resulted in more chores being assigned.) My dad was a freshman at the

ABOUT THE AUTHOR

Catherine "Kitty" Didion is executive director of WEPAN (Women in Engineering Pro-Active Network). From 2016 to 2018, Didion was a Vice President at Olin College of Engineering, with overall responsibility for the college's advancement efforts. Didion served from 2006 to 2016 as Director of the Committee on Women in Science, Engineering, and Medicine at the National Academies of Sciences, Engineering and Medicine (NASEM) and as a Senior Program Officer at the National Academy of Engineering (NAE). Didion was lead staff officer for more than a dozen publications. Before joining the National Academies, she was Executive Director of the Association for Women in Science (AWIS). During her tenure, AWIS won the US Presidential Award for Excellence in Science, Mathematics, and Engineering Mentoring. Didion has extensive experience in Washington, DC, including a staff position at the US Senate Commerce, Science, and Transportation Committee. In 2012, Didion was named one of "100 Women Leaders in Science, Technology, Engineering, and Mathematics (STEM)." Her honors include 2014 NAE Staff Award; AAAS Fellow; AWIS Fellow; Drucker Foundation Fellow; Texaco Management Institute Fellow; and Certificate of Commendation and Distinguished Service, Embassy of the United States of America, Riyadh, Saudi Arabia. Didion completed her undergraduate degree at Mount Holyoke College and her graduate work at the University of Virginia.

University of Wisconsin when he enlisted in the Navy during World War II and fought in Africa and Europe. He then completed his undergraduate and graduate degrees at the University of Wisconsin and moved to New York City to work for the US government.

My mother, Lillian Dosedel Jay, is first-generation American and spoke Czech before she learned English. Her parents immigrated to the US from what is now the Czech Republic, met in Wisconsin and married. My mother was the eldest of six children and my grandfather was the municipal band leader and owner of a hardware store. As a child I remember holidays as a time of music, dancing, and singing at my grandparents' home. Czech treats were often served.

Although my parents were from the same town in Wisconsin, they did not know each other well. My mother moved to New York as a graduate student in occupational therapy and my father also happened to move to New York for work. He would drop off the local Wisconsin newspaper at my mother's apartment as a courtesy, which soon led to courtship and marriage.

My father's work for the US Department of Defense required us to move frequently. I was born in Cleveland, Ohio; attended kindergarten and first grade in Chicago, Illinois; second grade in St. Louis, Missouri; half of third grade in one part of Virginia and when we moved later that year, the other half of third grade in another part of Virginia. I found that each school taught the subjects differently, and I'd be either behind or ahead—another intersection to navigate. It taught me to be resilient and it gave me a hint at how different experiences can be within one country, much less throughout the world.

I was always good at math and science and I enjoyed my classes. I attended high school in Arlington, Virginia, near the Pentagon; my father, along with most other parents of kids at my school, worked for the US government. As I was the eldest of five and I had turned down a scholarship to the University of Virginia to attend a private college, my father insisted that I needed to earn money during the summer to help pay for university. My first job was working for the US Senate Press Office on the third floor of the US Capitol—a patronage job that my father had arranged for me. I had just turned 18 and I did not appreciate my father's efforts on my behalf. He then gave me a good piece of advice: "Catherine Emily, I can get you the job, but only you can keep it." It was a transformative intersection in my life. I fell in love with the possibility and potential that good public policy could achieve.

I learned so very much that summer watching the senators in the press gallery banter and debate legislation with the reporters. My boss, Don Womack, the press gallery superintendent, took me under his tutelage and taught me how to run a press conference and count the votes during roll call on the Senate floor. It was my first occasion to see how women fared in the workplace. There were very few female reporters assigned to the US Congress or the White House at that time. The women reporters I met were tough, determined, and maintained a great sense of humor. I continued working at the US Senate for many years including for its computer center and its Committee on Commerce, Science and Transportation.

At college I studied arms control policy and international relations. My chemistry professor, Anna Jane Harrison, was the first woman elected as president of the American Chemical Society. I enjoyed my science and mathematics courses but my focus was on the policy implications. Through a professor's recommendation, I was invited to participate in a program at Oxford University. This led to an opportunity to live in Geneva, Switzerland, for two years. There I worked for Martin Kaplan, who was secretary general for the Pugwash conferences on disarmament. Pugwash is an organization founded by Albert Einstein and Bertrand Russell to reduce armed conflict and address nuclear threats; it eventually won a Nobel Peace Prize for its work.

Living in Switzerland was a challenge financially, and I learned how to survive on a modest salary while I explored the global framework of international organizations and the United Nations. I can still remember many meals of rice, bananas, and Knorr's curry sauce, and sourcing winter clothing in the local thrift shops.

Upon my return to Washington, DC, I worked for the Carnegie

Endowment for International Peace and then for the Arms Control Association. The collegiality of these organizations was amazing, and I was fortunate to work with many talented and committed public servants including two stellar men: Warren Zimmerman, who was the last US ambassador to Yugoslavia, and Spurgeon M. Keeny, Jr., who served four US presidents on issues related to military intelligence and arms control policy. At that time women were still relatively scarce in the fields of diplomatic service and nuclear disarmament, and many leaders were noted physicists such as Sidney Drell and Richard Garwin. This was a small group of dedicated scientists and engineers who relied on their network of relationships as well as their technical skillsets to accomplish their goals. It was a good lesson for me to understand how personalities can play a role in achieving success and that negotiations can be undermined by not engaging effectively with your opponents.

In 1987 I left the Arms Control Association when my husband and I decided to accept an invitation to live in Saudi Arabia. He was asked to become part of the US representation team at the Treasury Department to negotiate agreements between the two countries. I was fortunate to be hired as executive director for American Community Services, one of the first US nonprofits in Saudi Arabia; it was organized to support a growing population of thousands of American and other Western residents in Riyadh. I was given a four-story office building in downtown Riyadh to run, and

I helped start the first University of Maryland field courses in Riyadh. I organized classes, programs, and services for Americans and I was often the only woman at meetings with the Riyadh Diplomatic Authority when I was negotiating permission for programs.

I gave birth to my second child, Ryan, at the Dr. Abdul Rahman Al Mishari Hospital in Riyadh. I had to seek permission from the US Embassy doctor to do so, as the US embassy's policy at that time was for women to return to the US for the birth of their children. My son was 9.5 pounds at birth and was the toast of the hospital.

The experience in Saudi Arabia was transformative for me as a person, mother, and wife. It was an opportunity to experience a culture vastly different than the one I had been in. For example, when you meet someone in Washington, DC, they often ask you, "What do you do?" You are defined (and valued) by your job title and its importance. In Saudi Arabia, we were often asked, "How is your family?" There, the emphasis is on relationships. The fact that we had two young children, one born in Riyadh, gave us entrée to unique experiences.

I met many talented and educated Saudi women, including a significant number of female engineers and scientists. Their commitment and interest in using their education to further their society was always evident. After three years we decided we should return to the US so that our children could be closer to our families.

When I returned to the US, I had three job opportunities (including one on Capitol Hill, my old stomping grounds) and I approached one of my mentors at the Carnegie Endowment for International Peace for advice. I shared with him the opportunities, including one as executive director of the Association for Women in Science (AWIS), and he encouraged me to accept it, stating he knew that I enjoyed growing small organizations and having meaningful impact, and that it would be a good challenge for me.

During my tenure at AWIS the organization grew substantially in visibility and impact. It was awarded the Presidential Award for Excellence in Science, Mathematics, and Engineering Mentoring for its groundbreaking work on small group mentoring and its impact on female researchers. I co-chaired the first Science and Technology Caucus at the UN Conference on Women in Beijing and headed up a delegation of 12 representatives to the conference. I helped organize the gender component of the Organization of American States' Engineering for the Americas and led the discussions on gender and engineering. AWIS became more involved in international efforts to address the lack of representation of women in science and engineering globally. I was appointed to be one of four international representatives to South Africa's Department of Science and Technology to address issues of gender after the ending of apartheid.

My time at AWIS was an opportunity to increase my engagement in global science and engineering, and I was struck by two consistent observations. First, US science and engineering has much to offer in its partnerships with other nations and their efforts to develop their technology; however, we also have much to learn about how science and engineering is conducted in these countries, usually with fewer resources and greater constraints. Too often I found that US-based programs were eager to teach but not always open to new ideas. Second, gender is still a salient lens almost every female scientist and engineer I met has had to address in order to be part of their country's technical workforce. I recall an Eisenhower Fellow from Pakistan, who at the time was the highest-ranking female scientist in the Pakistani government, noting how she and I had much more in common than she had ever imagined.

After more than a decade of service to AWIS, it was time for a change for me and for the organization. I became the director for the International Network of Women in Engineering and Science (INWES), which was a Canadian-based organization looking to establish nonprofit status in the US. In January 2005 I was invited to attend a small private conference at the National Bureau of Economic Research at Harvard University on women and minorities in science and engineering. It was at this conference that Larry Summers, then the president of Harvard University, spoke. He noted that women's lack of representation in science and engineering was the culmination of several factors, including their reluctance to work long hours and "issues of intrinsic aptitude" for mathematics, given differences in test scores for boys and girls.

It was clear that Dr. Summers was trying to be provocative, yet I do not think he anticipated the response he would receive. In fact, none of us understood the impact this event would have in creating a global conversation on women in science and engineering. For his part, Dr. Summers noted that he was expressing his opinion as an individual and not as president of Harvard (even though during his presidency the number of tenured positions offered to women dropped from 36 percent to 13 percent). But the reaction of the media to his controversial words was huge; I was one of a handful of participants who met with a reporter from The Boston Globe early the next morning and responded to an overwhelming number of press inquiries. I was asked to handle the conservative talk show interviews including those with Bill O'Reilly and Laura Ingraham. It provided me an unusual platform to articulate the importance of diversity in securing new engineering and scientific discoveries. It taught me to be open to having discussions with any community. And it was another important intersection of my life—one where I realized that all leaders must acknowledge that their words as well as their deeds carry great weight and influence.

In 2006 I became the senior program officer for diversity, engineering education, and the workforce (DEW) at the US National Academy of Engineering (NAE) in Washington, DC. I was the project director for a $2-million grant from the National Science Foundation (Engineering Equity

Extension Services) that supported the efforts of engineering societies to increase the number of women earning undergraduate degrees in engineering. In 2007 I was asked to be the director of the Committee on Women in Science, Engineering and Medicine (CWSEM) at the National Academies of Sciences, Engineering and Medicine (NASEM, or the National Academies); this required me to split my time between NAE and CWSEM. The first CWSEM report I was responsible for was one mandated by US Congress on academic career pathways for female faculty in science and engineering. It was the first time that the top 100 institutions of higher education in the US had been surveyed about the recruitment and retention of women faculty in tenure-track and tenured positions in science and engineering. The report was seminal in that it collected new data that demonstrated where female faculty were being lost and how various disciplines fared.

During my time at the National Academies I was the staff lead on more than a dozen publications that focused on the engineering and scientific workforce. I was the representative for the National Academies' work on gender with the African Academies of Science, which led to collaborations with several national academies (including the Academy of Science of South Africa) and I worked with the InterAmerican Network of Academies of Sciences (IANAS) on their gender initiatives.

The opportunity to work with committed colleagues as well as members of the National Academies was tremendous. In particular, working with Norman Fortenberry, who was then the director of the Center for Advancement of Scholarship on Engineering Education (CASEE), was a crossroads for me. We were both committed to achieving change in engineering education and we often did not follow the normal pathways at the NAE, which emphasized publications. We wanted to impact the broader community of current educators of engineers and to engage institutions and organizations that often were not included in the National Academies' outreach, such as minority-serving institutions and community colleges. We, along with our NAE colleague Beth Cady, developed training tools, videos, workshops, and fellowships for educators and faculty. I firmly believe that this NAE effort through CASEE impacted an entire generation of engineering education faculty and educators. It is a legacy to the vision of Norman Fortenberry and then-NAE president Bill Wulf that is hard to overstate. The credibility of the NAE to highlight the importance and rigor of research in engineering education has led to the creation of engineering education departments, faculty positions, and research efforts globally.

I had many learning opportunities during my decade at the National Academies. One that stands out is when, in 2012, NAE president Chuck Vest (former president of MIT) persuaded the leadership of the NAE to sign on to an amicus (friend of the court) brief in support of affirmative action in the Fisher v. University of Texas-Austin US Supreme Court case. Chuck asked me to represent the NAE at the press conference at the

National Press Club to discuss the case. He later sent me a note that I was "an effective stalwart on really important issues." This gave me wind under my wings for months to come.

A cost-cutting reorganization at the National Academy of Engineering eliminated the Diversity and Engineering Workforce (DEW) office in 2016. In a moment of reflection, I had constructed a Venn diagram where the first circle was, "What am I good at?" The second was, "What do I enjoy doing?" as I had learned that one does not always enjoy what one does well. The third circle was, "Where can I have impact?" as I still wanted to make a difference in engineering education. I had discovered through my previous positions that working for a leader you believe in is critical to having impact. I found such a leader in Richard K. Miller, an NAE member and founding president of the Franklin W. Olin College of Engineering. I became his vice president for Development, Family and Alumni Relations, and moved to the Boston area.

Olin College is an undergraduate engineering college where 50 percent of the students and 40 percent of the faculty are female. Its focus is on design thinking and project-based engineering education with teams of students and faculty. Olin students complete an average of more than 20 portfolio projects by the time they graduate, and this experience has helped them successfully transition to the engineering workforce. It is a very young institution (founded in 1997) that is a compelling model for engineering education globally. It was my job to work with the president and the trustees to grow the external communities that would value Olin and its unique role as a catalyst for change in engineering education. I enjoyed my two years at Olin tremendously and learned a great deal from the faculty and students on how to experiment successfully in engineering education. The number of international institutions that have emulated aspects of Olin College is now in the hundreds. I believe that it is a critical part of the engineering education ecosystem, and we need more models that focus on how students learn and the importance of team learning in engineering education.

After a few brutal winters where my decades-old car was buried in snow, and given the declining health of my parents in Arlington, Virginia—my father died shortly before I left Olin—I decided it was a good time to return to the Washington, DC, area. I was encouraged to apply for the position of executive director for WEPAN (Women in Engineering Pro-Active Network), a nonprofit whose mission is to advance cultures of inclusion and diversity in engineering education and professions. I became executive director in the summer of 2018.

WEPAN aims to achieve its mission by empowering people and organizations who are catalysts for change. It works to sustain a strong network and has a long history of creating research-based resources that can be easily adapted for engineering classrooms or programs. Recent projects have focused on transforming engineering cultures to advance inclusion and diversity in engineering departments (TECAID) as well as providing resources to expand the capacity of engineering schools to retain undergraduate students by implementing proven strategies in engineering programs (ENGAGE). Examples include how to integrate these strategies into existing courses (Everyday Examples in Engineering) and the importance of improving student spatial visualization skills. As a small nonprofit, WEPAN must partner with other engineering organizations in order to achieve its goals. Recent collaborators have included the American Society for Engineering Education (ASEE) and the American Society of Mechanical Engineers (ASME). WEPAN will celebrate its 30th anniversary in 2020 and it is committed to continuing its work until there is no need to address the role of women in engineering, as parity will have been achieved.

Working for a nonprofit can be challenging and sometimes daunting, but I believe in the ability to create change and I am still excited about the next crossroads that will appear over the horizon. Many of the women scientists and engineers who worked for me at AWIS or the National Academies are now rising leaders in their own institutions. I am struck by their raw talent and their ambition to create change. My willingness to mentor, share contacts, provide advice, or just listen is often mentioned by them as a pivotal step on their current path.

My request to them is that they continue building the community by spending their most precious resource—time—with younger colleagues seeking guidance. When they do spend time giving advice, they will learn what I have learned: the mentor often learns as much, if not more, than the protegee. The ways one can conquer obstacles on their career path are limited only by one's creativity and determination. I am hopeful and excited to see the future of engineering and science as more women assume leadership roles.

The quote below is from Maria Mitchell, an American astronomer who in 1847 discovered a comet. It resonates with my firm belief that we are on a connected, living planet where we can tackle almost anything if we only work together.

> "We travel to learn; and I have never been in any country where they did not do something better than we do it, think some thoughts better than we think, catch some inspiration from heights above our own." —Maria Mitchell

JOURNEY 9

LEARNING AND LOVING STEM

BRENDA DISCHER

Senior Vice President
Business Strategy & Marketing
Siemens Digital Industries Software

UNITED STATES OF AMERICA

I have been graced with the gift of curiosity. As a child growing up in the 1960s and '70s about an hour northwest of Detroit, I was fascinated by how things worked, and it was quite common for me to take things apart and put them back together just to see their inner workings. Any device was up for grabs, including almost every toy my two younger brothers possessed. I would steal the crane they used in the sandbox, take it apart and reconfigure it to see how the arm worked. I would create elaborate Matchbox car tracks, using Lego blocks to build obstacles and to see how much of an incline the cars could take before they stopped and rolled backwards. I didn't know it at the time, but mechanics, physics, friction, and other aspects of engineering were taking hold.

On top of that, my leadership skills were developing. My mother recently reminded me that even when I was little, I would take on leadership responsibilities. If a family event needed planning, I was always the one organizing and assigning tasks to my family. "I'm not surprised that this became the course of your life," she told me.

There were two pivotal factors during high school that piqued my interest in engineering and set me on a path to becoming a mechanical engineer. The first was that I had a ninth-grade math teacher, Mr. Leckrone, who encouraged me and truly sparked my love for mathematics. Up until then, despite knowing full well that I could excel in math, I had never

ABOUT THE AUTHOR

Brenda Discher is a digital go-to-market strategist known for launching market leading products and brands that change the world. She is a thought and business leader with over 20 years of success in bringing products, brands, and businesses from inception to market. She is an accomplished global leader known for driving change, brand innovation and deep customer engagements that ensure customers use and expand their IT investment. Brenda's creative mindset, combined with her deep product management/marketing knowledge and powerful communications expertise, make her a valuable partner to CEOs looking to strategically transform their brand and position within the marketplace. Brenda currently serves as Senior Vice President for Business Strategy and Marketing for Siemens Digital Industries Software. In this role, Brenda is responsible for integrating and unifying the strategy and marketing organizations of Siemens Digital Industries Software. She manages global brand, communications and digital go-to-market strategies to establish Siemens Digital Industries Software as a market leader in the manufacturing industry for both enterprise and SMB customers. Before joining Siemens, Brenda held various business transformation and SaaS marketing leadership positions at Autodesk.

been comfortable in broadcasting my interest; I simply didn't want to be stereotyped as a geek at a time in high school when cliques were forming. So, although I got along well with all different kinds of students, and was a cheerleader and swimmer, I kept my math abilities a secret. That changed when Mr. Leckrone asked me one day, "Why do you see it as a bad thing to be unique and smart?" I didn't have a good answer—and from then on, I embraced my love of math and got over the stigma of being a "math geek."

The second factor was that my parents owned an automotive tool and die shop; my stepfather was in R&D and my mother was the company's accountant. The shop was located just a few blocks down the street from my high school, so I regularly went there in the afternoons. Instead of doing my homework, though, I spent most of my time hanging out in the shop with the manufacturing engineers who worked on lathes, milling machines and general fabrication. So, it was by this curiosity and ability that my fascination with STEM developed.

I went on to attend Eastern Michigan University (EMU) in Ypsilanti, Michigan, where I received a bachelor of science in mechanical/industrial engineering and a master of business administration in international marketing and finance. It was at EMU that my mechanical drafting professor inspired the next stage in my engineering journey. I had started in the computer engineering and science program. But one night, I was in our computer lab when I decided to check out the area that had funny looking computers—I would learn these are CAD computers. I watched as one of the students drew circles and squares.

"What are you doing?" I asked.

"I have a CAD class. I'm in the industrial engineering program," he said. He explained how he was building a program that allows people to draw different shapes and then make them different colors. He was basically drawing stick figures.

This was wildly different than my basic computer science courses and I could see the benefits of using math and science in such a visual way. Within 24 hours, I switched my focus, entered the technology program and never looked back. I was so thrilled with this newfound technology that I encouraged others to switch their focus as well.

Dr. Griess, my mechanical drafting professor, inspired me to pursue this passion and help bring more attention to the College of Technology, which included publicly speaking about the program, giving tours to incoming students and starting a new computer lab focused on CAD that was funded by the engineering program. My interest in the program never waned and it's because of these experiences that I'm a mentor at EMU today. (I'm also a board member and mentor for the business school at EMU.) I not only helped Dr. Griess expand the program, he helped me get my first internship and job after school.

Unfortunately, not all my experiences in college were as rewarding.

I had a welding professor who was very hard on the few women who took his course and it was abundantly clear that he did not support the notion of women in the plant/factory. He challenged many things about me and often criticized my clothes, my jewelry and my hair. For instance, I had gotten engaged during the semester I was in his class. After I had excitedly told everyone, he informed me that I couldn't wear my engagement ring—for safety reasons. When I noticed that several men in the class wore their high school class rings, I challenged him on it. He explained that they were "different kinds of rings." And it didn't end there. One day, I was told my scarf wasn't allowed in the lab. I could understand this "rule" if we were welding that day, and if we were, I would oblige. But we weren't welding—there was no reason for the "rule."

If there was one last insult from that welding professor, it came at the end of the semester when I received a C. I was confident my work was some of the best in the class and I knew he was grading me harder because I was a woman, and because I challenged him.

As much as it irritated me at the time, I didn't really raise this issue except to Dr. Griess, who told me to keep my head up and continue my hard work. I was determined to get through the class, so I didn't speak up. But I regret that decision. I suggest that if women were to encounter this hostility today from a professor, they should speak up and talk to counselors and others about the unfair treatment.

With the assistance of Dr. Griess, who had a good relationship with a company called Schlumberger, a global oilfield services company, I was able to procure an internship in my junior year. During that time, I developed a timekeeping program used in creating a chargeback model that could determine the cost and the time an engineer spent developing products versus time spent in meetings or at lunch.

Upon graduating, Schlumberger offered me a position in their CAD/CAM software training and technical documentation department, where I spent the next six-and-a-half years in their CAD/CAM division headquartered in Ann Arbor, Michigan. It was during this period that I experienced some of the hardest times being a woman in a male-dominated industry and workplace. I had been promoted into a management role quickly, and one of my tasks was teaching older men in the software and training/development group to use a new interface. There were constant rude jokes and inappropriate behavior towards me; for example, I heard from one guy comment, "How can a pretty little thing like you think you teach an old guy like me a new software tool?" There was little opportunity to talk to someone about the issue; I worried HR wouldn't take me seriously, or that it would affect my promotability. So I told myself, "Suck it up."

While I had developed a thick skin to deal with that sort of thing, the most unsettling time came when I was doing a presentation along with four men in front of a large group of executives. After I was introduced, one of the male executives in the audience shouted, "I don't need to hear what they have to say, I'll buy whatever she is selling!" I was horrified. But I bit my tongue, did my presentation—I killed it, by the way—and then left the room to call my mom. But not before this same man pursued me as I left, again giving me unwanted attention: He asked me if I wanted to go out for a drink.

When I spoke to human resources about the problem, I was told that this behavior was accepted in France (where the parent company was located, and where this executive was from) and nothing would likely happen. HR even told me that if I raised any red flags, it could reflect poorly on me. All I could do was tell my mother about the incident. She advised me to never be alone with this guy and request that he never be my direct supervisor or have direct contact with me.

I regret not making more of an issue with my company about this. I was so young and so worried about my job that I simply froze. I should have left the company when this happened, or at least been more vocal and formally documented the situation. It was a hard lesson to learn, but I know now that if women don't speak up, then nothing will change.

My career took a turn when I realized how much I loved working with customers and thinking about the value of the technology. I realized early on that moving from building software (R&D) to evangelizing software (marketing) would be more enjoyable and challenging. I wanted to work more on go-to-market strategies, rather than manage engineers who develop products.

By this time, I was married with two children, but that didn't stop my eagerness to pursue this new career path.

It started after I was hired at Autodesk, an engineering software company with headquarters in California, by a gentleman named Buzz Kross, who would become a great mentor and boss. I was at the Novi, Michigan, office. I started climbing the ladder right behind him: Whenever he received a promotion, I would be the one to take over his role or have increased responsibilities.

Buzz approached me one day to ask if I'd be interested in product marketing. This change request didn't come out of the blue. When I had started at Autodesk, I came in as a product manager because it was important that my new employer recognize that I didn't want the same role I held previously in R&D. I had remained in product management until, one day, Buzz decided to reorganize. He pulled me and a colleague into his office and flipped our roles, giving me the marketing director position and my colleague the product management position. While the change came as a shock, and there were growing pains in the beginning, within a few months Buzz had proven he knew what he was doing, and the change in positions was for the best. I have been happily in marketing ever since.

I stayed at Autodesk for 23 years, and in April 2018, I made a career change when I joined Siemens Digital Industries Software as their senior vice president of business strategy and marketing, based in Livonia, Michigan. In this role, I am responsible for unifying the strategy and marketing of a multi-billion-Euro organization, including managing their global brand, communications, and digital go-to-market strategies to establish the company as a market leader in the manufacturing industry.

Why Siemens, and why this role? Like most things in my life I love a challenge, and when my role changed at Autodesk and the opportunity for a new role required relocation, I decided I needed a plan B. I said to myself, before uprooting my entire family and moving, shouldn't I see what other opportunities exist in the market that would allow me to stay home?

With a plan B as well as a plan C in hand (plan C was leading the marketing for a small Ann Arbor-based startup software company), I was in the driver's seat: I was able to pick the role that met my needs and my situation, ultimately leading me to join Siemens.

At Siemens, my day-to-day job is to drive change and help the company evolve historical practices and programs. It challenges me to radically question if these practices will work for the next five to 10 years. As a change agent, I work to identify and evangelize a vision for change, and then develop the talent and processes to make it real for the organization.

Some men simply don't understand us. Take my father: When I was 18 years old and a freshman at college, he told me it was a bad idea as a female to attempt to get a mechanical engineering degree, since I also planned on being a wife and a mother. His exact words: "Getting a degree will be useless." Once I proved him wrong, he wondered why I even needed a boyfriend, especially since I had a great job offer. He couldn't see the point of a female needing a career if she wanted a family life, and conversely why she would need a husband if she wanted a career.

And then there was that professor who made life miserable when I was in his class. I'm sure there are people like him everywhere who go out of their way to make things harder for women by "testing" our conviction or questioning our capabilities. And while these poisonous thoughts and actions may be decreasing, they're still prevalent. Women want to be treated fairly and respectfully so it's important to recognize these as challenges we face, things we must power through. Throughout high school and college, while I had the support of my mother, I felt I had to prove to my father that being a woman didn't exclude me from a career in STEM—or preclude me from being a wife and a mother.

I've been fortunate that I found a husband who, through a series of events, took on the role of being a stay-at-home parent to our two boys and who has been very supportive of my career aspirations. It's wonderful to know that my sons have no preconceived notions about men who stay at home as a parent, or women who enter a male-dominated industry.

That's the funny thing, though; everyone has their own backgrounds that can aid or hinder their thinking. I grew up surrounded by men, always. I didn't have sisters, just brothers. I hung around the tool and die shop learning engineering by observing the men there. I was one of only five women in a mechanical engineering program among hundreds of male students. Now, I'm married with two boys. This has all played to my advantage; I'm comfortable around men.

So what does the future hold for women in male-dominated industries? And where does a girl begin learning and loving STEM? I'm a big supporter in FIRST Robotics, Lego Leagues and "maker" movement teams where girls can collaborate, problem-solve and use STEM skills in real-world applicable conditions. I encourage both girls and boys to get involved in these teams, even if they don't want to pursue engineering, or it's not one of their "skills." There are plenty of other opportunities, such as marketing, support fundraising, or even t-shirt designs. These teams are all about people coming together for a common cause for something that has meaning.

I currently mentor three robotics teams and I'm involved in female coding initiatives. I was fortunate to have learned and appreciated engineering because of the shop, but I recognize that not every student has that exposure. Robotics teams are great at teaching skills needed to fill in the growing skills gap. The initiative to support women in engineering is quite rewarding, and the more women that get involved with these types of activities, the more support and scholarship opportunities will become available. I've also sponsored and helped establish my sons' robotics teams while sponsoring additional teams in a school district that had relatively few options; this includes mentoring girls' robotics groups as well.

There is plenty of work that needs to be done when it comes to encouraging women to be engineers or to enter a STEM field. Overall, we need to build a better support system for very young kids to help them overcome the initial shock that comes with the introduction of the early traditional math/science programs. It's critical for girls to understand how math and science works around us. The more we cater to young kids and connect the real world to the learning, the more their interest will hold in the important STEM disciplines. Things are changing slowly for the better, but it's critical to change the way math and science are currently being taught.

Unfortunately, stereotypes still exist. In my personal life, when asked what I do, the reaction is almost always uniformly the same: they're surprised that I have a background in engineering and that I'm using STEM skills in a male-dominated industry. They say things like, "Wow, you don't look like an engineer."

Maybe I don't. I'm boisterous and outspoken, two qualities that don't align with the "math geek" stereotype. I like to drive change and solve the hard problems that require complex answers. You don't have to look a certain way or be a certain gender to love math and science. I believe the more practical exposure children have to STEM, combined with the consistent encouragement from parents, teachers, mentors, and an expanding circle of smart individuals, the more they'll strive to enter these incredible fields and achieve success even in the face of challenges.

To conclude, I want to share my three most critical career learnings.

1. **Have a great mentor and advocate.** From Mr. Leckrone to Dr. Griess to Buzz Kross, I was honored to have great mentors advocate on my behalf when I wasn't in the room. It is important that women engineers actively engage with younger women, encourage them, mentor them, and advocate for them. You can make a major impact if you mentor just one or two women who could eventually become an engineer. Best of all, it's a fairly easy thing to do, and it's very rewarding!

2. **Build a personal network.** Every position and job opportunity I had, including my current one, would not have happened if I didn't tap into my network. It's not about popularity; it's about having a network of people you trust and stay in regular contact with. You also must give back to them. I'm a big proponent of giving more than you take.

3. **Timing.** We live in a world where things are unpredictable. Carefully think about yourself and your goals, so that when an opportunity presents itself, you can take advantage of it. If I wasn't self-managing my goals, I wouldn't have been able to take advantage of ideas when they presented themselves.

JOURNEY 10

REAL SUCCESS IS IN TOUCHING HUMANS AND ADDING VALUE FOR HUMANITY

TUNCAY DÖĞEROĞLU

Rector
Eskisehir Technical University

TURKEY

Since my childhood, I have questioned what we expect from life: to be a successful student, to attend the university that we really want, to have a job we love, to advance in a professional career, to be a wealthy person.

Are these really the things we need to be happy? Or is it better to be remembered as someone who touched the lives of others and made a huge contribution to their improvement? Someone who has been pleased by the success of others who are touched by him or herself?

I think the second option is the best. Because I strongly believe that the more a person grows and improves in his or her career, the more modest that person becomes.

How a person chooses to live his or her life depends so much on their background. Like states and nations, people have their own history. They make that personal history only with what they leave behind. Scientists, especially, should focus on the starting point of their own history when they question the meaning of their lives.

The starting point of my history is when I began my education at age three. I wore a school uniform and carried a very big school bag when I joined the rest of the children to start elementary school. I know for sure that I was more into reading books than playing games like the other

ABOUT THE AUTHOR

Dr. Tuncay Döğeroğlu received her BS, MS and PhD degrees in chemical engineering from Anadolu University. As a professor at Anadolu University's Environmental Engineering Department, she taught graduate and undergraduate courses in air pollution control, environmental management, and engineering statistics. She conducts research, in both national and international projects, on the health effects of air pollution and passive sampling. She has coauthored more than 100 publications, which are cited in many studies, and owns a utility model. Between 2004 and 2010, Tuncay served as Vice Dean of Anadolu University Faculty of Engineering and Architecture and Dean between 2010 and 2016. She has served as Secretary-General of the Turkish Engineering Deans Council (MDK), and board member at the Global Engineering Deans Council (GEDC), the European Society for Engineering Education (SEFI), and the International Federation of Engineering Education Societies (IFEES). She is currently a faculty member of Eskişehir Technical University's Department of Environmental Engineering and has been Rector of Eskişehir Technical University since 2018. She is a member of the Higher Education Quality Council, Turkey's Presidential Education Policies Council, and the Islamic World Science Citation Center.

children. I spent all my pocket money on books, and I was happy whenever someone gifted me a book.

I still keep the signed book that was given to me as a gift by my primary-school teacher when I learned how to read. It was a children's novel called Away from Home. Inside the book was my teacher's handwritten note: "My little daughter, I wish you a successful and happy life. This is my gift to you, with my best wishes. Your teacher, Mistafa Yasatan, December 12, 1970."

Because of the nature of my father's job, I lived in several different cities throughout Turkey during my childhood years, from elementary school through to high school. I struggled with the challenges that come with repeatedly moving to new cities; it was hard at that time to realize there were advantages to it.

But when I think about it now, I can obviously see that being a child who frequently moves created certain talents, such as an awareness of people from different cultures and systems, and an ability to adapt to various conditions or positions. My efforts to manage human relations, to express myself, and to gain my place in society naturally began in my childhood.

※ ※ ※

As a child, I behaved just like a teacher; I used teach my friends math, science, and chemistry regardless of whether they were younger than me or not. My intense interest in chemistry, combined with my mother's respect for and interest in chemical engineering—she herself was really good at chemistry when she was at school, and her knowledge of it is still really good—are probably what led me to choose chemical engineering as a profession. And when I decided to enroll in university to study chemical engineering, the goal of a career in academia felt like the most natural thing in the world. The idea of searching, learning new things, and obtaining various points of view is deep inside me.

Immediately after I graduated with my bachelor's degree, I started to assist in the applied classes and the laboratory classes; I lectured ceramic technologies classes for vocational school students while I was studying for my master's degree. Afterwards, I decided to proceed into the PhD program on process and reactor design within the scope of chemical engineering. I gave lectures on reaction engineering, reactor design, and plant design, and some courses like environmental management, air quality management, and statistics of engineering in the department of environmental engineering. I feel lucky that I could do what I wanted.

The postdoctoral term is a crucially important period when academics can notice everything surrounding them. This is the point when a scientist can be face-to-face with the science in real life, when the structure that he or she has constructed with theoretical knowledge and experiences suddenly turns into concrete practices.

Right after I finished my PhD, I spent a period at the University of Pittsburgh's department of chemical and petroleum engineering, and I can absolutely define that period as the best chance I have ever had to practice "real-life experiences." This period added crucial value that I would benefit from for the rest of my life.

I went to the CNR Air Pollution Institute in Rome for 18 months, and this made a big contribution in my scientific and cultural experiences. The best part was the strong friendships I built during those days. Even today Rome is like a second home to me, and I always make sure to stop there if I am visiting Italy; I feel I will see someone I know around any corner.

※ ※ ※

My studies made a large and lasting impact on me. My post PhD topic was air pollution, within environmental engineering. One of the studies that left the most traces on me was the "Together Towards to Clean Air" project, which was supported by the Ministry of Foreign Affairs in the Netherlands within its Matra Program. The program's general objective is to contribute to the development of a plural democracy grounded in the rule of law, with room for dialogue between government and civil society; to build capacity and strengthen the institutions of civil society and government; and to strengthen bilateral relations.

I set much store on this project, carried out in collaboration with the University of Utrecht and Nijmegen University in the Netherlands and the Institute of Public Health; we were able to touch the lives of more than 10,000 of children. The project was really significant both for its scientific contribution and social responsibility, and its widespread impact on other people and groups. I carried out this project with students from different degree levels (associate, bachelor's, master's, and PhD) in collaboration with researchers from Holland's Nijmegen University and Utrecht University. It was about indoor and outdoor air pollution measurements, composing pollution maps, individual exposure measurements, respiratory function tests, biological sampling, determining the effects of air pollution on human health, and awareness instruction. It was carried out in two big cities (Eskişehir in central Turkey and Hatay-İskenderun in the southeast), and because its focus was both science and social responsibility, it made for a very satisfying and important project. It meant that we could give meaning to lives of many children and their families via our fact-finding reports regarding decision makers, and our goal of finding solutions to current problems. In this context, I would like to remind others that, no matter what you are studying, your primary aim should be to give meaning and sense to the lives of humans, for the good of all mankind.

I've learned that the success of a scientist can never be measured only by their contributions to the scientific environment; all scientists should be aware that we bear responsibility for all mankind. This was certainly the case in my science life; I continued to lecture at the undergraduate and graduate levels throughout my time in academia. However, I have been taking charge of preparing my country's plans for higher education quality and doing administrative duties for my university. It makes me sad that I am not able to lecture any more; I would like to. Basically, I am happy and satisfied when I am in close contact with my students and can witness their personal improvement.

As a result of my graduate courses and studies, I trained seven master's and three PhD students. These numbers have unfortunately remained limited over time due to my administrative duties, which I have done for much of my academic life. Over the past 15 years I have been spending the majority of my energy and time on quality assurance topics in higher education. This, to me, along with increasing the quality of engineering education, is a crucial objective.

Right after serving as a co-head of my department for more than three years, I served as an associate dean and then dean for 12 years. During this period, we achieved a lot: we provided high-quality teamwork on improving education and training processes and program accreditation; adopted a corporate performance management approach; implemented an EFQM excellence model in the faculty; and contributed to the faculty's institutionalization.

Since then, I have had some valuable duties, such as being a consultant to the Council of Higher Education (CoHE), member of the Higher Education Quality Council, and vice-president of Higher Education Quality Council. Thanks to these duties I had the chance to closely observe and contribute to Turkey's higher education system. I was also honored to have been entrusted with the role of founding rector of Eskişehir Technical University. While restructuring a new university is a difficult and painstaking process, it is also very exciting to be able to achieve something and leave a lasting legacy of that work.

※ ※ ※

To contribute to the development of engineering education by working with the Turkish Engineering Deans Council (TEDC), where I was elected as a board member in 2011, has given me an inutterable honor. We completed our first strategic plan work with engineering deans between 2013 and 2016, when I was secretary general of TEDC. During my tenure, we prepared a report entitled "The Problems of Engineering Faculties and Their Solutions" at the request of the Inter-University Council. We have presented three separate reports on the topics of minimum requirements for the opening of engineering programs upon the proposal of the Council of Higher Education; core curriculum implementation in engineering curricula; and the competency exam in engineering. With the support of engineering deans, significant contributions were made to the development of engineering education in our country. Although my executive committee memberships in TEDC came to an end in late 2018, I have honorary membership and I continue to make contributions whenever needed.

On the international platform, I am proudly following the global impact of IFEES, established in 2007 at the meeting hosted by Boğaziçi University (which I also helped manage for a period of time). It was priceless to have the experience of taking part in administrative bodies such as the GEDC and SEFI family. They are exemplary role models of positive interaction and cooperation at all levels, with the contribution of related organizations to the development and progress of engineering education.

I should remark that I am also very happy and proud to represent our country on the Board of the Islamic World Scientific Citation Center, which has 57 member countries across the globe. It is really exciting to be a part of this organization and its incoming tasks. Also, it was a great honor for me to be considered as a member of the Presidential Education and Training Policy Council. That committee is one of nine established by the Presidential Decree on the Presidential Organization No. 1, dated July 10, 2018; I am one of the nominated members. The duties and authorities of this council are as follows:

- To make policy recommendations on education and training activities in line with the objectives of Turkey.

- To make policy recommendations on identification and development of higher education strategies and objectives.
- To carry out studies regarding practice education and training activities.
- To make policy recommendations by developing needs analysis.
- To develop policy proposals to create an education system based on quality, equality, and effectiveness principles, and national and social values.
- To provide suggestions about strategic planning by making needs analysis about the faculties and departments to be opened in universities.
- To consider the country's workforce planning.
- To create education and training policies by considering the country's workforce planning.
- To develop policy recommendations on identifying implementation of European Union education and youth programs.
- To create policy and carry out research on European Union education and youth programs to determine implementation of them.
- To create policy and carry out research on planning of formal, non-formal and apprenticeship training, vocational and technical

training, schools and institutions and enterprises of all kinds, and degrees in which vocational and technical education programs are applied.

I am proud to be the only female member of this high-level council, where my country's policies on all levels of education are discussed. And it is more important than ever for our students to graduate from university as individuals ready for life, complete with 21st century skills. I feel their responsibility in this sense. Academic and administrative staff and students were very pleased when I was appointed as the rector of the Eskişehir Technical University, and I am very happy that the private sector and non-governmental organizations shared this joy. However, the happiness of our partners also put a heavy responsibility on my shoulders. Although this has been the biggest challenge of my life, I am pleased to see the development of the university every day.

There are 12,500 students in my university, where I have been doing rectorship duty. We have started to construct the basis required for students to transform themselves into heroes! I can proudly say that they will gain life skills as well as skills related to their own fields, so that they can be qualified researchers. Our students and staff members will do this with team spirit; it's their big chance to recognize their own success stories. We know that they will be able to do it, thanks to a well-qualified and organized team!

※ ※ ※

Being a woman academic and university administrator in Turkey isn't as challenging as it is in other parts of the world. The rate of female academics in Turkey is about 45 percent; this seems very good when compared to some other countries. Academic life isn't easy. It requires many steps to gain the required education, to carry out research and to build a career. Because doing research and satisfying other requirements to be an academic happens both at home and at the office, female academics in Turkey face, as they do in many other countries, some difficulties in sustaining both a family and a professional life.

Despite the relatively high number of female academics in my country, unfortunately the number of women in academic administrative positions is low. Although attempts by the Council of Higher Education to increase female managers in academic and administrative staff have yielded results in recent years, the numbers are not yet at the desired levels. Women comprise 216 of 1,388 deans in state universities, and 106 of 409 deans in foundation universities; 18 percent of deans are women. As for female rectors, there are 17 in 207 universities, including 11 foundations.

For me, it is too early to determine the difficulties or advantages of being a rector, but I know that even though women rectors who have had this experience for many years have had quite a hard time, they have achieved very successful works. Also, it is really important for me to be one of only six female rectors in 129 public universities. As a woman and a rector, I am always happy to say that we are not competing with each other in the world of science. In this sense, we will support each other, learn from each other and get inspiration from each other.

I want to finish with this thought: I consider my very large network to be my greatest wealth. It was built over time, starting with my beloved primary-school teacher, my teachers at secondary school and university, my schoolmates, many friends both from my country and in other countries, and people I've worked with during my service at various organizations and boards, including the Executive Board of Islamic World Scientific Citation Center (ISC).

I am very happy to know that I have spent a certain period of my life with many different friends, both in my country and in many parts of the world. The fact that these relationships are still going strong after so many years, and that I'm always building new relationships, is a great feeling. Touching lives and contributing to the growth of successful people is important work.

It is never possible to have the last word when it comes to human life, your personal history and science. Another person takes the flag over from where you left it, and moves it forward. That's why writing is the most important thing you can do; it is the flag you leave to be carried forward.

JOURNEY 11

REFLECTIONS ON MAKING THE MOST OF OPPORTUNITIES

JANE GOODYER

-

Dean

Lassonde School of Engineering

York University

-

CANADA

Let me share with you the story of how I ended up being dean of an engineering school in Canada. I came from very humble beginnings. My father was a tool-maker and the main salary earner, and with a wife and two kids to support, life was hard. It was the early 1970s, and we lived in a small terraced house in an inner-city suburb of Birmingham, UK, called Winson Green, which is famous for its prison. Our house had no inside bathroom, only an outdoor toilet. I can remember being bathed in the kitchen sink. We even had to put coins in the TV to keep it going.

We moved around a lot (by the time I was 13, I had attended seven schools and moved house nine times). When I was 10, we were devastated when my mother died of cancer, and it really affected my father. He didn't take it well, and after that my brother and I didn't see much of him. We were given to various family members and friends to be looked after. A couple of years later, my dad met this amazing woman, called Tina, who became my stepmother. She was a very interesting person because she didn't learn how to read and write until she was 45 years old. She gave me confidence and really taught me the value of education.

In a way, she was the main reason I pursued an education at all. In my world, education wasn't important to a lot of my family members. Most of the time we were simply trying to get jobs and earn as much money as possible, just to pay the bills. But my stepmother saw my potential. She was an assembler operator at a local company that manufactured relay

ABOUT THE AUTHOR

Jane joined Lassonde School of Engineering in October 2018. Prior to her arriving in Toronto she worked at Massey University in New Zealand for 12 years, where she was a professor and, from 2017 to 2018, served as head of school in the School of Engineering and Advanced Technology. In this position, she was a member of the College of Sciences' executive team. She led strategic planning to reposition organizational structures, teaching, and research in the school. Prior to this appointment, she served as the school's associate dean for undergraduate teaching and learning, with responsibility for curriculum, and student success and welfare. In that role, she led a redesign of the curriculum, incorporating blended learning and project-based learning, resulting in improved student satisfaction and retention. Before her appointment at Massey University in 2006, she held an appointment at Coventry University in the UK, where she was part of a research center working with automotive businesses to apply cutting-edge research in advanced joining technologies for body-in-white manufacture. Jane is an advocate for the advancement of women in engineering. While in New Zealand she launched a national engineering outreach program for girls aged 10-14 to encourage girls to consider a career in engineering.

and power transmission systems, and one day she said, "Why don't you come over and see what we do? Maybe you could become an apprentice."

I took her up on the offer and was amazed that you could actually make things that transmit electricity into homes. I just took it for granted that electricity magically appeared. So, at the age of 14, I went to my school and told them I wanted to be an apprentice engineer. They told me, "You need to make sure you do your math, but you will also need to learn Latin." Clearly, my school had no idea what I needed to study to become an engineer, and neither did my stepmother. I know it sounds crazy, but I just went along with what the school said and dropped my physics course and did Latin for about a year. However, at some point someone told me, "Jane, you need to study physics if you want to work as an apprentice engineer." I had one year to catch up on two years' worth of physics classes, all because I had no idea it was required to study engineering.

At 16, I got my exam results—they were good—and I was ready to join that company as an apprentice, but they said to me, "Jane you did really well in your exams, so why don't you stay on at school for another two years?" This time I got the right advice and studied math, physics, and chemistry. During those two years I found math and physics to be really difficult; I struggled. The way they taught us at school was so theoretical that I had no idea what I was doing. Luckily, my stepmother got me a tutor.

I had it in my head that I wanted to be an engineer, but I didn't really know which discipline, as there were so many. Then something amazing happened in my last year of school when I was 17: I joined what was called the Young Enterprise Scheme, which is a UK national charity specializing in enterprise and financial education. I ended up on a team with 12 school friends as managing director. I absolutely loved it. I loved working under pressure, staying organized, and motivating people. During that time, I discovered the discipline of production/manufacture engineering, and to me it resonated because I could do some technical work while working with people.

I never did become an apprentice at that local manufacturer. Instead, I began to apply to universities in production engineering during my last year of school. That year, however, my dad left Tina and began divorce proceedings. I was devastated, but I still loved my dad, although I didn't see much of him due to his 12-hour work shifts. It was terrible for my stepmother; we believe stress triggered something in her, because she was taken to hospital and subsequently diagnosed with a rare auto-immune disease. She died just six weeks later. This was a lot for me and my brother to handle; we had now lost two mothers.

So at the age of 18, I had graduated from high school and had to leave the family home, as my father wanted to begin a new life with a new family. Luckily, at that time in the UK I didn't have to pay any fees to attend university, and I could apply for a grant for living expenses.

Unfortunately—and probably not surprisingly, given all of the changes going on in my family—I didn't do well on my exams, so rather than going to university I ended up going to a polytechnic in another city. At the time, I was really upset about it, but it ended up being the best thing to happen to me. The first year was amazing. I had small classes, and real engineers teaching me mathematics and actually putting everything in context. It left me wondering why they made math so hard at my previous school.

I was about to complete my first year when more bad news came, just before my exams: my father died of a sudden heart attack. I knew I had to sit the exams, because if I didn't pass them, I was going to be exited from my studies, without a home or a job.

I don't know how I did it, but I came top of the class. I had even bested someone who was being sponsored by his company to study for a degree. Apparently, his training manager asked him, "How could you have been beaten by a woman?" The training manager then asked me to see him, as he wanted to meet this woman who had beaten his top apprentice. I went to the company to meet him and, on the spot, he offered me a place in the engineering training program, where I would be paid and could still finish my degree. I couldn't believe it. I was really struggling financially, and it was just awesome to have this opportunity.

I did my degree in four years, including a year working in industry. I also graduated top of my class and went to work for the company that sponsored me during my degree, an automotive supplier that made brakes, clutches, and steering systems. There were about 5,000 employees at the company and 400 engineers of all types. I think I was one of two women engineers.

I'm a manufacturing engineer and the majority of work was with men. One of my early jobs was being a team leader for 15 men with an average age of 45 to 50 who were highly skilled setter-operators. It was quite something when a 22-year-old woman straight out of university was telling them what to do. It was the early 1990s and at that time I had to be chaperoned during the night-shift, as there were no women who worked that shift. That said, I had really found my niche. My idea of what production engineering should be played out perfectly: It was all about people.

My manager was a mechanical engineer, and very supportive. He actually said to me, "Jane, you are one of the best engineers I've ever come across." I never forgot that, and I've always treasured his support as it gave me strength and confidence. In fact, only very recently, I met with him after not seeing him for nearly 20 years. He is now 78. I told him what he said to me all those years ago and what that meant to me. He just couldn't believe what an effect he had on me and how that kept me going. He was instrumental in my academic career, too. I remember one day he said, "You need to go back to university. Do your PhD, do research."

After spending three years in the automotive industry I did go back to university to do a PhD. It was one of the hardest things to achieve, but it made me realize that I thoroughly enjoy teaching and working with people, and being able to share my experience with the next generation. After I got my PhD, I became a lecturer teaching manufacturing systems design. At that time, much of teaching was for mature learners who wanted to get a degree part-time. Hence, I did a lot of teaching in the evenings. I learned so much from these students, who brought their experience to the classroom.

Things were going well in my professional life, and I had married at age 24. But then another personal tragedy struck. When I was 35 a good friend of mine died of breast cancer; she was just one month older than me. She left behind a husband and two small children, and it really made me and my husband think, "Life is short. Sometimes you have to take a pause in life and reflect on what it is you are doing and whether it's meaningful or not."

It also got us thinking about those who have gone before us, and the fact that they didn't get the opportunity to live a full life. This gave us the impetus to make our lives as full as they could ever possibly be—to make sure we have rich, diverse experiences and fully utilize our capabilities in the process. We had traveled a lot, and were not fazed about living abroad.

And so, our next chapter began. We started looking for opportunities overseas (for example, in Cape Town), but I ended up obtaining a position as a senior lecturer at Massey University in New Zealand. My husband accompanied me without a job to go to, and we knew it would be a challenge for him to find appropriate work as he was also in the manufacturing industry. (New Zealand's strength is in the primary sector, not manufacturing.) We knew it would be quite a change to be living on one salary, at least initially, but we thought the opportunity overcame any financial uncertainty. We intended to stay for only three years. However, we ended up loving New Zealand and within a year I had an opportunity to become the university's associate dean of teaching and learning, and my husband settled in to work, too, albeit he took a job that didn't utilize his experience and skills. We ended up staying in New Zealand for 12 years.

A key part of my role was to transform the school's engineering curriculum. This was a huge challenge as any change is very difficult to get academics to align forward. But, again, I love working with people, and change is all about the people. I spent the next six years working on that program development and implementation. The result was a fantastic degree and I'm pleased with the work done by all. It wasn't just about seeing the students graduate, but also seeing my fellow colleagues so engaged in the process.

During that time one of the professors urged me to become a Fellow of Engineering New Zealand and also of the Institution of Engineering and Technology in the UK for my work in engineering education. I would have never thought of doing something like that. At first, I didn't see the benefit, as I already had a lot to do in my daily life. Plus, I'm not very good at promoting myself. However, my husband is such a driving force, and he strongly encouraged my nomination.

I've never been one to seek impressive titles or spotlight; I've just never been that status-driven. But looking back, these things have actually been very important for me in advancing my career, because for others looking at you, who don't really know you, "titles" show them what you are capable of. As someone who cares deeply about what's happening around me, and who wants to make change for the better, I learned that sometimes you need the promotion or the title to create change.

Then something big happened. I arrived at the university at the start of 2017 prepared for another year of teaching, but it became clear the school was potentially in trouble. They'd been looking for a new head of school for a while but couldn't find anyone. I went to the provost and told him my concerns. He asked me what I would do about it and so I told him, in no uncertain terms. Before I knew it, I became the head of school—and I quickly learned that this was the job I'd always wanted. It was amazing. Again, it is all about the people, and that is my greatest motivator in any job.

Eighteen months later I was approached by York University in Toronto to become dean of the Lassonde School of Engineering. I wasn't interested, as I loved living in New Zealand, but agreed to have a telephone interview; I was intrigued by their vision to create the Renaissance Engineer (a term that they had trademarked). But shortly after they approached me, my husband suffered a heart attack and went into cardiac arrest. Luckily, when it happened he was with someone who knew how to do CPR and use a defibrillator. He survived! He spent a month in hospital and then had another six weeks of recovery. This was a life-changing event: After living in New Zealand for 12 years and even becoming New Zealanders, we knew we needed to be closer to our family. We made the decision to go back to the UK.

However, life, it seemed, had other plans for us. The week after we made the difficult decision to move back to the UK, York University contacted me again and asked, "Could we convince you to visit us? We are still interested." This time, without reservation, I replied, "Yes. I am ready to leave New Zealand." After all, I thought, Toronto is much closer to the UK than New Zealand is.

When I visited York University, what struck me the most were the people I met. They wanted to transform engineering education to equip graduates with the empathy and perspective to tackle global issues. York convinced me to join, and I was very excited at the prospect. My husband and I left NZ in October 2018 to begin working at York University: I as Dean of Lassonde School of Engineering, and my husband in research support services. In fact, if it weren't for York's spousal hiring policy, it would have been difficult for us to have considered the move as we both needed jobs to support our living expenses in Toronto.

I still can't believe I'm in Canada. Sometimes I miss New Zealand, but Toronto is such an incredible city, and it's very culturally diverse. Also, the people I initially met have lived up to my first impressions. I work with an awesome group.

I am happy to say that in this moment, I feel that my life so far has been very fulfilled. My job is amazing, and I get to work on interesting projects and meet some wonderful people in the process.

Despite this, I can't forget all the low points I have experienced. I have been through a ton of personal challenges that have left me grieving, angry, frustrated, and financially stressed. I have collected a lot of memories, experiences, and successes, but I've lost a lot, too—my parents, and my best friend. These are realities of my lived experience, which is uniquely my own. I haven't let these struggles define me, but they are part of who I am and whom I've become, and are part of the path I've taken. Even in my darkest times I remained focused on the bigger picture, cultivating opportunities for myself because I knew no one else would.

Many people don't get the opportunity to live a full life, and being on this earth is not a privilege I take lightly.

I can pass on this wisdom: In times of hardship or happiness, always try to find time for reflection. Ask yourself, "Am I making the most of what I'm doing at this very moment?" And if you are not, do something about it!

JOURNEY 12

THE DIFFERENCE THAT PARENTS CAN MAKE

MARIA JOÃO VIAMONTE

Dean
Instituto Superior de Engenharia do Porto
President
Engineering of Porto

PORTUGAL

I was born in the coastal city of Porto, Portugal, in 1969. When I was three years old, my parents decided to move back to their home town of Vila Real, a little town in Portugal's interior. My brother was born there, and we grew up in a happy, healthy, and very peaceful environment. Those years were wonderful. Portugal has always been a relaxed, easygoing country, and, in a way, old-fashioned. Yes, I lived in a small town that was traditional and conservative, but in spite of that I had a lot of freedom and was surrounded by many friends.

My parents, well-known people in our town, were teachers in the fields of history and literature. They brought me and my brother up to be good students, responsible and happy. My brother and I received an equal education; there was no difference. Unlike other girls at that time, I didn't have what was considered the "traditional" upbringing for girls—the kind of upbringing that prepared you to marry and live for your family. On the contrary, my parents raised me to become independent, strong, and professionally fulfilled.

I returned to Porto, alone, to study at the university when I was 17, and graduated in the field of computer science. Those were wonderful years during which I experienced what it was like to be completely free, and with the weight of responsibility. Fortunately, I had always been responsible and able to manage my time. For this reason, I was both a good student and able to enjoy all the perks of the academic life. During this period, I made lifelong friends.

I finished my degree and went to work in industry; I joined the informatics department of a Porto company that was part of the international

ABOUT THE AUTHOR

Maria João Viamonte is a Professor of Computer Engineering at the Institute of Engineering of Porto (ISEP), and has been Dean there since April 2018. ISEP is the oldest and one of the leading reference-engineering public institutes in Portugal. She has also been Vice-President of the scientific council for nine years. Maria received her PhD in electrical engineering in 2004 from the University of Trás-os-Montes and Alto Douro, Portugal, and works in the area of Artificial Intelligence with special interest in multi-agent simulation, agent-mediated electronic commerce, semantic web technology, and decision support systems. She has been involved in several projects involving the development and use of Knowledge-Based systems, Modelling and Simulation, Multi-Agent systems, Emotional Behavior, Data Mining, Ontology Matching Services, and Social Network. She has been published in more than 60 international publications, including in journals and book chapters.

group Hoechst AG. There, I met many engineers from different fields and had the opportunity to grow professionally, and to awaken to the world of engineering. Although the company's environment was industrial, it was also very friendly. There were many more male engineers than female (which is still the case today in most of Portugal's engineering companies), but I never felt any gender discrimination.

As I was still young—it was 1994 and I was 25—my parents believed I should continue my education, and advised me to keep studying. Although I was independent, living on my own, and free to make my own decisions, I knew my parents were well-informed people who always gave me good guidance, so I followed their advice. Besides, I was also missing the academic life, and wished to go further in my studies. But I couldn't decide whether I should enroll in another bachelor's degree, in either economics or management, or get a master's degree. In Portugal in the 1990s it was unusual to do a master's degree, especially if you had already chosen a career in industry. In the end, my choice was to enroll in a master's course in systems engineering.

Today I realize it was one of the best decisions of my life. I was in a new academic atmosphere, the University of Minho, and living in a new city, Braga, in the north of Portugal. There, I deepened the knowledge I had acquired when I did my bachelor's degree. My thesis work was in the field of communications networks and information systems. I undertook a study that analyzed the feasibility of integrating internet information services. This was done using different protocols (e.g., Gopher, News, Archie,

WWW, anonymous FTP and WAIS) in a single application, creating a system that provided its users with easy access to information, and made transparent the interoperation between those services. As you can see, that was a very different time: those technologies are now outdated, as all IT changes very quickly.

When I was developing my thesis, I took advantage of some free time by teaching at the university, discovering a fondness for teaching. Paradoxically, at that time it hadn't crossed my mind that teaching could end up being what I would do full-time in my future professional career.

During the years I worked in industry, I had the opportunity to work abroad. I really enjoyed it, so it was great when, after finishing my master's degree in 1996, I started working for a Barcelona-based company, called Herberts Barcelona, that was associated with the one I'd worked for before. It was a great period, because it tested my limits: On the one hand, I had an enormous desire to have new experiences, but on the other hand, I had a fear of the unknown, and I was homesick. I needed to have family and friends around me. So, working in a different culture was a very important personal-growth experience for me.

When I returned from Spain in early 1997, I continued to work in industry, but I also became an assistant professor at Instituto Superior de Engenharia do Porto (ISEP), an engineering school. My fondness for teaching had grown and I saw both activities as complementary: I felt that my experience in industry could benefit the students. Over the course of one semester I divided my time between industry and teaching in higher education.

My time working in industry may be described as an experience full of challenges and emotions that made me grow professionally and as a person. At a certain point the desire to embrace teaching as a full-time career began to grow, and staying committed to both became difficult. Although it was not an easy decision, as both career paths were full of opportunities, I ended up choosing academic life.

In September 1997 I became a full-time professor at ISEP, and a member of the research group in computer integrated manufacturing, in the field of applied artificial intelligence. I developed activities related to the engineering of knowledge and decision support systems. Later this research group became a new research group in engineering of knowledge and decision support systems.

Between 2001 and 2004 I was fully committed to developing my PhD, with a scholarship. My PhD thesis was focused on the field of artificial intelligence; I proposed a multi-agent model for an electronic marketplace in a business-to-consumer context. I defended my PhD thesis on December 22, 2004. I loved this period of my life. Full-time research is rewarding when you are deeply involved with a project. When I have more time, I'll probably go back to research.

In November 2009 I was invited by the president of the school to become vice-president of the Technical Scientific Council (TSC), a position that I occupied until March 2018. The TSC is one of the management boards that plays a big role in the daily life of my school's staff, and has important interactions with external entities. This position has given me great personal and professional satisfaction, not to mention valuable experience and a deep knowledge of the school.

When the right moment came, I took some time to quietly reflect on and decide what I wanted to do next. The appointment to ISEP's presidency became obvious; I felt ready and motivated to hold such a position, but above all I believed I could return, with added value, everything that ISEP had invested in me over the 20 years that I was a teacher, researcher, and manager.

I was elected in March 2018 to lead ISEP from 2018 to 2022, and I took office on April 4, 2018. I am grateful to my parents for having supported my choices, even when they differed from what they had dreamed of for me. I always felt their unconditional support. I am the first woman to be elected to lead an engineering school in Portugal, an institution with 167 years of history. This has been a great point of pride for my parents, especially for my father, who had been ill; sadly, only 22 days after I assumed ISEP's presidency, he passed away.

I cannot finish without saying that the man I choose to be by my side is my biggest supporter, and Tomás, our fantastic little son, gives meaning to everything. I hope I can pass to him my commitment to my job and to the joy of living. I truly believe that today's woman can be a mother, can embrace love—and can also be a successful professional.

JOURNEY 13

A LETTER TO SOPHIE

GUDRUN KAMMASCH

Professor
Beuth Hochschule für Technik Berlin

GERMANY

This letter is addressed to all young women who are interested in natural and engineering sciences. I have listened to their questions in hundreds of talks throughout my professional life. Here is how I would answer one of these women. I'll call her Sophie.

※ ※ ※

Dear Sophie,

We have had a long chat about your career choice. Your father has managed to spark in both children a great enthusiasm for his own profession, and your mother, for her part, rejoiced in the way both you and your younger brother inventively and perseveringly engaged in craft-making, and designed audacious constructions—ones that you were also able to implement. From an early age you became fascinated with being able to meet and overcome challenges. And now the time has come that you have finished school and are facing the decision: Should you become a woman engineer in today's world?

Dear Sophie, you have already discovered through your own experience that nowadays, here in the centre of Europe, this choice of profession will open doors everywhere, in particular for young women. And yet, at first you hesitated, then you paused, and now the questions have started to emerge:

- Why indeed do so few women study STEM subjects?

ABOUT THE AUTHOR

Gudrun Kammasch, Professor of Food Chemistry and Analysis in Food Technology at Beuth Hochschule für Technik Berlin (UAS), is president of IPW e.V., Ingenieurpädagogische Wissenschaftsgesellschaft / Scientific Society for Engineering Education, and also a member of the German UNESCO Committee. She has more than 35 years of teaching experience in food and packaging chemistry and analysis (with comprehensive lab education), in nutrition sciences, and in general subjects such as sustainability and women in technical careers. She has delivered workshops on lab didactics in Europe and other continents and worked as consultant in curriculum reform in Ethiopia and Central Asia for more than 12 years. She is the author of numerous papers and book chapters and has edited several proceedings of international conferences in engineering education. For almost 20 years she organized the integration of international students at her university. In her academic career she held the position of vice president of the university, dean, and others. In 2010 Dr. Kammasch received the Bundesverdienstkreuz 1. Klasse award from the president of the FRG especially for her engagement in implementing the "dialogue of the cultures of the world" as well as improving the situation of women in technical studies and professions, both in industry and academic careers.

- And, once I have finished studying, will I be taken seriously? Will I be welcomed into the still mainly male-dominated world of technology and science? Will my wish to start a family be met with understanding?
- And looking at the world, does not technology above all play a significant role in the ongoing destruction of the environment, the ghastly destruction wreaked by war? With all these questions, will I find my own career path?

Your questions have touched me deeply and even after our conversation, they have continued to occupy my mind; they are of fundamental importance. During the course of my life, these questions had in fact also become my own questions and I kept coming back to them. We will not be able to answer them once and for all. Your questions have now spurred me again to reflect on my own experiences, with the benefit of hindsight. In doing so, I found myself wishing to write this letter to you.

WHY IS IT THAT SO FEW WOMEN STUDY STEM SUBJECTS?

The fact that women have gained access to higher education is only a recent development of the past 100 years. Even nowadays, this is not a matter of course everywhere in this world. Certain socialist countries are—or were—the exception, even though the choice of career was often directed by the state. During the period of reunification of the two German states,

I got to know established, experienced female engineers, charming and self-confident women from the GDR. One of them, for example, was a passionate specialist of wheel suspension for rail vehicles. In actual fact, she had wanted to become a shoe designer; when the time came to choose her course of studies, however, there was no available university place.

The engineering profession developed in the 19th century, at a time when bourgeois women did not pursue a career. And even when subsequent access to universities became available, technology in general was not a subject offered in the schools preparing for university studies (this partly prevails to this day). Girls otherwise also had hardly any contact with technology; there were no role models. In Tübingen, a university town where I grew up, I was exposed to a plethora of stimulating ideas from the fields of culture and science, but came into nearly no contact with technology. I had gotten to know solid craftsmanship to be sure, but no industry, and no engineers. Back then, in the 1950s, female engineers were quite unheard of.

HOW DID MY PATH UNFOLD?

In my family home, there was a dearth of natural sciences, no technology in sight. History, art and music, in addition to sport, were my favorite subjects—in my first chemistry exam I actually "achieved" an F (a fail). Then my future brother-in-law stepped into my life: as a student of palaeontology, he had also studied chemistry as a minor subject. He pointed out, encouragingly, that it was rather easy to understand! Thus he introduced me to the secrets of atomic structure and the periodic table. I was enthusiastic about how I could deduce the properties of all the elements by virtue of my own thinking, yes, even "create" the elements. I learned by the process of reviewing and checking to trust my own thoughts. Dear Sophie, perhaps at that time I glimpsed something that Immanuel Kant had noted in 1786:

> "Thinking for oneself means seeking the supreme touchstone of truth in oneself (i.e., in one's own reason); and the maxim of always thinking for oneself is enlightenment." (I. Kant, "What does it mean to orient oneself in thinking?" 1786, Footnote 7, transl. Allen W. Wood, in: *Immanuel Kant, Religion and Rational Theology*, transl. and edit. by Allen W. Wood and George di Giovanni, Cambridge University Press, 1996.)

My teacher in grammar school, a genuine pedagogue, caught this change in *statu nascendi* (roughly, "in the course of being formed"), and his reaction was encouraging. And at home, my always curious father asked during lunch, "And, what have you been up to in chemistry? I have been out of touch with it for a long time." I loved relating news from my chemistry lessons and he took an avid interest. I was attending a girls-only grammar school at the time, which certainly also contributed to my development and my later choice of studies. In this situation, my new passion for chemistry was certainly noticed.

THE DELIGHT IN FACING AND OVERCOMING CHALLENGES

Yet there is something else that is decisive: an inner bearing, an attitude, which is essential for following a path less trodden and arriving at the goal. I am curious to know your thoughts about this, as I could sense the same attitude in you. I am referring to the delight in new challenges and the perseverance and resilience, occasionally even the tenacity, to follow something once begun through to the end result.

In order to acquire the extensive fundamentals in scientific-technical areas—a prerequisite for thinking through the mathematically or "merely" qualitatively construed connections and for developing true understanding—you will need plenty of stamina. As when doing training pull-ups or when climbing mountains, you will start to sweat and be in doubt, sometimes almost in despair, as to whether you will make it, and then you will experience the breakthrough, often with your last strength. You've done it, you've arrived, and you've got a great view.

A colleague of mine told his students that the Latin word for "study," *studere*, derives from endeavour (to dedicate oneself to something). The reward is the deeply felt joy of understanding, of entering into the world of knowledge. But this attitude is also of paramount importance during the whole course of studies, up to and including professional qualification.

What are my roots of this approach, of this inner attitude? I have reflected on this a lot. Was it the experience from sports, the combined competitions in gymnastics—with the insight gained here that training makes it possible to master what was supposedly unattainable, to overcome one's own limits? Was it the basic attitude of refugees like my father in the post-war period—the indomitable will to rebuild, to lead a better life?

Or was it the many people who accompanied me here and enjoyed my progress? There were quite a few of those: fellow students with whom I spent long nights discussing technical issues and questions and long days surviving the daily ups and downs in the laboratory; the teaching staff, the doctoral supervisor, "mountain guides" who blazed the trail into the world of science; my older sisters who encouraged me to follow the path, still unusual at the time, to a doctorate and professorship; and even with my little family and offspring.

All of them cheered me along this journey, and I am ever so grateful to them. I believe and know from experience, Sophie, that one thing is incredibly important: we need people who value our path and encourage us, especially when we feel dispirited or even encounter people who express their skepticism at a young woman on a path of life that is still somewhat unusual today. Usually I was able to take note of this in a slightly amused way, though sometimes it hurt me.

THE WAY INTO THE PROFESSIONAL WORLD

Today, as a woman, you too have access to the most diverse opportunities around the globe. Basically, this was also true for my generation, but on the way there, the obstacles were even more abundant and harder to overcome. What soon became clear to me, however, was that as a chemist, a doctorate was indispensable. I was the first woman to pursue a PhD with my doctoral supervisor. During these years I gained extensive experience in analytical and organic chemistry, and I also supervised student laboratory exercises—and made a big discovery: I discovered that I had great pleasure in introducing inquisitive young people to the highly complex world of chemistry and its applications, in leading them step by step to knowledge in conversation. This was to become my world!

Against the background of my practical professional experience, I soon received as one of the first women a call to the University of Applied Sciences in Berlin in the field of food technology. Now I had arrived in the world of engineers; all fields of engineering sciences were and are represented at my university. Originally a natural scientist, I now got to know the point of view of engineers.

WHAT IS SO FASCINATING ABOUT THE ENGINEERING PROFESSION?

Being able to solve problems! I love those people who face reality head on. A problem? While other people often shy away, they take on the challenge almost like an adventure, as a matter of course. They consider the problem, analyze it—and get down to it. And when they can't progress any further, they involve others, ask others. Working in a team, cooperating is familiar to most of them. That's the engineer, female and male: accepting challenges courageously, mastering them with knowledge and ability—and not shying away from effort and sweat. Just as you are today, I felt drawn by this world of action, of what is feasible!

But my post-war generation was profoundly influenced by the exploration of the causes and consequences of World War II and the industrial extermination of human beings that was possible in the concentration camps. The discussion of the aftermath of the atomic bombs on Hiroshima and Nagasaki was also a fundamental childhood experience. The reflex that not everything that is doable should be done is deeply rooted in me; it has become my professional ethos.

And there I was in this world, a young woman with a little son, a family, with predominantly male colleagues and already with some female students—and they asked me the question you ask today:

DOES THE WORLD OF TECHNOLOGY, WHICH IS STILL DOMINATED BY

MEN, WELCOME ME WITH GOOD WILL? AND WILL IT UNDERSTAND MY DESIRE TO ALSO START A FAMILY?

Oh Sophie, what can I say; this question has remained the central question for the decades. In the meantime, the professional world has opened up more to this issue and nowadays, young men who consciously want to devote more time to their families are also asking the very same question.

When I was a young professional, there were no family-friendly legal regulations. In my case as I was a civil servant there was either a full-time position—or none. If I have one regret in my life, then it is this: not having more time in the precious first years of seeing one's child grow up. Even today, this phase of life demands difficult decisions from young parents, because engineers in positions of responsibility are often tied to ongoing production and have an "international schedule"—there simply are no easy solutions. Nevertheless, we must do everything in our power to ensure the compatibility of family and career, including in the professional world of engineers.

YET ONE FURTHER QUESTION

But there is another question that has preoccupied you when looking at the world: our world today is full of "technical creatures." As never before in human history, the world is shaped by human inventiveness. But strategies from the world of economics and business management, as well as politics, often intervene directly in their implementation, based on non-technical motives, based on the lust for power and the pursuit of profit. In this context, has technology not also played a significant role in the environmental destruction that has occurred? Was it not technology that made it possible in the first place for us to develop high-tech weapons with a vast destructive potential, enough to wipe out humanity several times over? Should we not, today, before it is too late, face up to our responsibility towards humanity—towards those who live today and towards future generations?

BEING AN ENGINEER IN THE 21ST CENTURY: RESPONSIBILITY FOR OUR PLANET EARTH, HUMANKIND, NATURE AND CULTURE

Our world needs young people like you, Sophie, who enjoy the possibilities of technical developments and who focus their attention on the whole, on the interaction of man, nature and culture. It is important to respect the "planetary boundaries," as the renowned scientist Johan Rockström said. It is important to show that we can solve the problems of this world without wars, as the preamble of the Constitution of UNESCO stated in 1945: "That since wars begin in the minds of men, it is in the minds of men that the defences of peace must be constructed."

To this end, the countries of the world have set 17 Sustainable Development Goals in the context of Agenda 2030 (UN, 2015). But there is one thing in particular we should bear in mind: the unconditional absence of war is a prerequisite for achieving these goals. We need wise and prudent strategies for conflict resolution worldwide if we are at all serious about achieving a reversal. It is not just the joy and fascination for what is feasible that are now required, but also the joy in conserving and preserving the precious natural and cultural heritage around the globe—for all people and also for future generations. This joy is the source of motivation for using technical inventiveness to solve the problems that have arisen. It is important here to cooperate with all like-minded people, with men and women together, around the globe.

WILL YOU FIND YOUR WAY IN YOUR PROFESSION?

Many coincidences as well as unpredictability play a part in shaping your path into the professional world. When, at the beginning of my studies, I was offered one of the extremely scarce laboratory places at that time in the specialization "food chemistry," a dear older relative said: "Oh Gudrun dearest, that's something quite wonderful for a woman." I felt a surge of protest. I truly wanted the same recognition as my male fellow students. But soon, when questions of cultivation methods and livestock husbandry, of gentle processing methods (e.g., to preserve the valuable secondary plant substances) were discussed, a rethinking of agriculture and food technology as well as their economic organization arose.

In 1973 came Ernst Friedrich Schumacher's book *Small is Beautiful: Economics as if People Mattered*; then in 1980 there was the impressive documentary *September Wheat*; in 2008 the International Assessment on Agricultural Science, Technology and Development (IAASTD) released the *Global Report: Agriculture at a Crossroads* (initiated by the UN and World Bank); and in 2018 came the UN resolution, *"United Nations Declaration of Peasants and Other People Working in Rural Areas."*

I witnessed these things happen, and so I felt I was part of them. Many of my students took up these ideas and later founded their own companies. I was invited to advise universities on various continents and to set up corresponding courses of studies. And the inquiry into the question of how to kindle independent thinking in people's minds led me into the world of engineering education. I discuss these topics with colleagues around the globe, for example at international conferences.

My best advice to you, Sophie, and to any woman aspiring to the engineering profession: It is always a matter of boldly grasping new situations and making decisions where we can act—and finding people with whom it is possible to shape projects together. In a variety of situations, I have repeatedly brought women together and motivated them to open their eyes to possible perspectives, and to shape these with courage.

However, I was privileged in one thing: a lifelong secure position with great freedom of design, for which I am deeply grateful. I have never had to compromise on anything I found intolerable. And that is what I wish for you too, Sophie: to be able to use a certain economic security, a degree of freedom, in order to be able to defend your own standpoints without fear of penalty.

JOURNEY 14

CAN A WOMAN ENGINEER A BETTER WORLD?

MARLENE KANGA

President
World Federation of Engineering Organizations

AUSTRALIA

Engineers have the skills and abilities to change the world. But I didn't know about the power of engineering when I was a young girl with the strange and extraordinary ambition to become an engineer.

I was considered an oddity by my family and friends: I was good at mathematics and science, but I had no desire to become a teacher or nurse—the "women's jobs"—or even a researcher or a doctor. I simply liked finding out how things worked. So, engineering was my career choice. Although I grew up in India, had a very sheltered, privileged life, and attended an all-girls school, no one told me that very few girls go into engineering. It never occurred to me.

I decided to sit the highly competitive entrance test for the Indian

Institute of Technology, the best engineering education institutions in India. More than half a million sat the entrance test for just 2,000 places. The vast majority of students taking the exam were male, and most of them had attended coaching classes; I did not even know these existed! However, I did very well in the exam, ranking in the top 50 nationally, and getting my choice: chemical engineering at the Indian Institution of Technology (IIT) Bombay, located in Mumbai.

When I arrived at IIT Bombay, I was a naïve teenager who thought she knew what engineering was all about. I excelled at mathematics and science; my father was a leading engineer and had been involved in many exciting projects, and I had heard that IIT Bombay was the place to be. I had no idea that engineering would provide me with the tools and capacity to actually change the world.

ABOUT THE AUTHOR

Dr. Marlene Kanga is President of the World Federation of Engineering Organizations (WFEO), the peak body for engineering institutions; it represents some 100 engineering institutions internationally and approximately 30 million engineers. A chemical engineer and a fellow of the Australian Academy of Engineering and Technology, she was the 2013 National President of Engineers Australia. Marlene has been listed among the Top 10 Women Engineers in Australia, the Top 100 Women of Influence in Australia and the Top 100 Engineers in Australia. She is a Member of the Order of Australia, a national honor in recognition of her leadership in the engineering profession.

Engineers have been innovating and changing the world for millennia, and that's especially true in India. Civil engineers thousands of years ago built the early urban settlements in the Indus valley at Mohenjo-Daro, around 2600 BC. They created rectangular street grids, grand buildings, and public baths. In the third century BC, the Mauryan Emperor Ashoka built the city of Pataliputra, the largest city in the world at the time; it controlled a large empire that covered most of India. And, around 1569, the Mughal Emperor Akbar built the planned city of Fatehpur Sikri as a new capital to enable control of his vast empire.

The Industrial Revolution in the 19th century in the UK and Europe was driven by inventions like the steam engine, which reshaped the world, yielding massive productivity improvements and wealth. Steam engines led to rail networks and industrialization; jet engines led to global travel; and the early computers eventually enabled global connections and access to vast amounts of information. All of this has been made possible with science, technology—and engineering.

Engineers continue to be at the forefront of shaping our world in the 21st century. In the last 30 years alone we have seen the rapid rise of computers and communication technology. The invention of the iPhone, which celebrated 10 years in 2017, transformed our world. The smartphone has facilitated political upheavals around the world as well as economic empowerment—for example, enabling cashless payment in remote and rural Africa and Asia, even for those without a bank account.

We need engineers like never before. Rapid urbanization requires solutions for better transport, air quality, food security, water supply and sanitation, and energy and telecommunications; all of these problems will need engineers. For cities exposed to natural disasters and rising sea levels, engineers are needed to develop sustainable solutions to mitigate these risks and build resilience. These are just a few examples of the enormous economic and social benefits of engineering.

However, technology has not reached everywhere. It is estimated that approximately one-sixth of the world's people do not have electricity in their homes and one-third lack access to basic sanitation. Nevertheless, changes are occurring, and it is engineers who are making them.

I know first-hand of the impact of engineering. My father, an electrical and mechanical engineer, led projects to electrify the west coast of India in the 1970s. In the same period, my father-in-law, a civil engineer, developed water supplies for Bombay and later developed four new cities including Navi Mumbai, now with a population approaching five million.

My ancestral home, some 400 years old, in a remote village in Goa, has changed as a result of engineering. It received electricity in the 1960s, and our first tap supplied from the public system was installed only in 2011 (we had previously accessed untreated water from wells; we still do not have a public sanitation system installed). Our telephone number comprised just two digits in the 1970s and has now grown to eight digits; a couple of digits have been added in each decade as the communications network expanded. Now, with smart engineering, this village is part of a global village thanks to access to high-speed broadband and mobile communications. These developments have had profound implications on the local economy and on the quality of life for those who live there.

One of the greatest revolutions of the past 60 years has been in computing, information and communications. When I was an engineering student, I had to walk into the library building and submit a pack of punched cards to run a small program on a large computer that filled the entire ground floor. The computer's memory was just eight kilobytes. It took about a day to successfully run a small program of 100 lines of code. Today, most personal computers have a memory of 100 times larger, and we all have a powerful mobile phone in our back pocket or a smart watch on our wrist. This demonstrates how far computers have come—made possible by, of course, engineers.

I was at school when James Watson and Francis Crick published the sequence of a gene at Cambridge, UK, and won the Nobel prize for it in 1962. I did not understand the implications at the time but over the past few decades, the cost of genome sequencing has fallen dramatically, even faster than the cost of microprocessors. This had led to the development of medical technologies and advancements in health diagnostics that have huge impacts on us all—thanks, again, to doctors, scientists and, yes, engineers.

These are just two examples of the remarkable impact of engineers and engineering on the modern world.

※ ※ ※

I've always been grateful for three great unforeseen legacies of my undergraduate years: the challenge, the opportunity, and the inspiration. These developed my critical thinking abilities, my capacity for work, my leadership skills and my resilience.

At IIT Bombay, I was in a very tough academic environment, especially in the first few years when I had to grapple with subjects like applied mechanics—never my favorite! It was also a challenge to be one of just 20 female students among more than 2,000 males and with only one or two female academics.

The role of "mess secretary" of the ladies hostel (this was on the committee that ran the food and beverage area of the hostel) was an opportunity for my first leadership position, and it took courage, integrity and tenacity. In those days, the student halls of residence, or hostels, were run by a student committee who were responsible for planning and managing costs for all the students. I didn't know it at the time, but we were effectively running a small business. I had complained about the high cost of the food bills, which was shared among the student residents, and had observed that staff generally produced about three times the required amount of food for each meal, taking the rest home or selling it at the local food stalls outside the campus. In the role of mess secretary, which I was elected to at the end of my first year (and continued in until I graduated), I found I could make a difference, and that was empowering.

I set about analyzing what was utilized, and attempted to converse with the kitchen staff in what was a foreign language to me (there are approximately 300 languages spoken in India). They split themselves laughing. Nevertheless, I established a strict regimen, handing out oil and other staples from a locked store room before each meal. This cut costs by half. I adopted a "command and control" style with my fellow residents, posting rules on the board—that were all ignored. I quickly learned to lead instead through collaboration and influence. The changes came slowly, but everyone recognized them, and some even appreciated them.

That was my first leadership position and it taught me not only to balance the budget but to work with people. Previously a shy, quiet person, I learned to speak up, and I worked to be of service to everyone—all while enjoying the challenges.

I also became adept at bargaining with the residents in the male student hostels for extra rice when our ration quota ran out, in exchange for my lecture notes in a particular subject. (I was a very diligent student and everyone knew I had the best lecture notes.) These tactics have enabled me to negotiate at an international level with member nations at the United Nations as we worked toward declaring March 4 of each year as World Engineering Day. No mean feat. More on that later.

Professor Indira Madhavan was among the few women academics on campus who taught environmental engineering as an elective in my fourth year. She inspired me to think about the social and economic impacts of engineering and how it can make a better world. Engineers are changemakers. We can create tangible solutions out of concepts and ideas; we create the future. I went on to study process safety engineering at Imperial College at the University of London because I saw it as socially responsible engineering. It was a time of great change in the chemical industry, with a recognition of the need to manage risks in hazardous industries to keep workers and communities safe from explosions, fires, and toxic chemical releases. The UK Health and Safety Executive led the world in this area.

When I moved to Australia, the area of process safety had not even begun to develop. It was a decade later before I was able to participate in a project of managing hazards in the chemical industry at the Warren Centre for Advanced Engineering at the University of Sydney. I was among their first women to participate in this project. I was also pregnant with my second child, definitely a first for them!

This led to a long career in process safety risk engineering in Australia and New Zealand. In my own career as an engineer, the changes I have been able to make have been empowering and sustaining. For example, I developed the first Land Use Safety Criteria for Hazardous Industries for the State of New South Wales, which were later adopted throughout Australia and in New Zealand in 2016, and Singapore in 2017, without much change. These criteria guided government planning on the siting of hazardous industries in sensitive and populated areas. I am proud of my contributions to process safety engineering, as it has made a safer world.

As a woman engineer, I have been at the leading edge of change. I was the second woman to graduate in chemical engineering from IIT Bombay, and I am sure I forged a pathway for others to follow. In Australia, I traveled to various remote areas, where I was a curiosity; people had never actually seen a woman engineer until I arrived. I had to set the terms of engagement to ensure that I could get my tasks done, and always to a very high standard. Making a mistake was never an option. I even had to argue the case for the most basic facilities such as toilets for women in remote work sites, and for child care close to work. I have visited every chemical plant, refinery and gas treatment plant in Australia and New Zealand. Even today, there are very few women doing the risk assessments for the hazardous chemical industry in Australia and New Zealand; there are probably fewer than five.

I continue to face barriers even today, where I often have to challenge the assumptions about my ability to do the job. This takes patience, tenacity, and resilience. However, in the 21st century in a developed country, it really shouldn't be this hard. I could have achieved much more and am constantly underestimated.

The number of women in engineering in Australia speak for themselves. The proportion remains below 10 percent because of the extraordinary pressures of balancing family and work, a top concern for women engineers, and because of harsh work cultures that are ever present. Despite the stated commitment by leaders in engineering to diversity and inclusion, progress has been slow. Less than 20 percent of engineering students in Australia are women. About half of these leave engineering on graduation; that number is halved again in the first five years, and continues to reduce thereafter. Less than one percent of engineers in Australia in the 50-plus age group are women, and most of them are in universities, not industry. This is a huge loss. However, the situation is very different in countries that are developing fast, especially in Asia and South America, where there are high proportions of women students—up to 50 percent in some cases—and high proportions working in industry and academia.

I became involved in issues relating to attracting, supporting and retaining women engineers approximately 15 years ago, at a time when my children had grown and I had more time to give back to the profession. I became chair of the Engineers Australia National Committee for Women in Engineering, and developed and led the Year of Women in Engineering in 2007, the first time in the world that a year-long program of events had been held to showcase the achievements of women engineers. As a board member of Engineers Australia in 2008, I introduced the Career Break Policy for Chartered Engineers, enabling flexibility with Continuous Professional Development (CPD) requirements while on a career break, irrespective of reason. This was a world first, and it has since been included in legislation for the registration of engineers, in Queensland, for example. I also lobbied successfully to include diversity as a leadership value in the Engineers Australia Code of Ethics in 2010, another world first for an engineering institution.

I went on to host an international conference for women engineers and scientists in Australia in 2011, which brought together women engineers from across Australia and around the world. The Asia Pacific Nation Network of women engineers and scientists was also established at this conference, and went on to support groups dedicated to the development of women in engineering and science across Asia, including India, Nepal, Sri Lanka, Mongolia, Vietnam, Taiwan, and Malaysia. This is an active and vibrant network that has supported hundreds of women engineers and scientists. In 2008, I became a board member of the International Network for Women Engineers and Scientists (INWES), leading changes for a diverse and inclusive engineering profession internationally.

My leadership roles in engineering also led to my election onto the

National Board of Engineers Australia. I became the second woman to be elected national president in 2013. This position enabled me to make changes for improved governance, with the development of the first consolidated member regulations. A vision statement was developed for Engineers Australia in 2013, another first, and it is still in use today. This set the compass for the organization, articulating and activating its values. I was proud to be recognized for my leadership in engineering with a national honor in June 2014, when I was made a Member of the Order of Australia on the Queen's Birthday Honours List.

I have also played a role on the world stage, starting when I attended my first meeting of the World Federation of Engineering Organizations (WFEO) in 2007, advocating at its general assembly in New Delhi for the establishment of a Women in Engineering Committee. I went on to mentor and support this committee, which has also helped to increase the number of women engineers participating in the federation.

My election as president of the WFEO was quite remarkable. It involved my personal representation and commitment to every member without incurring travel or other expenses to garner votes, and I had widespread support, especially from Asia, Africa, and Europe. I felt humbled by the outpouring of joy when I was elected in a huge majority vote in the first round, a clean election. It was a mark of the trust placed by the mostly male engineering leaders of the world that I could do the job and do it well.

As president of the WFEO, I have a unique opportunity to lead change by engineers. This federation is internationally recognized and trusted as the leader of the engineering profession; it can work with international bodies at the United Nations and World Bank to apply engineering to constructively achieve the UN Sustainable Development Goals. My goals are for capacity building in engineering where it is needed most (in Asia and Africa); improving the standards of engineering education; and continuing professional development through shared action. Another priority is to ensure that engineering is a diverse and inclusive profession that provides opportunities for participation by all, irrespective of gender, ethnicity, or age, so we have the best intellects engaged in engineering. During my term I have provided opportunities for women and men from every region and continent. In particular, engineers from Africa and Asia have increased, like never before, their participation and contribution to the organization.

In March 2018 the WFEO signed a declaration with UNESCO on the shared commitment of engineers to advance the goals of sustainable development. This vision has led to remarkable partnerships, including with the International Federation of Engineering Education Societies (IFEES), in our shared goal of improving engineering education standards and building capacity for engineering in developing countries.

※ ※ ※

I mentioned earlier in this piece the success of another seemingly impossible challenge: to annually declare each March 4—the founding day of the federation—as World Engineering Day for Sustainable Development, starting in 2020. Remarkably, there had been no global day to celebrate engineers and engineering! I took up this challenge despite never having dealt with the UNESCO system and its member states before. Nevertheless, the proposal was approved unanimously by UNESCO's executive board at its meeting in April 2019, with the support of 40 member states and 80 international engineering institutions representing more than 22 million engineers. I felt that I had moved a mountain! This day will be a huge opportunity to celebrate engineering and the change that engineers can make to achieve the goals of sustainable development.

To sum up: I am grateful for a remarkable career that has had many challenges as well as many opportunities. I am empowered by the change that I can make as an engineer, and I want all young people to consider engineering as a career. My student years transformed me from a shy, quiet young woman to someone ready to take on global challenges. There is, of course, still a great deal to be done. However, I have a clear vision of the task ahead and the role of engineers to continue to make change for a better, more sustainable world. Engineers have the force to do that. We have the dreams and the skills. Let the future begin.

JOURNEY 15

WOMEN IN ACADEMIC LEADERSHIP, FROM AN INDIAN PERSPECTIVE

SUSHMA S. KULKARNI

Director
Rajarambapu Institute of Technology

INDIA

According to a 2013 UNESCO report, women account for 53 percent of the world's bachelor's and master's graduates, 43 percent of PhDs, and 28 percent of researchers. Whereas women have achieved parity in life sciences in many countries, they still trail men in engineering and computer sciences.

The country of my birth, India, has long been a male-dominated society. Women were supposed to be homemakers, whereas the men were assigned the task of earning the bread. However, the scenario today reveals a newly emerging picture, one in which many women have broken these barriers and joined the workforce in almost all industries. Still, the numbers are not so rosy: India ranks fifth-lowest in having women in top leadership positions as per the global diversity survey. According to a report conducted by the organization Community Business, "Gender Diversity Benchmark for Asia 2011," of the jurisdictions included (China, Hong Kong, India, Japan, Malaysia, and Singapore), India has the smallest number of women in the workforce, and the largest pipeline leak, around 48 percent. In other words, almost half of women leave the workforce when they are still young.

The report shows that gender equality policies are abundant and widespread, and the education sector is not an exception. Most of the educated women in the countries studied aspire to a career in education. Higher education in India attracts a number of women. Of almost 13

ABOUT THE AUTHOR

Dr. Mrs. Sushma S. Kulkarni is Director at Rajarambapu Institute of Technology, Maharashtra, India. She received her PhD in Civil Engineering from Shivaji University, Kolhapur, India. She has 32 years of teaching experience in Civil Engineering programs, and her areas of interest are Concrete Technology, TQM, Quality Circles, Construction Management, Watershed Management, OBE, and Women's Empowerment. Dr. Kulkarni has contributed to more than 85 research papers and has two patents provisionally registered (on "Pond Ash" and "Academics with ICT"). She has guided six PhD students and more than 57 UG & PG students for projects. Dr. Kulkarni has visited universities around the world to study engineering education systems. She was invited to be a jury member for the "GEDC-Airbus Global Diversity Award" in Australia in 2015, a keynote speaker at the Asian Engineering Education Conference in 2016 in China, and she presented as panellist at the GEDC Conference in Canada in 2017. She is on the executive committee of GEDC. Dr. Kulkarni has contributed to various professional boards, including the IUCEE, ISTE. She is a fellow of the Institution of Engineers. Dr. Kulkarni won the ISTE's Best Engineering Principal Award in 2011, and the ISTD's Emerging HRD Thinker's gold medal.

million teachers here, about 42 percent are female. At the all-India level, there are merely 72 female teachers per 100 male teachers. Also, there are 60 percent females at the level of demonstrators (similar to the level of a lab assistant), which gets reduced to 30 percent when the level of professor or equivalent is achieved.

So what about engineering specifically? Women comprise around half of students across almost all fields of engineering around the world. Yet the field is very much a man's world: only around 20 percent practice engineering, and the pipeline leaks at such a rate that only three to four percent end up in senior positions. As for India, according to a 2018 survey of higher education by India's Ministry of Human Resource Development and the Department of Higher Education, the number of women educators at the level of assistant professor is 67 per 100 male educators, which drops by almost 50 percent to 35 females per 100 males for associate professor.

This scenario is forcing us to think about what is going wrong; what challenges are creating these leaky pipelines? Industries have started giving thought to this. For example, in 2008 Google launched the Google India Women in Engineering Award to "encourage women to excel in computing and technology" and "recognize women in the field of computer science and engineering." But the challenge is so formidable that despite such efforts, there has been little improvement. There is a dire need to design development programs to bring more women into leadership roles.

I feel that leaders cannot be abruptly made; it is a gradual and continuous process that starts in childhood and evolves as the person grows up and moves from one role to another. Nurturing a girl from childhood makes a significant impact on their transformation into leaders. I am a living example of that. Today, I am the director of the Rajarambapu Institute of Technology (RIT) in Maharashtra, India. The journey was full of challenges, surprises, ups and downs and, finally, successes. The following reflections from my life experiences provide glimpses of the sincere efforts and passion required, and will show how leadership is something that evolves on the path to achieving your goals.

※ ※ ※

I was born in the 1960s to a family with a military background. I was third born, and had one brother and two sisters. Importantly, my parents never treated boys and girls differently, both in our family and outside of it (though of course I always helped my mother in household work like cooking and cleaning). I think the fact that my father was an Air Force officer was influential for me in terms of my ability to adapt to new places and people and to have a disciplined work ethic. Also, my parents exposed me to many "worldly" people, such as station commanders and officers; one of my aunts was based in Hong Kong and worked for the United Nations. In this way, from a young age I was able to connect with highly educated people who inspired me.

My parents insisted that I should be ambitious and consider a career that would contribute to the development of people. They were very supportive of higher education and they knew very well that education can make a difference and improve our lives. Although it was financially difficult for them to provide higher education to all four of us, they were determined to do so, and took out loans.

My father had a diploma in electrical and mechanical engineering, and used to involve me in repairing small appliances at home, and his Vespa scooter, which he taught me to drive at age 15. Such things gave me hands-on learning. Plus, my elder brother, Sanjay, who was also in engineering, helped spur my interest in the field. When I was in secondary school, he would show me engineering equipment and machines that he was studying at various sites and explain to me how they work.

I did my schooling at Kendriya Vidyalaya, part of a system of central government schools, and there was a good blend of students from different communities. The school was co-ed and there was no discrimination based on gender. In secondary school, I was interested equally in biology and mathematics. My mother wanted me to become a doctor, but unfortunately, I didn't get admitted into medicine. But I did get into civil engineering at Visvesvaraya National Institute of Technology, one of the most reputable engineering colleges in India. I did my engineering degree from Regional

College of Engineering (present NITs); there were only 22 in India at that time. In college, there was a boys-to-girls ratio of around 80 to 20. There were 40 girls in our hostel, and we took part in cultural activities, volleyball, basketball, and badminton.

However, we had no influence in college elections as there were only three girls in my course. And, initially, we had some other challenges. For example, many times when we were out in the field doing land surveys—which were supposed to be a team effort involving cooperation of the whole group—the boys in our class did not help with collecting readings, nor did they work with us on preparing the drawings. (I think it was a cultural thing; if a girl talked to a boy, it became fodder for him being teased by his fellow male classmates, so the boys steered clear of us.) It meant that we girls were essentially on our own in what was intended to be a group learning effort. However, after I engaged the boys in conversation and they got to know me a little, they started involving us.

Thankfully, all of the professors were supportive, and they inspired me. I did an internship under an architect in Pune who was also very supportive; I observed and learned the importance of building drawings with specifications and dimensions, how to interact with clients, how to make field notes, etc. I still remember the surprise I'd see in the eyes of engineers, contractors, and clients when they realized that a girl can be a civil engineer.

After graduation in 1987, I joined a small road construction company as a junior engineer, carrying out surveys. Soon I got a very different opportunity: to become a lecturer. I had never considered a career in teaching; my only aim was to work in industry. But when I heard by chance of a lecturer position at RIT, I decided to go to an interview. I was asked challenging questions mainly focused on my project work, but I could answer them confidently. I got the position. In my appointment letter, it was a condition to complete post graduation within five years. I was sponsored by the institute, where I was working, to do my post-graduate work at nearby Shivaji University. Three of my academic colleagues were also doing this post-graduate work and we all supported each other for our seminars and projects. My dissertation for my master's program was at Afcons, a construction company in Mumbai. It was on design and construction techniques of diaphragm walls as the foundation for a 10-story hospital that was being built; advanced techniques were being applied for construction of the diaphragm walls.

This gave me deep insights into labor management, project planning, pre-stressing techniques, tremie concreting using bentonite slurry, etc. It provided a lot of exposure to the world of construction as a civil engineer. However, there were many challenges. There was no women's bathroom facility at the site. Initially, I was hesitant to talk about this with our site engineer. But after two days, I had to talk to him, so he made an arrangement with a hospital near the site. Because of this incident, I learned that you must voice your concerns with others if you want a solution.

Our RIT principal, Prof. M.V. Joglekar, was very supportive. He believed in women and in my leadership. He encouraged me to take up my PhD and helped me to identify the subject of research. By then, I was married, and when I started my PhD, my daughter was eight years old and my son was six. There are always challenges at every phase of life, but balancing family needs, my job and studying for my PhD has been one of my life's greatest tests. It is your own determination that helps you to find a way through difficulties. And I must say that whatever I am today is because of good support from my husband and mother-in-law: thanks to family, I had no worries about my children.

I loved the academic world. Preparing for lectures, working on course material, learning innovative methods for engaging lectures... these things were always enjoyable and I had no problems. I always got encouraging feedback from students. And I learned that as a woman, I was able to earn the trust of students and fellow colleagues; cases of disputes in the department were referred to me to resolve. I think this is because women typically have the right traits for this. I have patience, an ability to earn students' trust so that they feel comfortable approaching me, and a focus on mentoring and counseling.

I remember an incident when I floated an elective course to be considered for the program. At the same time, my department head, a male, had also floated an elective. When the students selected mine and did not opt for his, he was so annoyed that he closed my elective the next year. Maybe he could not accept my supportive outlook towards students, the way that I could counsel and understand them, and nurture their abilities.

I feel all women can achieve heights for a few reasons: they are able to multitask; their emotional quotient (EQ) is consistently higher than men's; they tend to have more patience; and they often pursue a holistic view of development. To younger women I say this: You should believe in your abilities. It's a shame when we miss out on opportunities because of fear. For example, when a woman on our faculty was offered the position of department head, she was reluctant to accept it, unsure whether she could handle both work and family life at par. She took two or three sessions of counseling, and ultimately declined the offer; she said she feared that her family would suffer.

Parents often come to discuss with me which branch of engineering is good for their daughters. They insist that it's inappropriate for girls to take jobs in the field, far from their homes. In some areas, such as sales and marketing, recruiters even discourage female candidates. For things to change in society, perspectives need to change. Yes, women's security is very important, and working in the field, in particular, poses dangers (even if sometimes they are only perceived dangers). There is a lack of washroom facilities for women, and there is shift work. Plus, many men view it as wrong for a woman to be away from her husband and family, and they even have difficulty accepting that a woman can be a colleague. But you should be bold enough to be on your own. You should have a strong belief in your abilities as an engineer and as a leader. Today's workplace is equally demanding for both genders. Women should think of their own identity and recognition, and hold on to their self-esteem.

✵ ✵ ✵

RIT was started in 1983 in Rajaramnagar, a city south of Mumbai. It has emerged as a leading technological institute in western Maharashtra, through its dedicated and disciplined approach to providing quality technical education over a period of more than 35 years. In 2011, RIT was awarded academic autonomy by India's University Grants Commission and Shivaji University in Kolhapur. In line with the changing scenario of the industry, the introduction of changes in curriculum focus on R&D, industry internship, the culture of entrepreneurship development and startup, international exposure to students, and international admissions. The results have been satisfaction and enjoyment, both for students and teachers. RIT has ranked among India's top 75 private self-financed institutes in various ranking surveys.

As engineering is a very much a man's world, it was difficult in the early days, after I took charge in 2005 as principal, to work effectively as a leader. (The challenges are still there, but they are not as intense.) When the principal position was offered to me, I didn't have much experience in administration except for a few months as department head and a few years as coordinator of Quality Circles. And to help me decide for myself whether I should pursue the position, I met with two or three other principals (males) so that I could understand the job profile. When the board of governors showed their belief in me and selected me as principal, it was difficult for my colleagues to accept a woman's leadership, especially in the rural location of RIT. However, my leadership really evolved out of those challenges. I found wonderful mentors—Chairman of our BOG Mr. Bhagat Patil, Secretary of Society Prof. R. D. Sawant, and Member of BOG and Minister Mr. Jayant Patil—who supported me through demanding times.

The leadership labyrinth has been full of challenges. Here are some that I feel all women academic leaders in India face, and some possible solutions:

- In India, more women leaders end up leaving their jobs or not realizing their potential in their chosen career because they say no to promotions. Typically, their thought process is that they will need to devote too much time to the profession, and that it will be difficult to manage both family and work. To overcome such challenges, we need family support; we need to delegate household work and manage our families so that they become more independent rather than relying solely on the wife and/or mother. Aspiration and ambition within yourself are important because that will only drive you to overcome these stresses and obstacles, which are part of everyday life as a leader. Women leaders must play many ever-challenging roles in a competitive environment that is just as demanding as taking care of the home front. And both of the roles are equally important.

- To manage the home front, it is important to take members of your family into your confidence and share that what you are doing is very important for you and your career, and you value it as much you value your family. Delegate the routine, day-to-day tasks at home with domestic support. This helps make your children feel more independent, since they are not being overprotected in many aspects of their lives. Fortunately, I had the support of my mother-in-law, who valued education, and my husband, who respected my aspiration.

- When you are the head of an institute, nurturing and developing it is important, and you must challenge yourself every day to overcome difficulties. In my experience, there will be faculty who are onside with your plans, and others who are not ready to accept you, or who would stand in your way or ensure that your plans fail. Therefore, understanding the psychology of people—their behavior and attitude—is essential in a leadership role. You must select the right person for the right place, practice what you preach, and be passionately certain that the execution of whatever task or project you work on is essential to your role as leader. Respecting the human capital (students or faculty) and empowering them is the path to removing fear and creating faith in themselves.

I feel that women need to be physically and mentally strong to be able to balance family and work life. A leadership role demands more time to be spent on travel, both national and international, to attend things like meetings, conferences, and workshops. Independent thinking, the ability to endure stress, commitment, inner drive, and self-confidence—all are necessary to overcome any challenges faced. Let me share one experience I had. In 2005, one of my papers was selected for a conference in South Korea, and I was asked to travel there to present it. It would be my first time out of India. My family was not willing to permit me to go; they were very worried—that I wouldn't be able to travel alone, and that it was too far to go to a place where the people were different and spoke another language. But I really believed that I should be able to go and present my paper, and I was able to convince them that there was nothing to worry about.

Finally, they relented. I went to South Korea and successfully presented. This incident made me realize that we have to believe ourselves first.

In general, there are not many role models for women. Yes, there are some women leaders in education, but the data needs to be compiled. Thus, aspiring women have very few leaders from whom they can take inspiration and continue to climb. For me, my PhD guide, Dr. K.T. Krishnaswamy, was the role model. Seeing the quality of his work and observing how efficiently he handled high-profile meetings inspired me to become a leader, and what I learned under his mentorship helped me a lot. Other mentors I'd like to make special mention of include: professor M. V. Joglekar, who motivated me to do my PhD; Dr. Suhas Sahsrabudhe, who developed my managerial skills; professor Krishna Vedula, who introduced me to the world of engineering education outside of India; professor Hans Hoyer, who connected me to deans through GEDC and inspired me to present my views on a global platform; and professor Lueny Morell, who is my role model as a global woman leader in engineering education.

Working long hours results in women having feelings of guilt that they are neglecting their family, home, and children. Women always have the burden of fulfilling their family's expectations, such as attending family functions and caring for a sick member of the family. But women must learn to balance cultural challenges with ambition. I would like to share an incident that illustrates people's perceptions of a woman principal. About six to eight months after I took charge as principal, I was in a meeting with some visitors to RIT. Suddenly one of the visitors asked me, "Are you principal of this building only, or all of the buildings at RIT?" The visitors could not imagine that a woman could lead such a big institute. To me, it confirmed the stereotype they had.

But I'd also like to share the memory of an incident that gave me the confidence that women leaders are accepted and equally respected. Soon after taking charge as principal, we had to make a presentation to the managing director for Industry Institute Interaction in a high-profile industry. The MD listened to me with full focus and attention, appreciated our initiative, and signed a memorandum of understanding with us that is still active 12 years later.

To conclude, I feel that with the right mentoring, self-aspiration, and confidence, women educators can definitely occupy top leadership positions. At the same time, formal training and retraining through optimally designed leadership development programs are essential to develop them as leaders. The role is obviously very demanding, hence the right balance of work and personal life is the key to performing well at both ends. But success will be yours if you can find it in yourself to strongly deal with all the negative forces and convert them into positives. Of course, you will meet mentors on your journey who will support, guide, and develop you to help you reach your goals. But it's your own determination and willpower that will inspire you to take this journey to success.

I feel very happy about the job I have. I love what I do, and I am passionate about developing my institute. I wish to continue to develop women engineers and nurture new leaders. Join me. I truly believe that every woman has the potential.

JOURNEY 16

PROBLEM-BASED LEARNING AND ME

ARCHANA MANTRI

Pro Vice-Chancellor
Chitkara University

INDIA

My career has spanned more than three decades, and for one third of that I have been in a leadership position at a highly ranked university in India. Having risen from the position of lecturer to my current position of provost, I enjoy unrelenting support from my team of researchers and faculty members, my PhD scholars, and my students. We are like a family: we have fun together but also work very hard because of a strong sense of duty. I believe in leading from the front; we share the credit, but I must take responsibility for our failures.

My journey wasn't always smooth; it's been filled with challenges along the way, for I was neither a girl born blessed nor with a golden spoon in my mouth. Rather, it's been a perfect combination of chances and choices. I can tell you first-hand that being of modest means and having mediocre schooling are no obstacles to shaping the achievements of a girl nurtured in an environment filled with love, compassion, respect, and equal opportunities—that is, for the most part. Because being a woman in a patriarchal society, in a leadership position in STEM, came with its set of obstacles. But they were obstacles I was able to overcome, thanks to an unrelenting support of family and mentors. Countless women might achieve the same if they only had more belief in themselves.

I was born and raised in the small town of Guna, on the banks of the

ABOUT THE AUTHOR

Dr. Archana Mantri is a PhD in Electronics and Communication Engineering with 29 years of experience in academia and research organizations. She has worked extensively in curriculum development, specifically for making engineering curriculum project-, skill- and apprenticeship-based. She has created and copyrighted several blended learning models to support modern pedagogical practices, and puts a lot of focus on enabling and rearing technologies and repositories for online, blended. and flipped classrooms. Dr. Mantri also works on evolving adaptive assessments to support newer pedagogical practices. She is a senior IEEE member and is on the advisory board of Indo Universal Collaboration of Engineering Education (IUCEE) along with 35 other international experts from the United States, Australia, and Europe. She has conducted numerous workshops at national and international platforms for educators' training. Having traveled extensively, she brings a truly global perspective to education. At Chitkara University, Dr. Mantri is a thought leader, enabler, and functional head of Chitkara University Research and Innovation Network (CURIN). She is spearheading all initiatives related to research and innovation. Under her leadership, CURIN has been able to collaborate with leading research organizations across the globe, truly putting Chitkara University on the path of research.

Parbati River in central India. My father, one of nine siblings, was lovingly raised by my grandparents. Some of my fondest childhood memories are of evenings spent with members of our large extended family, who would gather from wherever they were at our ancestral home to celebrate festivals and spend summer vacations. We would play in the twilight of the setting sun and then, after a sumptuous dinner, snuggle up together and listen to our grandmother's stories. She chose to tell stories from mythology and pauranic literature, which taught us lessons of ethics and morality. And then, competing to count the stars and spot new constellations, we would fall asleep.

Living in such a big family, I watched, learned and appreciated that it is okay to disagree and win assertively on a valid point. I also learned that even the biggest of differences could be resolved over dining table discussions, and how important it is to listen to others' viewpoints before making a decision.

In retrospect, I realize what a difference it makes to just let kids be kids, regardless of gender. In my immediate family, I did not see—and so I could not even think of—a child being repressed just because she is a girl. Case in point: my uncle Anil and I each got an engineering degree (he in 1986 and me in 1989) from the same college in Gwalior, also in central India. Later, he and I both earned gold medals, too.

Growing up, I drew my first lessons in simplicity, sincerity and hard work from my father, Justice R.C. Lahoti. He is a vivid observer and an avid reader. Commencing his career as a lawyer, he was chosen as a judge in a High Court, and later went on to hold the highest judicial office in the Supreme Court of India. Yet he never let any of his kids have any attitude that "I'm-the-child-of-a-man-in-power." Instead, we learned from him the importance of learning well and doing well to strengthen and shape ourselves and our family. These instincts became deeply ingrained in our minds; they guided our activities, and then became traits of our character.

My mother, Kaushalaya, was, and still is, my first woman role-model. She is multitalented, including being a prize-winning sportsperson and acclaimed dancer. Even though she was married off at the age of 16, just after she finished high school, she remained a life-long learner despite her formal education ending early. Not only would she teach us, but she would also teach herself from our textbooks. She was a disciplinarian and did not tolerate any nonsense, but she also taught us to have a hearty laugh whenever we can. She taught my siblings and me to have a deep and unmoving faith in God and grab the smallest opportunity and turn it in our favor. It's thanks to my mother that I even became an engineer: she and Uncle Anil helped me to get over my fear of mathematics, a subject essential to pursue engineering.

Life can take such unexpected turns; it amuses me to think back to when I took my engineering entrance test. I went into it blissfully unaware of what it really was; I thought it was just a test of my knowledge of physics, chemistry and mathematics, all of which I had studied well. And—surprise!—I passed, and gained admission in 1985 into a college for pursuing electronic engineering.

On my first day, I found myself to be one among only nine female students in a class of 60. As we became good friends, my eight women classmates helped me in getting over many of my complexes (including being from a small town, and having inferior language and interpersonal skills). It is from them that I learned to dream BIG. I graduated in 1989 at the age of 20.

Soon after, I took up my first job; it was at a fibre optic telecommunications company. I did not realize it then, but it must have been very difficult for my parents to let me take up a corporate job. I was the first woman to do so in our family—ever! But not once did any of my family members raise an eyebrow, and they probably turned away many who wanted to.

While there were many women at my workplace, I was soon made acutely aware of the effects of the gender imbalance in STEM when I was working on a product for the Indian Armed Forces. I had to go to the national capital, New Delhi, for a few months to run the product trials and tests. The test site was large, spanning a few square kilometres, and it didn't have a toilet for women. In this difficult situation, I felt I had no choice but to drink less water so that I wouldn't need the toilet during the day. When I was about to finish this posting and leave New Delhi, a Colonel who was in charge asked for my feedback. He was shocked to learn about the absence of toilet facility for women. He apologized, and ordered the immediate construction of toilets for ladies. No female worker had ever raised the issue before, and men simply were unaware of the problem. I realized then that I could make a difference, because I chose to express myself, even if it was too late to make a difference for me.

Within a couple of years, I became engaged to be married to a wonderful man, an engineer named Neeraj; I assumed that after our wedding, I'd have to give up my job and stay at home, just as my aunts and female cousins had done. Little did I realize then that, after my parents, my husband-to-be would become my biggest strength. His parents assured me that I would be able to continue in my career, and that my husband could make adjustments so as to be with me in my city instead of the other way around.

It was the support of my in-laws (especially my mother-in-law, who volunteered to do all the household chores herself) and my husband that allowed me not only to remain united in the family but to continue working. And later, it was my father-in-law who insisted that I do a PhD in 2002. While contemplating my PhD topic, I came across two highly influential personalities: Dr. Krishna Vedula, Dean Emeritus, UMASS, Lowellu; and

Dr. Veena Kumar, Rutgers University. They would become instrumental in enabling me to explore my love for engineering education and pedagogical innovations. Soon, I would end up doing my PhD in "Problem-Based Learning." In a way, these two people, along with another woman (about whom I'll share more later), became my mentors-in-profession.

In 1995, two years after I had my first child, I decided to quit my full time job to spend more time with my daughter. I did some teaching part time at various engineering colleges. It was only after my second child turned two that I decided to return to work full time, and because the part time work had made me realize how much I loved teaching, I knew my full-time work would have to be in the field of engineering education. It was the turning point in my life, leading me on the path to my current organization and position.

I joined Chitkara University in 2004, which was then a college affiliated to a state university. It was there that I met another woman of substance whom I came to admire; in fact, to this day, my admiration continues to grow. Dr. Madhu Chitkara, who with her husband Dr. Ashok had co-founded the university, became my chief mentor and the principal architect of my professional life ahead. It was from Dr. Madhu, who became Vice-Chancellor in 2010, that I learned all that I know and all that I practice about administration and being a leader today.

Thanks to her, I began to sense the difference a woman in a leadership position brings to the workplace. It may not be a universal experience, but in my case, a woman being in power ensured that employees were treated with much love and respect—almost as though they were family. Paying attention to the details, emphasizing cleanliness, and going the extra mile to make the women employees feel safe were just a few of the many things that I noticed. Things were positive there—simply because the leader was a woman! It continues to be so even today.

The female leadership at the university helped encourage many other women in the organization, too. Today, almost half of the academic and support units under the university scope have women leaders. If there are any men who bring biases to the university, they quickly learn they cannot afford to sideline their female colleagues. This, and the fact that I had so many women colleagues and mentors to look up to, played a vital role in my becoming a provost in 2010.

Life went on as it does, a joyful ride yet at times a challenging one—especially starting in 2014, when my husband was diagnosed with cancer. He went through painful treatment spanning over a year. Yet he neither made any adjustments in his work life nor did he expect me to do so. Neeraj managed his occupation, illness, treatment, and later rehabilitation with outstanding courage and positivity. He is an inspiration; a man possessed of the power of positivity, and bubbling with wit and humor , he has taught me how to steadfastly sail in hostile winds.

So there you have my story. I could have brooded throughout those years on the sad moments and the hard battles, but I chose to either ignore them or to take them in my stride, because I preferred to stay focused on the opportunities. There were challenges, certainly, and not just from outside—they also came from within. That's because, as I realized somewhere along the way, gender roles can be so deeply ingrained—like when I just assumed, despite having great family support, that I would have to give up my job after I got married, and when I chose to move from a full-time to a part-time job to take care of my kids.

There's so much guilt involved when we women make our choices: I felt guilty when my elder daughter volunteered to take care of her younger brother so I could go to work. I felt guilty that my husband would have to do the cooking while I attended my evening classes to complete my master's degree. And I told myself that it was not correct to socialize with my colleagues in the evenings because I should instead go home to compensate for my absence. None of these feelings of guilt were necessary, because my family was so supportive. It was not a favor they were doing for me, despite my guilt. And it took time for me to realize that. Now that's what I call another kind of problem-based learning.

Being a woman in STEM in a leadership position can be very lonely. At times, we tend to make mistakes, simply because there is nobody in whom we can confide or share. My advice is that women should develop relationships—even if it's just one—with someone who will empathize with your journey without being judgmental, and who will, most of all, lend a listening ear. I'm fortunate to have my sisters for that support: My elder sister, Pankaj, and my younger sister, Vandana. These women, both of whom are also successful professionals, have always extended me the emotional support, even when nothing else worked.

I was privileged enough to have people telling me that I can step outside my comfort zone, that I can be more than a wife, a mother, a caretaker. Today, I am a mother of two loving, caring, and fiercely independent adults. And while I adore my roles of wife, daughter, and mother, I feel that as women, we tend to fit ourselves into a picture that others paint of us. Many times, our surroundings are a reflection of us. So, if you're privileged enough to be presented with opportunity, I'd urge you to take that leap of faith, and you will be rewarded sooner or later. You can be a successful career woman, a leader—and even a pioneer.

Most of all, remember that a woman is no less than a man in vision, wisdom, or wits. She need not think even for a moment that she is competing with a man. No, she is aiming at occupying the place that rightfully belongs to her. Every woman engineer—in fact, every working woman—should remember this: all that emerges from within remains invincible.

JOURNEY 17

WOMEN IN ENGINEERING, FROM THE MALAWI PERSPECTIVE

THERESA MKANDAWIRE

Dean Emeritus
Faculty of Engineering
University of Malawi – The Polytechnic

MALAWI

I was born and raised in Mzimba district in Malawi, and am the eldest of six children. I did my secondary school education at Lilongwe Girls' Secondary School from 1984 to 1988, where my favorite subjects were mathematics and sciences. I was always enthusiastic, focused and very hard working, and to this day I get a lot of satisfaction when I have contributed to solving a problem or challenge.

Malawi is one of the poorest countries in the world, with 50.7 percent of the population living below the poverty line and 25 percent living in extreme poverty. Its population is estimated to be 17.6 million, with a density of 186 people per square kilometer. (By comparison, in the US that figure is 35, and in the UK it's 272). About 84 percent of the population is rural; agriculture accounts for about a third of the GDP. Agriculture is the mainstay for the country's economy, with subsistence and smallholder farming being prevalent among the rural population; agriculture production contributes more than 90 percent of foreign exchange earnings.

Like so many other people in my country, my parents were farmers. Growing up in our small village, the only role models around me were teachers and nurses, and I dreamed of one day becoming a nurse. But my late father played a big role in motivating me to always aim higher in life. He taught me to be strong, and as a result I grew up looking at

ABOUT THE AUTHOR

Theresa Mkandawire is an Associate Professor and a Registered Civil Engineer with more than 22 years of experience lecturing at the university level. Dr. Mkandawire also has experience in managing projects targeted at low-income countries for different development partners. She leads and works effectively in partnerships with other institutions and has been effectively managing large donor financed projects. She has experience in the monitoring, evaluating, and reporting of project outputs and outcomes including influencing policy and practice. Theresa served as Dean of Engineering from 2013 to 2018 at University of Malawi – The Polytechnic. She has led program development for both undergraduate and postgraduate studies. She also led the development of a new mining engineering department at University of Malawi -- The Polytechnic. Theresa led the development of an international Master's program in collaboration with Leeds Beckett University and University of Botswana, which is currently running. Dr. Theresa Mkandawire is a co-founder of Women in Engineering in Malawi and has been supporting and motivating girls in science, technology, engineering, and mathematics (STEM). Next Einstein Forum (NEF) awarded her for her "outstanding valuable contribution and dedication to science, engineering & technology and overcoming adversity" in 2018.

life positively and knowing I should never give up. This is a good thing, because not everyone is able to complete their schooling, especially girls. In Malawi, the number of boys and girls in primary school, which spans eight years, is more or less equal, especially in lower classes (up to fifth grade). Then, the number of girls starts to drop in larger numbers than boys, and the disparity increases in each successive grade. There is hope; the National Education Sector Plan (NESP) has a mandate to promote education in Malawi irrespective of race, gender, ethnicity, religion, or any other discriminatory characteristics.

In the culture I grew up in, we always listened to advice from our parents, and both of mine were very supportive of my education; they were excited that I would study engineering. This was no small goal in my country; while access to higher education around the world averages 25 percent, and 6.3 percent across southern Africa, in Malawi, that number is only 0.4 percent of the eligible population (between 15 and 25 years of age). Of those, females account for 30 percent of students who enroll in public universities, and among the programs that universities offer, enrollment in science and technology programs remains low (around 4.3 percent each of the total enrollment); enrollments in engineering are among the lowest.

I was selected to study engineering at University of Malawi (UNIMA)—The Polytechnic in 1988, and graduated with a BSc degree in civil engineering with distinction (the only distinction for the faculty of engineering) in 1993. I was the only female student in a class of 20. My strength was that I considered myself as any other student in class, not necessarily as the only female. Fortunately, my fellow male students and my professors were very supportive. I obtained my MSc degree in 1996 from Oklahoma State University, US, and later obtained my PhD in 2012 from Leeds Metropolitan University in the UK.

Today, UNIMA—The Polytechnic as a whole has a 50:50 selection policy, but women remain under-represented in STEM programs in this country. In fact, between 1965 (the year of the institution's inception) and 1987, there was not one female student in engineering; it was the only institution offering engineering programs at the time. When the university registered its first group of females in 1987—four of them—the perception from males was that the girls would not make it and that they would be withdrawn. Fortunately, all four girls excelled and one even graduated with a distinction. I believe this changed the male perception of females studying engineering. The percentage of female engineering students at the institution—which offers five-year Bachelor of Engineering programs in civil, electrical, mechanical, and mining engineering—was 30 percent by 2018, a huge shift.

In another sign that things are progressing, Malawi University of Science and Technology (MUST), a public university established in 2012, has 24 percent females in its engineering programs. MUST offers metallurgy and materials engineering, chemical engineering, and biomedical engineering programs. MUST's first engineering cohort is currently in its final year.

Although just nine out of the 210 engineers registered with the Board of Engineers in Malawi are female, this could be attributed to the fact that there were no female graduate engineers until 1992, when those four female engineers graduated. So it's likely this imbalance will change over time.

* * *

In the 22 years I have been at UNIMA, I have moved ranks from lecturer to associate professor, the position I currently hold. Administratively, I have served as deputy head of the civil engineering department, deputy dean, and dean of the faculty of engineering from 2013 to 2018. When I joined that faculty in 1997, I was the only female in the department.

As dean of the faculty, I led four departments (civil, electrical, mechanical, and mining engineering) in addition to lecturing and other obligations. I managed a 65-member faculty that included just five female members, representing eight percent. The majority of faculty members were very supportive of my leadership and this contributed to my achievements as dean. I relate well with female co-workers and have also been supportive of them.

We need more female engineers. They excel once empowered, and they know what they need to do. They bring a diversity of ideas that they relate to their daily life. They are procedural, flexible, and intuitive in their approach to work. According to 2011 research by Kacey Beddoes of San Jose State University, female engineers have certain inherent characteristics that are advantageous to them. Beddoes said that women are conscientious and they pay attention to detail.

There are definitely challenges in being a female engineer, but they can be overcome. Being the only female student in my class during the BSc in civil engineering could be lonely, and you tend to stand out. Nonetheless, this drove me to work even harder to succeed (hence the first class award result that I got). Another challenge is in meetings, when some men are oblivious to my contributions or underrate my capabilities. Often, men suggest that I take the minutes; many men think women should be secretaries. Or, sometimes I'll say something in the meeting and no one bothers to pay attention. Then, a few minutes later, when a man says the same thing, people are suddenly paying attention and agreeing with him. Over time, I have learned to speak up and tell everyone in the meeting that I had just said the same thing.

To counter this kind of behavior, women need to be proactive and offer to chair meetings. As a woman, you have to work twice as hard to prove that you are worthy. So, believe in yourself. It is what is inside you that matters.

I am married and a mother of three children, so I know firsthand that balancing work, family, and other activities is the biggest challenge for women. In some cases, I was forced to go to work on holidays and weekends so that I could meet deadlines and also advance my career. Sometimes I work late so that I can accommodate my children's needs. Luckily, my family has been understanding and very supportive.

So what does it take to increase the number of female engineering students and engineers?

There is a need for a change in the mind-set of the parents, the girls themselves, teachers, and society on how they view females in engineering. Discrimination starts from the types of toys parents buy for boys and girls and also the roles and tasks they are given. It will require education and coaching for this perception to change.

Role modeling and mentoring, which is something I started doing in 2013, play a big role in motivating girls and female engineers. As a successful female engineer, my passion is to reach out to primary and secondary school students to raise awareness that females can also excel. Female students need to be informed about opportunities in engineering careers. During my term as dean of the faculty of engineering, we made this happen, and doing so contributed to the number of female engineering students at the Polytechnic increasing from 15 percent to 30 percent.

There is also a need for follow-up meetings to encourage female engineers who are in industry. Experience-sharing can help female engineers learn how to approach challenges and remain in the profession. Female engineers also need to be empowered with soft skills such as leadership and management, which would boost their confidence as they move up the ladder of success.

My advice to girls and young women is that they should have self-belief, and be courageous and independent. They should be focused and hardworking. What makes society feel that men have an upper hand is nothing but perception; the British writer William Golding once said that women are foolish to pretend they are equal to men, as they are far superior and always have been. Girls should create a purpose road map, and their parents should help them do that. On their road map, they should define what they want to achieve, and work on what it takes for them to get there, whether it's academic qualifications and/or other skills.

Life is about making choices. We are the product of what and how we think. If girls put great effort into mathematics and science subjects, it can only increase their chances of excelling in life.

JOURNEY 18

IT'S ABOUT MAKING A DIFFERENCE

KHAIRIYAH MOHD YUSOF

–

Director
Centre for Engineering Education
Universiti Teknologi Malaysia

–

MALAYSIA

Hello; my name is Khairiyah. In addition to my role at Universiti Teknologi Malaysia (UTM), I'm also president of the Society of Engineering Education Malaysia. My entire post-secondary education—bachelor's, master's and PhD—has focused on chemical engineering, and I've enjoyed learning about this field. I've had short stints in industry, mostly as part of my research work, and I constantly keep track of what is happening in the engineering world and stay connected with those from industry. That's because, as an educator, I think it is important to be armed with the information you need to best educate students for the future. In fact, my engineering research work on modelling is in collaboration with industry.

But learning about different aspects of education has always run in parallel with my learning in engineering. When I have conducted training workshops or given presentations related to teaching and learning, or on research in engineering education, some members of the audience ask how I came to focus on the intersection of engineering and education. And it took a while for me to realize that engineering education is my passion.

I was the only girl in our family, between two brothers, and there was no difference in the way we were treated by our parents. Growing up, I was close to Zikri, my older brother. We shared our toys and books, we played with our Matchbox cars and we played house together. We'd roam

ABOUT THE AUTHOR

Khairiyah Mohd Yusof is a Professor in the Department of Chemical Engineering and the founding and current Director of Universiti Teknologi Malaysia's Centre for Engineering Education. She is President of the Society of Engineering Education Malaysia, was Vice President for the International Federation of Engineering Education Societies from 2014 to 2018, and was Board Member of Research in Engineering Education Network from 2010 to 2017. Khairiyah is passionate about implementing and promoting meaningful learning. After seeing the impact on students in her own classes, she began disseminating these practices through publications, and training and mentoring educators. Khairiyah has conducted workshops throughout Malaysia and many countries around the world. As part of her efforts to learn and contribute to the scholarly engineering education community, she serves on the editorial boards of several academic journals. Khairiyah is the recipient of the 2018 Duncan Fraser IFEES Global Engineering Education Award; she has also won other awards, including the Global Student Platform on Engineering Education Mentorship Award in 2017, and the Frank Morton IChemE Global Award for Chemical Engineering Education Excellence in 2015.

around outdoors, exploring the nearby orchards and rubber plantation together. Later a physics enthusiast, my brother introduced me to science TV programs and magazines, and that is what sparked my interest in science. My parents never told us to devote ourselves to studying, but they made sure we were surrounded by books: once a month, my father would take us to the bookstore to buy any books we wanted. We really enjoyed reading them. I understand now that it was the environment that my parents set up for us while we grew up that helped us develop a love for learning and seeking knowledge.

In school, I have always liked science; to me, it was fun. And I really found it interesting when I could connect what I learned in the school laboratory with the world around me. Although I liked getting good grades, I appreciated even more the idea of learning by doing experiments and discovering how to make things work, and this led me to choose engineering.

I studied in a girls' school in Johor Bahru that was well known for academic and leadership excellence, and throughout those five years in secondary school, mathematics and science (divided into physics, chemistry, and biology in the last two years) were taught by both male and female teachers. This reinforced my belief that gender has nothing to do with being good in science and mathematics. In addition to academic excellence, the positive environment at the school developed girls' confidence and leadership abilities.

In the mid 1980s, after I graduated from secondary school, I was sponsored by Petronas, the Malaysian oil company, to study chemical engineering at the University of Alabama in the US. Apart from the technical knowledge, I appreciate the problem-solving and computing skills that I gained from my undergraduate years, and even today I use and develop them. I hardly noticed that the number of girls in our engineering courses was much smaller compared to boys, because that was never an issue for me. I liked that there were other Malaysian girls taking the same courses as me at the University of Alabama, since we could study and do our homework together.

I'd never worn the hijab (a scarf for covering my hair) in Malaysia, but shortly after arriving in the US, I decided to do so. While I have always known that covering my hair is required in Islam, being on my own in the US forced me to think about my own identity. I believed that knowledge is to be practiced, so wearing the hijab is about me practicing my faith and pleasing God. Although I did worry it might be a problem and make me stand out in a lecture hall, to my surprise, I did not face any discrimination from my professors. Yes, there were incidents in which a random person would shout at me on the streets outside the university area, but there were many who were friendly, or who would politely ask why I wore the hijab; most of the attention I received was out of curiosity. (That was in the 1980s and 1990s, but sadly, these days when I travel in the West the questions and stares can be quite hostile. This has led me to be extra careful, especially when I travel alone. It has also made my husband worry for my safety.)

I graduated during Malaysia's late-1980s economic slowdown, and there were no jobs available at Petronas. However, I was able to get a position as an assistant lecturer in the newly formed department of chemical engineering at UTM in the capital, Kuala Lumpur (the main campus would move to Johor Bahru in the 1990s). This enabled me to obtain a scholarship from the government of Malaysia for university academics in the 1990s to pursue a master's degree in chemical engineering at Clemson University in South Carolina in the US, and later a PhD in chemical engineering at the University of Waterloo in Canada. Furthering my studies to the highest possible level had always been my dream since I was in school; I even made it clear to my fiancé that it was my goal to study for a PhD after getting married, something he wholeheartedly supported.

My journey in engineering education can be divided into four phases, some of which overlap:

1. The discovery phase.
2. The learning and scholarly implementation phase.
3. The research and dissemination phase.
4. The leadership and transformation phase.

※ ※ ※

In the discovery phase, my early exposure to scholarly aspects of engineering education was during my graduate studies. When I was at Clemson in the early 1990s, my research was on time-optimal control of distillation columns. I was working with dynamic simulation of a 32-stage methanol-water distillation tower on the fastest personal computer in the lab, which had an 80386 microprocessor. It took about five hours for the simulation to run for every control structure that I tested. In between running the simulation, reading and writing for my research, I would go to my favorite shelf in the chemical engineering department library to read a journal called Chemical Engineering Education. As I was reading the articles, it dawned on me that there are many chemical engineering professors who are concerned about understanding learners, helping students to learn abstract concepts in the field, and various aspects of the curriculum. The best thing about this was that I realized there were resources that I could refer to in teaching chemical engineering, just like in the technical part. While working towards my PhD in Canada, I signed up for the Tomorrow's Professor e-mail list run by Rick Reis from Stanford University. Every week, I looked forward to reading the short article that summarizes research on issues related to college education. Looking back, these articles formed my early knowledge in teaching and learning, and showed me the importance of taking the scholarly approach in engineering education.

  The learning and implementation phase started after I obtained my

PhD, when I taught process control and dynamics, a subject notorious for a high number of failures, no matter who was teaching. It was very difficult to get students to understand the meaning behind the modelling equations; they were not able to relate what is physically happening to what is being represented in the mathematical models. I was also developing the process control laboratory, but it was not helpful for students in the course because they took the lab after taking the course. We have three to four parallel sections of the same course, each with a maximum of 60 students. By the end of the semester, each section had failure rates of 30-40 percent, which forced us to create another section for students repeating the course. I was thinking there had to be something that can be done to help students to learn and have an interest in the subject. My colleagues assured me that it was not my fault that students were not doing well in the course. However, I knew there were strategies that I could try to improve how I teach.

There was another reason why I had to try something to help my students. I was born to a family of educators; both my parents were teachers in a government secondary school located in Pontian, a small town in the state of Johor. The school served a large surrounding rural area, with hostels for boys and girls who lived far from the school. Being the founding principal, my father set up a lot of pioneering programs to help students who were mostly from low-income families. Our house was on the school compound, so I witnessed how my parents really cared about students and how committed they were in ensuring that all of them were nurtured in the school. They even temporarily took female students from rural areas into our home when there were no more beds available in the girls' hostel, to allow them to continue schooling.

I used to go with my parents when they visited students' families in the villages; they did this to gain the trust of parents to permit their children to stay in the school hostel so that they could get an education. Lack of funding did not stop them from establishing innovative programs such as textbook loan programs and the purchase of sports equipment, including two large rectangular trampolines (which my siblings and I used to jump on, too!). They held school charity fairs with other teachers to raise funds for the school, and their efforts brought about opportunities for upward social mobility for many students. My parents and these teachers became my role models for taking action to make a difference in the community—and that even small efforts can have a positive impact on other people's lives.

My upbringing and the wealth of support that I experienced throughout my studies made me realize that now was the time for me to give back. The knowledge I've gained based on what I have read all these years about engineering education nagged at my conscience. I just knew there had to be something that could be improved, something that I could do to help students learn. My engineering training cried out, "This is a problem, and you need to solve it!"

Yes, engineering can be tough, but it's not impossible. So I started to try out active learning, and grouping the students together. It did not work out very well initially. It was also necessary to motivate and reassure the students that the subject was interesting and not impossible to learn. I searched online for articles on how to conduct active learning and cooperative learning (CL) better—and I started to see improvements. In the semester of my first proper attempt at CL, the failures dropped drastically to 17 percent from the usual 30 percent, and the number of students with As went up to 10 percent! I began to see the power of utilizing existing educational principles and research in my class.

I was so happy to see the improvements that when I saw a call for papers for a conference on engineering education in Kuala Lumpur, I wrote one about my first attempt in CL and presented it at the conference. This was the first time I had written a paper on the implementation of teaching and learning in class. However, I was disappointed when I went to the conference, because many of the papers presented were on technical engineering research instead of engineering education. I wished that I could attend good engineering education conferences and meet the authors of the articles that I had been referring to, but it was just too expensive, and I did not have the funds. However, writing that first paper forced me to read more and reflect on my own implementation, and this gave me more ideas for improvements that could be made.

My attempts to implement active learning approaches caught the attention of UTM's director of the Centre for Teaching and Learning (CTL). UTM was attempting to introduce outcomes-based education, which requires alternative teaching approaches. With his encouragement and support, I started to explore problem-based learning (PBL) in 2002. We formed an active learning (AL) and PBL task force under the CTL to move forward and create an interest in UTM. Since the budget was limited, we could invite speakers only from Malaysia or neighboring Singapore to conduct PBL workshops, and went for observations within the two countries. It worked out well because we could find experts in PBL among the medical faculty (Prof. Azila from Universiti Malaya) and the education faculty (Prof. Tan Oon Seng from the National Institute of Education in Singapore).

I harbored hopes of having an engineering education community in Malaysia, and bringing in global experts to learn from. Initially, it seemed futile since there was no budget available, and my application to attend a conference on engineering education was rejected. Then, the late Professor Duncan Fraser from the University of Cape Town came to our university as an external examiner for the department of chemical engineering, and we held a seminar for him to talk about his efforts in engineering education. His talk not only inspired me, but I realized that there are other ways to bring in experts in engineering education.

In 2004, UTM held its first conference on engineering education, marking the start of UTM's interest in national level engineering education involvement. The following year, I offered my services as the secretary of the committee to support our dean as the chair of the conference at the regional level. We agreed to rename it the Regional Conference on Engineering Education (RCEE), and invited Prof. Richard Felder and Dr. Rebecca Brent as keynote and workshop speakers. As the person in charge, I had a lot of work to do, but it was worth the effort because I was able to learn, to verify my knowledge and to do classroom practice with them. Most importantly, I was able to disseminate valuable scholarly knowledge and gather local and regional practitioners to create a network. By this time, I realized that conferences could generate enough revenue to fund the cost of invited speakers, and that I could invite experts as well as form a community of practice.

    The RCEE became our signature event. Through it, we have managed to host various experts to learn from, such as Karl Smith, David Radcliffe, Ruth Streveler, Anette Kolmos, Johannes Strobel, Duncan Fraser, Erik de Graaf, and many others, depending on our need in engineering education at that time. For example, in 2007, Karl Smith was the right person to give input when we started our PhD in engineering education program, and he gave an introductory workshop on engineering education research to all potential students and supervisors in UTM, as well as a workshop on cooperative learning.

The launch of UTM's PhD in engineering education program in 2007 marked the third phase on research and dissemination. Although we had conducted action research and training courses since 2003, this marked the start of doing rigorous research on engineering education, as well as proper design and a high scholarly level of training workshops. UTM also provided funding for me to visit Purdue University, where I met with the late Professor Kamyar Haghighi to learn about its PhD in engineering education program, and most importantly, to learn about the need and standards for such a program.

The leadership and transformation phase started when I was appointed as head of the chemical engineering department in 2006, which was a critical transition period to the outcomes-based approach for all engineering curricula in Malaysia. Two years later, just a month after my term as department head was renewed, I was assigned to the position of deputy director for Advancement of Teaching and Learning at the CTL, where I oversaw training programs for academic staff in UTM. A couple of months after my term at the CTL was extended in 2010, my position was again changed: this time, I became director of the Centre for Engineering Education (CEE) under the School of Graduate Studies, mainly to take care of the PhD in Engineering Education program. Together with CEE's deputy director, Dr. Fatin Phang, we shaped CEE's activities into a scholarly centre of excellence, and CEE's achievements exceeded everyone's expectations.

✳ ✳ ✳

I am thankful for the blessings that God has given in my life. Although much of what I have described may make it seem as if it was all smooth sailing, there were various challenges that I faced. I did not start out feeling so confident about what I do; there were always doubts, and I made mistakes. I had to put in a lot of effort to attain the good academic results that I achieved; believe me, there were a lot of sweat and tears. However, I pushed myself to be consistent and thorough when learning, and I was not afraid to ask when I did not know something, even in a big lecture hall. There were episodes when I cried because of frustration with my research during my graduate studies, but with my husband's encouragement, I chose to go on after taking a break for a day or two. I learned that for all the trials and tribulations, there are rewards and achievements waiting. I knew I needed to focus on my goal and be positive about whatever happened, and about the effort that I needed to put in.

The support of my family has also been very important. My daughter was just eight months old when I started my studies in Clemson. By the time I was at Waterloo, my two sons had been born, so we had three children while I was pursuing my PhD. There was a lot of sacrifice on my husband's part, too; he came with me to Clemson and to Waterloo, where we took turns looking after our children and figured out the best way possible to bring them up within the constraints that we had. My ever-supportive parents did their best to help us with the children. I am thankful that my children could see the importance of what I am doing and would always be very helpful at home; they have also kept me up-to-date with the trends of today's youth.

I am fortunate that I had colleagues and bosses who were mostly supportive. The deans and department heads I had worked with always give me the chance to participate when they saw activities or opportunities in engineering education. The directors and deputy directors of the CTL at UTM were also supportive in allowing me to bring in experts and develop activities in engineering education. This made the challenges of developing something new in UTM and Malaysia possible, and even enjoyable.

Nevertheless, I had doubts about what I could do, because some of it was new and not that well-defined. Thus, I had to define it myself the best that I could with those around me, and modify my aim as activities took place, knowing that what I was going to get may not be perfect. This can be scary at times, but I had to forge through so that the next time around, things would be better. Mistakes will be made, but at least I can say that I did my best and made the best decisions under the circumstances.

Having mentors from all over the world was a very big blessing. That includes my supervisors at Clemson and Waterloo, my PBL mentors in Malaysia and Singapore, and my mentors in engineering education. They taught me the importance of scholarly practices and persuaded me to write what I had done in my classrooms. They knew that what I did should be shared if it was going to make an impact that went beyond the four walls of the classroom.

Learning and conducting rigorous research in engineering education was challenging, although I was really interested in it. I had to force myself to learn, because I was supervising students and taking care of the graduate program. All the while, I thought that my English was pretty good, but when I started to learn the field, I felt like I was pulling my hair out every time I had to read research articles. Initially, it was difficult to learn the language of educational research, thinking about questions on the bigger picture beyond the classroom and understanding the paradigm of educational research. However, this experience enabled me to have empathy for engineering educators as I guide and train them in this area, and most importantly, it has deepened my own understanding of research.

Sometimes, I do feel that opportunities may have passed me by because I am a Muslim woman. However, I do not dwell on them, because despite all the lost opportunities, there is so much more out there that I can contribute. And, I believe that not getting something is a blessing, too; the most important thing is to do my best and be thankful.

From all these wonderful experiences, I realize that God has given me a precious gift: to mentor other engineering educators and develop good engineering students. I am thankful that, through quality teaching, providing training workshops, and developing and sustaining a community of practice in engineering education, I have the opportunity to inspire others to make a difference in this world.

I know that what I am doing can never equal the gifts that I have received, but this is the least I can do in return for all the love and kindness that so many others have given me.

JOURNEY 19

ENGINEERING: IT'S A WAY OF LIFE

NAADIYA MOOSAJEE

Co-Founder
WomEng

SOUTH AFRICA

Some people are born knowing exactly what they want to do in life. My sister knew she wanted to be a doctor, and today she is a specialist. I unfortunately did not have such clarity and direction when I was a girl. I went through life climbing trees and exploring. I thought being a firefighter would be a cool job... until I watched a replay of the 1976 Olympic Games and saw Nadia Comaneci, the Romanian gymnast who scored perfect 10s. I was convinced that, as a Naadiya, it was in my name to perform. I would do routines on my bed until I was barred from jumping on the bed.

Growing up in Johannesburg as one of the middle kids among four siblings, there were always other options and avenues to explore. I started playing with my brothers' toys along with my own, decided that my Barbie doll needed a car, and at some point it came to me: the clarity that girls and boys should be equal. I once asked my father why girls had to do the dishes and boys washed the cars. Washing cars sounded like way more fun; plus, you could be outside. And it needed to be done less frequently. All in all, it just seemed that the chores were designated unfairly. After a few minutes of pondering, my father decreed that boys should help with the dishes, a decision one of my brothers loathed me for (but one that I am sure his wife is very happy about today).

Coming from a traditional Indian/South African household, my parents truly valued education. They were in high school during the 1976

ABOUT THE AUTHOR

Naadiya Moosajee is an entrepreneur by passion (she owns a restaurant group) and a civil engineer by training, with a Master's degree in Transport Engineering and a Bachelor of Science in Civil Engineering. She is Co-Founder at WomHub, an entrepreneurship incubator and advisory firm, and WomEng, a global social enterprise developing women and girls for the engineering and tech industries. In 2017, she received a special award from the Government of China at the BRICS summit for her contribution to girls' education in Africa. WomEng, which works across 19 countries, launched a commitment in partnership with UNESCO to empower one million girls through STEM education. Naadiya is a management consultant and serves as an advisory board member for the University of Cape Town Faculty of Engineering; is a Global Future Council Member with the World Economic Forum: Gender, Education and the Future of Work; and is an Aspen Institute New Voices Fellow. A renowned speaker, she was named one of the "Top 20 Young Power Women in Africa" by Forbes magazine. She is a global leader in gender, inclusion, and innovation focusing on the engineering and technology industries. Naadiya is passionate about fostering prosperity in emerging economies and engineering better societies.

riots, when non-white school students across South Africa rose up against having to learn the Afrikaans language under the apartheid regime. Many young people were killed for their beliefs. And disruption in schools meant that protesting students could not finish the year as planned.

In my family's case, my father, the eldest, had to leave school to work for a few months to support his six siblings and his parents when my grandfather became ill. My father sometimes reflects on the opportunities lost. He is one of the smartest people I know, and he became successful working in IT for a large retailer. But he didn't have the opportunity to go to university, and he didn't want the same fate for his children. My mother, who was a teacher, always said she was hard on us over our homework because she wanted us to succeed, to build ourselves, and never be reliant on a man. Together, they pushed me to be excellent. I remember when I was in the fifth grade and came home with a report card mark of 84 percent. I was so happy with myself, smiling from ear to ear. Upon looking at my marks, my father asked, "What happened to the other 16 percent?" I was shattered, and blurted out, with tears in my eyes, that my friend's mother would be ecstatic with these results. My father calmly looked at me and said, "Well, she is not my child, but you are, and there is always room for improvement." (I still got a reward for my report card; my parents would take us to a huge toy store once a year after our reports came out, as a special treat.) That memory has stayed with me and that mantra has guided and pushed me towards excellence, to achieve and also acknowledge that there is always room for improvement.

I was that person who loved school. I could be as sick as a dog but still go, and was proud to receive school awards for never being absent. They gave out awards for the top student in class, and I received those trophies with a sense of pride. I loved my friends, and my school; it was my happy place. So when my father told us he was being promoted to head office and that we would be relocating to Cape Town, I was devastated. It was just before I was to enter seventh grade, and I couldn't understand why we needed to leave everything behind. I remember the goodbye party we had, where we made so much food that we ate it for days. Then my family moved to Cape Town.

It's horrible to be the new girl in the final year of primary school in a new place. Kids can be brutal. I faked being sick because horrible girls and boys would laugh at me for my accent—the accent in Cape Town, on South Africa's southwest coast, is very different from that of Johannesburg in the northeast. I was teased for being smart, for being polite to teachers, for wearing glasses... all the things that had made me popular at my old school. I learned that a stomach ache was the easiest to fake, and in the mornings at home I'd be bent over crying in fake pain, or locked in the bathroom pretending to be dying. I hated school, and those who laughed at me.

Deep down, I was angry about having to move, not understanding that it was a better life and a better place for us, and that on the plus side our new house had a pool. I didn't appreciate small joys like going to my grandmother's house after school and having cheese sandwiches with my great grandmother, who would tell me such interesting stories of when she was younger. And my grandmother, who was a rebel of her time, would share with me how she traveled the world by herself. I would realize later that these two women, who were both abandoned by their husbands and had to fend for themselves, were the reason my mother wanted my sister and me to be self-sufficient.

For high school the next year, my parents put me in an all-girls school. It was the best decision they could have made. There was no name-calling or laughing at my accent. It was a fresh start, a place where I could thrive. Where being smart was valued and I could be me. I was back.

High school was filled with so many different experiences. I would go on to excel in my classes, and I also played tennis. I had vague dreams of becoming a Serena, but upon reflection, realized that I was better at math and science than I was at tennis. I joined many clubs and societies, and was thriving. For being the top student in a subject, I received class prizes of book vouchers. I bought some of the most amazing books and got lost in a world of literature.

I loved watching the TV series Ally McBeal, about a female lawyer who would fight cases in court along with a cast of really quirky characters. Because I, too, was someone who would never stop talking, I decided that I wanted to be a lawyer. Television made the profession look so glamorous, and I wanted to stand up in court, too. In the 11th grade, when one must make a choice about careers and apply to university, I decided I'd apply for law—until my mother said I would be wasting my talent.

Going back to the drawing board was so difficult. What would I study? Our school had career guidance speakers and it was usually about going to beauty school, secretarial colleges, or law school. I was stumped. I looked at my marks again. I did well in geography, and I loved it, so I asked Google for its wisdom on what career I could do. It said geologist. I was excited, and went back to my mother—who said no, because geologists worked in the mines and it wasn't safe. So, back to Google I went, and discovered geotechnical engineering, which was under the umbrella of civil engineering. This seemed a better option, and my mother gave her blessing.

I applied to only one university, the University of Cape Town—the best in the country—for civil engineering. When I received early acceptance, I decided it was a divine sign that I would be a civil engineer, and off to UCT I went. I remember sitting in orientation and the dean of engineering said, "Look to your left, and look to your right. The person on either side is not going to make it through this degree." I was terrified. As the top student in my high school and the first in my family to study engineering, I couldn't fail.

After the first semester, the test scores came out, and indeed I was failing. The only course I was thriving in was the Introduction to Civil Engineering. One day I was walking around campus wondering how I would get through it when my sister's friend spotted me. She must have seen the look of sheer terror on my face when she said, "Don't worry, I have seen really stupid people pass the course here. You will be fine." She made me laugh, but she also made me realize that I needed a change in strategy. I decided to befriend the smartest guy in our math class. Marlin was the kind of student who would ask questions that stumped lecturers. I got him to tutor me in math in exchange for muffins my mother baked. To this day, I still say that the only way I passed math was because of muffins, Marlin, and loads of prayer. I ended up passing my first year, scraping through in some subjects. But I also received the class medal for civil engineering. That was how I knew I was on the right path. The first two years of engineering were tough, but after that it got better.

Engineering is an interesting field to be in. It can challenge you on so many levels. Just when I thought I got the hang of engineering, and the technical nature of the beast, I had to learn practical application through work experience. In third year, I worked in a local steel fabrication plant for a few weeks. I was one of very few women there, but that's not unusual in engineering. In fact, it's the norm.

What happened next was, sadly, the norm as well. First, I was told I wouldn't be paid because it was a learning experience. That was fine, as I wanted to grow as an engineer, and I tried to volunteer for work projects so I could learn more quickly. I was paired with the technician and had to stamp drawings, but what I really wanted was to be on the floor of the plant. So I convinced one of the engineers to send me to the plant. It's a hard environment, and cold, especially in Cape Town during winter. The foreman showed me the ropes and I learned a lot. But the week after I left, that very foreman began to cyberstalk me. He emailed me constantly, and got hold of my university transcripts and commented on them. I had to block him. But when I did, he found another avenue to communicate with me; he also blamed me because I had smiled at him. I told no one about it. But I wanted to leave the industry. Then came the worst part: When I returned to university, I learned that my male colleagues who worked at the same firm were paid for the same job.

I was ready to leave, and while I loved engineering and wanted to complete my degree, I knew there were many other options out there for me; I didn't have to take this. Yet, the activist in me couldn't rest. The little girl who understood gender equality in chores wouldn't let this gross injustice go. I started to speak to a few friends, and suddenly a pattern emerged: we all had the same story. And something needed to be done. This is how we founded SAWomEng, or South African Women in Engineering, in my third year of my engineering degree. The organization supports female engineering students as they transition to the workplace.

It was an exciting time: not only had I decided to continue in engineering by pursuing a master's degree in transport engineering (as it turns out, I had hated geotechnical engineering, but I loved the challenge of dealing with the services that urban engineering provided to humanity),

SAWomEng was helping to change the world. We were bringing together female engineering students for training and skills development. We gave them industry mentors and we got companies to fund the organization. In short, we provided female students with everything they needed to succeed in engineering.

I was nominated for a UCT outstanding leadership award for my work forming SAWomEng. I hoped to win as the prize money would go into my organization. I waited with bated breath—and someone else's name was announced. But I did get third prize, which was an international exchange at a partner university for a semester abroad. I chose Germany, and a city I had never heard of, Stuttgart, mostly because it wasn't too far from Italy; it was my dream to visit Italy.

The night I left, I was so scared. It was my first time away from home, in a strange land, where most people, I assumed, didn't speak English. I heard Germany was really cold, so even though it was August, I wore my boots and warm coat on the flight—and when I arrived in Stuttgart, home of iconic engineering from Mercedes-Benz, Daimler, and Bosch, it was 32 degrees Celsius, a glorious summer day.

Germany would teach me independence and freedom. I tested my own boundaries. I traveled to Italy and ate loads of gelato and pizza, and I made friends with fellow engineers from all around the world. When it was time to head home at the end of the semester, I'd been completely changed by the experience. The one thing I regretted was not studying longer in Germany. But it was time to come home, because South Africa was hosting the 2010 FIFA World Cup. And not only was I a huge football fan, I had a plum job waiting for me.

The 2010 World Cup was one of the most exciting times ever for my country. There was so much euphoria, and I felt like I was at the center of it all, as I was running FIFA's VIP transport operations. It was the coolest job to be at the stadium, making sure the VIPs, match officials and FIFA representatives got in and out safely. I was supporting Spain for the win, and was there to say "Hola!" when the Spanish team arrived and to see Cristiano Ronaldo up close when the Portuguese team arrived. And Spain won! It was a surreal experience involving very little sleep, and eight months of preparation and execution, but I had the best job in the world.

After the World Cup, I focused on SAWomEng. We were now running development programs for high-school and university students, as well as supporting women in the engineering industry. We had teams all around the country, and committed partners. I was headhunted by a niche development consultancy working on interesting transport projects. So now I had a dual career of working in a social enterprise developing the pipeline of women and girls in the engineering sector, on top of an exciting day job working with the public sector on transformation engineering projects. Both careers allowed me to travel around the world, and I truly felt I was making an impact and changing lives.

One of these trips was to Turkey. I was dining with my business partner and soul mate, Hema, whom I'd met through SAWomEng, at a restaurant overlooking the ancient part of Istanbul when my fate would change once again, though I didn't realize it at the time: there, I met a persistent and charming Turkish man, who after one dinner decided that he wanted to marry me. I was not so easily convinced, and after a sad departure, flew to my next destination.

The work we were doing for women in engineering was gaining traction, and we started to expand to Kenya. It became demanding, and Hema realized that we would have to quit our jobs and work on our venture full time. This was 2014, and the timing was horrible as a recession had hit and many funders could no longer support us. It forced us to be creative and inventive, leaning on our engineering skills to derive a solution from first principles. We pivoted our business and started working in more countries, driven by large clients who saw the need to increase the number of women in their engineering businesses. We were developing and training women for the sector and working with the sector to embrace diversity and inclusion. We created global partnerships and committed to empowering one million women through STEM education at the United Nations. There are women engineers in industry today because of the programs we have run to empower them and change their paths.

Life works in mysterious ways. There have been so many important moments in my life when Hema was there, and we have been through so much together. I ended up marrying Veysel, the persistent Turkish guy.

He moved to South Africa and we decided to open a restaurant together; today, we own two restaurants and have a toddler.

As for Hema and I, beyond SAWomEng we now also have WomHub, a female-founder accelerator for women in engineering and technology businesses. We are also building a co-working space, and our Imagineering Lab to foster entrepreneurship. We have moved from creating women engineers to helping women own the engineering industry. We grow entrepreneurs and look at ways in which we are able to transform the sector.

Entrepreneurship is not for the faint-hearted, especially in engineering and when you are trying to bring about systemic change. But I'm up to the task; I've always believed that I became an engineer because of divine intervention (and maybe a few muffins). And as I go through career changes—from engineer to consultant to entrepreneur—I'm so thankful for my engineering degree because it prepared me in ways I could never imagine. If I had to do it all over again? I'd definitely go into engineering.

JOURNEY 20

SUDDENLY, THE IMPOSSIBLE!

LUENY MORELL

Founder & Director
InnovaHiEd;
Vice Dean
School of General Engineering
Beihang University

-

PUERTO RICO (USA) & CHINA

I don't consider myself a road warrior, but admittedly I'm a frequent traveler. I travel across the globe trying to bring together individuals, educational institutions, governments, and industry partners in an effort to innovate and transform engineering education. Throughout my younger years and as a professional, along the way I have faced many challenges and difficulties, but I have been sustained and propelled by the conviction that your life and mission can make a lasting difference in others' lives. If nothing else, that is our reason for being on this Earth.

That irresistible motive and driving passion for believing in something and acting on it is all one really needs. Although I recognize that it has not always been particularly easy, the positive and satisfying impact of my endeavors has grown continuously throughout the years—and will keep doing so as I face the future. Each day I'm amazed to see how a series of small steps always ends up bringing forth so much! Let me tell you about how I got here.

I grew up in the town of Camuy, Puerto Rico. Both of my parents had been university educated—my father was a pharmacist and my mother a university math professor—and so they expected my younger sister and I

ABOUT THE AUTHOR

Lueny Morell, MS, PE, Ing.Paed.IGIP is Founder and Director of InnovaHiEd, and Vice Dean of the School of General Engineering at Beihang University in China. With a BS and MS in Chemical Engineering from the University of Puerto Rico and Stanford University, Lueny is passionate about STEAM education and innovation as pillars to develop talent to better serve society. After successful careers at HP Labs and the University of Puerto Rico, she has catalyzed the creation of two new schools of engineering: one in Silicon Valley, US, and one in Beijing, China, and currently offers capacity building and certification programs in engineering (and other STEAM areas) education and innovation as principal foundation to support regional and national economic development efforts. She is a member of several professional societies and international boards and has received various awards for her work, including the prestigious US National Academy of Engineering Gordon Prize for innovations in engineering education in 2006. Recognized as one of the Engineering Education Pioneers in the US in 2014, Lueny is author of Essentials to Innovate Engineering & Related Disciplines, as well as many papers. She maintains two blogs on topics associated with innovation and engineering education and her consulting/mentoring activities: www.luenymorell.com; www.innovahied.com.

to also go to university. When I reached high school, the Catholic Colegio San Felipe in Arecibo, in the mid-1960s, I entertained the possibility of engineering as a career. When I brought the idea to my career counselor, a nun, I was bluntly told that engineering "was not for ladies." Rather than detouring me, that authoritative opinion sparked in me a fire to prove her wrong. Growing from this original seed of accidental motivation, I ended up spending decades in engineering, teaching new generations and aiming to transform outdated educational paradigms.

I went on to the University of Puerto Rico at Mayagüez (UPRM) to earn a bachelor's degree in chemical engineering. As the only woman in the class—engineering was a male-dominated discipline in the 1970s in my country—and having an extremely shy personality, perhaps due to a very dominant father, those years were not easy for me. I never dared to question my professors nor speak in the classroom. And I always sat in the front row to avoid others. But UPRM was where I met and married my husband, Waldemar, in 1973, and from there we both went on to Stanford University, where I earned a master's degree in 1977 in chemical engineering and had my first two children.

It was at that point that I was recruited by the University of Puerto Rico at Mayagüez (UPRM). (I live in that city to this day.) At the time, there was a strong focus on the industrial economic activity on the island and an emphasis on developing STEM professionals. Thus, there was a strong need for educational reform to address the country's needs, even if those needs were not readily apparent to the naked eye. So, at 26 years old, I began my professional journey, in a department where I was the only woman (and remained so for over 20 years). Given the economic development priorities and development of the chemical and pharmaceutical industry in Puerto Rico at the time, chemical engineering had the highest admissions requirements across the university's 11 campuses of 65,000 students. So, we were catering to la crème de la crème of the island.

I started my teaching career enthusiastically, not once thinking that I was less capable than anybody else, although I later learned that some experienced professors questioned whether a woman could do the job. Research was not required then, so I had a full-time teaching load. Even though I carefully prepared all my lectures, homework, and tests (sometimes in partnership with my colleagues), my style of teaching emulated that of my predecessors: I'd stand in front of students and do all the talking. And guess what? No matter how much work I put into these efforts, the students were apparently not learning! For example, in the Mass and Energy Balances course, the pass rate was a mere 40 percent. True, this was not the traditional plug-'n-chug kind of course; it required a lot of analysis and critical thinking skills. So, colleagues told me not to worry, that this was historically expected.

It would seem that although industry's need for a new breed of engineers was growing and evolving, and the admissions requirements for students were ever higher, teaching methods and pass rates had not changed. I wondered how the best and the brightest students could do so poorly. Bottom line: I was not happy, and the students were not happy.

A general sense of shame overtook me and remained for several years—until I reached the conclusion that the problem was not the students at all. The problem was me and the way I was teaching. So, I started to read about teaching and learning, and attended ASEE conferences to learn from others. Around 1985, I registered for one of Richard M. Felder's teaching workshops. He's an expert in learning styles and teaching strategies from North Carolina State University. Suddenly a new world of possibilities opened my eyes. I was getting answers to my questions:

- How do people learn?
- How can I teach so that students learn what they need to?
- How can I create a classroom environment conducive to learning?
- How can I assess learning in a fair way?

Richard Felder and others inspired me to incorporate novel and sometimes strikingly odd or unusual ideas into my classes. Many of the changes were simple and were implemented promptly. For example, one of the homework assignments I gave students was to define and solve a problem. I would collect all of them and put one in the test (what a miracle: all 30 students learning 30 problems together!). I would have them take quizzes (not for grade) to learn how ready they were for the real test, then I had them exchange the quizzes and grade their peers. This would also help them to learn the importance of organizing solutions and writing clearly.

As I became more creative with my teaching, a little miracle occurred: my students began to perform better, with passing rates as high as 90 percent! And I hadn't changed the content. They were simply learning more effectively. My teaching "revolution" was already yielding positive results.

By 1989, students were contending for spots in my courses. Due to restrictions in class size, some students would attend a course taught by me instead of attending that same course they had registered for but that was taught by another professor. But notwithstanding my satisfaction and the happiness of my students, all was not rosy, because despite these results, I had not yet earned the support of my colleagues. Instead, they regarded me with suspicion and doubt. One of my colleagues abrasively told me, "Either you're telling the students what problems are going to be on the exam, or you're telling them the answers during the exam." My response was simple: "Well then, I won't come to the meetings where we write and prepare the exams, I won't be at the exams when they are administered, and I won't grade the exams." I did just that—and still my students did better.

On another unforgettable occasion, a senior professor member of the Personnel Committee, which oversaw tenure and promotions, called me to his office and sounded off. "Lueny, you have a fan club among the students, and this is unacceptable! I don't know what you are doing, but the Mass and Energy Balances course has had a historic failure rate of two out of three students. This happens here and elsewhere and will continue to happen. You had better stop!" Admittedly, this did cause me to be fearful, but more than that it gave me more encouragement to prove I was doing the right thing. I remember leaving his office pleased that he'd heard what was going on in my classes—and that a small revolution was happening!

In 1993, I decided to document the outcomes. I invited the two colleagues teaching the course that semester to do some research on the effects of teaching/learning styles. One of them was head of the department, a very experienced professor. The other was a young professor who had asked me about mentoring him in teaching methods. We were able to document and correlate the "little things" that had been implemented in the class with the outcomes of the course. This process resulted in a paper sharing these experiences. The document was presented at the ASEE conference in 1996. These efforts, all documented in peer reviewed papers in journals and at conferences, was evidence that the teaching and learning methods were working! And these documented outcomes gave me the strength and motivation to continue making innovations in other courses and participating in curriculum and teaching projects funded by the National Science Foundation (NSF) and the National Aeronautics and Space Administration (NASA). Working with colleagues has been, and continues to be, a very rewarding learning experience.

Eventually, peers in the faculty stopped doubting me, and stopped troubling me. I was given tenure, promoted to full professor, and offered various leading roles in energizing, critical projects. But the most rewarding part for me was the satisfaction of making a difference in students' lives, and in having done what needed to be done for them to be able to learn the fundamentals through unforgettable experiences.

Attending the commencement parade became a sort of personal challenge to not cry, but I couldn't win that challenge. I cried tears of joy that "my kids" had learned, and even enjoyed it along the way, and that they were now taking a little bit of me with them. They were moving into successful engineering careers of their own. And I was on the road to a very fulfilling journey—starting with my original baby steps in engineering education that had led to successful innovations. My work, and that of my colleagues, was even recognized by the US National Academy of Engineering: the Gordon Prize (viewed by many as the American version of the Nobel for innovations in engineering education) confirmed that what I went through to help my students learn was worthwhile.

Looking back now to some of the things I have done—and beyond my journey in education, my husband and I have proudly raised three children (Juan Antonio is an engineer; Ana Carolina is a psychologist; and Gabriel Antonio is also a psychologist)—I feel God has given me a marvelous opportunity to pay forward all the blessings I have been given. Beyond my faith and my family, friends, and colleagues, I am deeply grateful for the opportunity to be a part of teams who have founded, and continue to strive to change the world through, organizations like the International Federation of Engineering Education Societies (IFEES), the Global Engineering Deans Council (GEDC), and the Student Platform for Engineering Education Development (SPEED). I also feel privileged to be helping universities all over the world transform their programs to better address their economic and social well-being.

Often, our will and determination falter, as one has only 24 hours in a day, and our human body can only take so much. But what keeps me going is my philosophy of life, which is something St. Francis of Assisi said: "One only needs to start doing what needs to be done, then what is possible, and suddenly, the impossible happens."

At this point in my career, when I am focused on sharing with others my experiences, mentoring colleagues and helping them catalyze their own innovations, and after having received various awards and recognition for my work in transforming and re-engineering engineering education—all of which I am honored by and grateful to have received—I could never have imagined that doing what I love and believe in could have turned into something that has positively impacted so many people.

And to think it all started with a high school career counselor's doubt. When I think about that nun telling me that, basically, women should know their place—advice that in fact led me to my place on the path I was meant to be on—it just reaffirms to me that God does indeed work in mysterious ways!

JOURNEY 21

INCREDIBLE OPPORTUNITIES ON AN UNLIKELY PATH

TAGWA AHMED MUSA

Dean
Petroleum Engineering
Sudan University of Science and Technology

SUDAN

I was born in the 1970s in Algazira State, an agricultural area in the middle of Sudan where most residents work as farmers. My small village, Hillat Abbas, was a poor one, and I was the fifth eldest of eight children. We enjoyed our days running around the neighborhood, and other times sitting under a big shady tree in front of our house along with other children from my village. We spent a lot of time under that tree, especially during holidays, and I still remember that we were fond of making toys from old clothes, and building small houses and animals using mud and shale.

Although my mother, Aziza, was illiterate (and remains so), my father was able to read and write Arabic well, despite the fact that he didn't go to school either. Even though I was one among eight children, I used to enjoy special attention from my father. He always asked me to come along when he went to visit his friends and relatives, and he used to encourage me to sing famous local songs to his friends, whom he bragged to about my school grades and academic excellence. He really believed in my capabilities and he was certain that I would be the best among his kids academically.

Sadly, when I was only eight years old and in grade three of primary school, my father passed away, leaving my mother, me, and three brothers and four sisters. Even though I had lost him, I would never forget his encouraging words and his belief in me. In fact, I think that's what inspired me to build my future as a successful student, and to later create a career as a professor and scientist.

ABOUT THE AUTHOR

Dr. Tagwa Ahmed Musa is an Associate Professor of Petroleum Engineering at Sudan University of Science and Technology (SUST), as well as Dean of the College of Petroleum Engineering and Technology. She has extensive research and teaching experience in addition to being a significant contributor to academic, research, and community service programs both locally and internationally. She is the first Sudanese woman to receive a PhD in the petroleum engineering field. In 2017 she received the Women in Industry and Academia award from the Industrial Engineering and Operations Management (IEOM) Society. Dr. Musa has served in leading committees of several professional societies and published many papers in peer reviewed journals. She has participated in organizing many conferences and has served on technical committees for others. Dr. Tagwa is a member of the editorial board of several scientific journals, and she has worked as an external examiner for several universities around the globe. Currently she is serving as director of the Sudan section of the Society of Petroleum Engineers. Dr. Tagwa has a Bachelor's degree with First Class Honors from the Sudan University of Science and Technology, and a Master's and a PhD from China University of Geosciences (all in petroleum engineering).

I continued my primary school in the same village and passed all my exams with flying colors; I was the top student. My academic excellence encouraged my mother to move me to another village to join middle school, where I stayed with my uncles. I was fortunate to continue my schooling, because during that time, Sudan and the whole of Africa lacked good schools in small villages and rural areas, so education opportunities for village kids were scarce—and unfortunately, educating girls was the lowest priority. Families in my village at that time were mainly looking for a husband for their teenage daughters.

I completed my three years of middle school and scored first place in the district in the General Qualifying Exam. So, when I was 15, I joined a high school in Almanagel, the nearest city to my uncle's village. Only cities had high schools, and since school was far from even my uncle's home, I spent three years living in that school's dorm before going to university.

In Sudan's academic system, being accepted to a specific major for post-secondary education depends mainly on how well you perform in a national exam. If a student aims to go to medical school, he or she needs to enroll in the biology stream in high school, while those whose aim is engineering college must enroll in the high-level mathematics stream. My major interest was to study engineering; however, because my mother wanted me to study medicine, I enrolled in the biology stream, and I also took all of the high-level mathematics classes. This was not commonly done because it was very difficult.

My results were equally excellent in both streams, but I elected to study petroleum engineering; I was fortunate to be in the first batch of students studying this major in Sudan. The program is five years of study, which my mother considered too long; she supported my education but wanted me to get married. Nevertheless, I was accepted to Sudan University of Science and Technology (SUST) and was the first among my siblings to go to college.

The institution is in Sudan's capital, Khartoum, where life is totally different from the village I grew up in. Of the 26 students in my class, only two were female. Later, two more women transferred to the program. I liked university life very much and enjoyed my field of study. More importantly, I liked the volunteer work: for three years I served as the vice president of a student association that represents students from my district, and for two years I served as social affairs secretary of the Association of Petroleum Engineering Students.

There was no gender bias in class, but the challenges started when we were semifinalists, as we were required to go for training in the oil fields in western Sudan. The university arranged for the trainees to travel there by bus. Since this trip takes more than two days, the university decided the two females shouldn't go; they said we were to join them when the Ministry of Petroleum found us seats in an aircraft in a couple of days. We didn't believe this would happen, and refused to lag behind our colleagues. So, we ignored the department's decision and took the bus with the rest of the class, who were very supportive. (Upon our return, we would be reprimanded by the university and given a warning letter.) We stayed for 45 days in an army camp, and the entire experience was a very good one, marred only by the fact that I fell sick in the last 10 days and underwent an appendectomy.

I was one of only two out of 42 in my class who graduated with a First Class (Honors) and was selected to join the university as a teaching assistant. I then received, along with two of my colleagues, a scholarship to get a Master's degree in the People's Republic of China through the Chinese scholarships program allocated to the Government of Sudan.

One of those two colleagues happened to be my fiancé, Ahmed Elrayah. We got engaged during the last year of my BSc studies, and were married in China during the first year of Chinese language courses, before we even started the Master's program. I gave birth to our first daughter while in the Master's program. Our second daughter was born during my PhD studies at the same university; I had received a scholarship for the program, and became the first woman from Sudan to receive a doctorate degree in oil and gas engineering.

Having two babies while studying was very challenging for me; however, nothing could stop my ambition to complete my graduate studies. It was not so difficult to find a babysitter; I found that the Chinese people were very helpful to me in this regard.

✳ ✳ ✳

When my husband and I returned with our little family to Sudan in August 2005 after seven years in China, we had to leave our daughters with my husband's family in the city of Madani until the two of us could get settled in our jobs as assistant professors at the petroleum engineering department at SUST, our alma mater in Khartoum. Four months after starting, we welcomed our little girls to our new rented apartment.

My main work in the university was teaching, research, services, and administrative duties. I went on to teach eight different courses related to petroleum engineering for undergraduate and postgraduate students at SUST and other universities inside and outside Khartoum. I have also supervised many student projects and theses at different levels. My work resulted in the publication of more than 25 papers in peer reviewed journals.

The fact that I was not much older than my students when I began at SUST helped me to build excellent relationships with them while receiving excellent ratings in all of their assessments. After two years I was assigned to serve as department head for the petroleum engineering department, the first female to serve in this role since the establishment of the program 14 years earlier. Female department heads have become much more common at SUST and other Sudanese universities since that time: As per 2018 statistics, of SUST's 117 departments, 42 are headed by women; that's more than one third of the positions.

Since the petroleum engineering department was where I graduated from, I was familiar with all the challenges it faced, and this helped me to do well in its management. Although sustaining the performance of my program is not an easy task in my country, I did my best, and tried to find sustainable training opportunities for my students in the oil fields. This was achieved through an agreement with the Ministry of Oil and Gas, which is still in effect today.

After three years as department head, I was appointed manager of the Training and Oil Consultancy Center, and in 2014, I assumed responsibility as dean of the College of Petroleum Engineering and Technology. As of 2018, the college has 38 faculty members, 20 administrative and assisting staff, and 25 laborers; females represent 36 percent, 65 percent, and 80 percent respectively. However, of the 1,003 undergraduate students enrolled in 2018, only 96 are females (that's less than 10 percent).

Based on my experience as dean at one of my country's most prominent universities, I have witnessed the leadership of the university take interest in recruiting and retaining women for management positions, and supporting them. I have had a very positive experience with the opportunities the university leadership has offered me to lead many initiatives and to represent the university locally, regionally, and internationally. These incredible opportunities allowed me to build character, reflect my strength, develop an excellent network of contacts, and establish key relationships.

However, such tremendous commitments have also represented significant challenges in my personal life and family commitments.

Establishing the required delicate balance between family obligations and work requirements is quite challenging, requiring me to juggle responsibilities. In my case, my husband has been working in the same college; that's an advantage in that he understands my work and this makes him a big supporter of it. But it's also a disadvantage in that it often leads to us bringing work issues to our dinner table at home. Perhaps this has been a good thing, however; it does serve as an example to our daughters that it's perfectly "normal" for both parents to have fulfilling careers. My older daughter, Samar, is 19—and very smart. She is doing quite well in her second year of medical college in Khartoum. Suha is 14 and just starting secondary school. I don't think she is interested in a career in engineering, but she still has more than a year before she must choose a stream.

It's true that the nature of a job in academia is, in general, quite flexible, especially in the area of teaching and research; however, management duties are incredibly exhausting, particularly when staff and operations require frequent follow-up. The staff I manage are culturally diverse and come from different educational and social backgrounds. I'm fortunate that all the males in my college are helpful and supportive.

The pressing challenge for women in the engineering field, especially in petroleum engineering, is that it's an industry that requires fieldwork. Some duties and long-term job commitments, specifically in oil and gas fields, are perceived as unsuitable for women in our culture and represent severe challenges for married women and others.

Based on my experiences, the judgment of women in leadership roles depends on the impressions of staff and peers. Typically, a woman in such a position will be exposed to many tests. Some will describe her as an "iron woman," while others refuse to accept her leadership role and assume that she is too weak and soft to be a dean.

Despite these challenges, I have been quite successful in creating a healthy work environment and maintaining productivity while working with many male leaders. I gave much attention to university/industry collaboration, and have tried to make significant contributions to the community, both independently as well as through my college and my university. I got involved in many different activities and committees nationally, globally, and internationally, and led committees of several professional societies. I'm currently a member of the Society of Petroleum Engineers (SPE), Sudan Association of Petroleum Geoscientists (SAPEG), and Global Engineering Deans Council (GEDC), among others. Also, I've participated in organizing many conferences and served on technical committees for others. I'm on the editorial boards of several scientific journals, have worked as an external examiner for many universities around the globe, and acted as a reviewer on the promotion dossiers for some universities. Every year since 2010, I have held a different position in SPE Sudan Section. Furthermore, I'm a member of the Consultancy Council of Sudan's Ministry of Oil and Gas and many other committees in the ministry. I'm the only female dean working in the body of the ministry that is responsible for all engineering education strategies and policies in Sudan.

The reason I mention my work in all these societies and committees, and my participation and engagement in related activities including international meetings, seminars, training, workshops, and conferences, is that it has been the main platform for building my career. The exposure I got has given me a good opportunity to learn from expertise around the world—different cultures and countries—and has helped me build very good personal relationships that are really helping me to fulfill all my work commitments inside and outside Sudan.

I try to reflect any experience I get from these global activities to my people in Sudan. For example, my attendance at the Industrial Engineering and Operation Management (IEOM) conference in Morocco in 2017 inspired me to establish the IEOM student chapter in my university. This became an excellent platform for linking engineers from all five engineering colleges at SUST in carrying out joint activities across colleges and departments. Last year, I was fortunate enough to join Texas A&M University in College Station, Texas, US, as a visiting scholar for a period of more than two months. This opportunity allowed me to observe and understand the mechanisms behind the academic, research and education excellence of Texas A&M, one of the world's leading engineering education institutions. This was particularly useful since my work there was in the petroleum engineering department, which is globally known as the best such program in the world. I presented the outcome of this unique exposure to my faculty at SUST and have tried to adapt some of the Texas A&M models in all areas.

Another example of how I try to reflect my own global experiences when I'm back home is my attendance at the 2018 World Engineering Education Forum (WEEF)–Global Engineering Deans Council (GEDC) conference in Albuquerque, New Mexico. There, I discovered the relationship between peace and engineering. I also learned about the United Nations' proposed Sustainable Development Goals (SDGs). And in early 2019, I was a part of an international training program in Stockholm, organized by the Swedish International Development Cooperation Agency (SIDA), called "Intellectual Property for Least Developed Countries—National Technological Capacity Building." There, I proposed a project to establish a Technology and Innovation Support Centre (TISC) at SUST, which I'm working on now. Although there are so many challenges in a country like Sudan, I never give up when I'm working on these projects, even after setbacks.

And my country is a difficult place to work. There is so much instability due to economic collapse, which is the result of corruption, sanctions, poor management, and political upheaval. I have witnessed the damage on all Sudanese institutions due to two decades of comprehensive economic sanctions by the United States and other Western countries. There was a time when I didn't understand the reason for the sanctions on Sudanese universities, which negatively impacted our education system and our connection to the modern world. I used to feel very sad when, every time I tried to open a website or download software, I received this message: "Access is forbidden in your country." Or when I'd receive a warning e-mail from the Society of Petroleum Engineers informing me, and anyone from the student chapter or section offices, that Sudan was not to contact them. I felt helpless when one of my students asked me why it was not possible for him to participate in a specific international conference or any kind of competitions. I never understood it: Why should we Sudanese people suffer in this way because of political issues we are not part of?

In the search for answers and to better understand the political issues in Sudan, in 2014 I involved myself in activities of the National Congress Party, which led the government at that time. I didn't object when they assigned me the role of the party's director of Asian affairs in 2015, an unpaid position I stayed in for three years before I stepped down in order to dedicate my time to technical, scientific, and academic matters. Although my work in politics took a lot of my personal time, I gained many insights and lessons from this experience. I now understood the importance of international lobbies, how Sudan has a chance to be part of the world if we manage our international relationships in a good way and pay more attention to the quality of our negotiation representatives.

✽ ✽ ✽

Women in my college are very helpful and always support me; however, just like women around the world, they struggle to find better ways to balance their work and personal lives. Often, there is a feeling of guilt that stems from social pressures; it comes from their husbands, families, and communities. My leadership has sometimes left me feeling helpless to defend the women in my college because there are so many challenges. These include:

- Frequent requests for leave. In Sudanese culture, requests can be made for things like marriage festivities, family issues such as illness in the immediate family, and maternity. The law here also supports women escorting her husband if he goes to study or work abroad, even if it's for several years.
- Staff requests for me to engage in marital disputes; e.g., a female staff member is expected to obtain a permit from the husband if I need her to do additional work.
- Staff and faculty are required to get their husbands' permission to travel. Such restrictions limit access to training opportunities and delay promotion.
- Women at all levels of employment and all levels of the workplace are affected by sexual harassment—especially students and younger female teachers.
- The Sudanese oil fields, which are located far from cities, are not equipped with sleeping and toilet facilities for females, so the training opportunities for girls is limited to an office, with

only a one-day visit to the field. The challenge for leaders is to search for another solution to meet the needs of female students.

- Unfortunately, some of my colleagues, both male and female, are not keen to take advantage of opportunities. Perhaps because of the bad political situation in Sudan, it's as if they feel helpless, and therefore don't like to do anything beyond their duties.
- External partnerships, especially participation in activities of the Ministry of Oil and Gas and petroleum companies in Sudan, are considered a platform to bring the views of the industry and academia together and therefore develop cooperation. Yet there is a lack of interest among my colleagues (especially females), despite my personal interest, diligence, and work, to seek these partnerships.

In my opinion, women are more than capable of doing any kind of work if they are empowered and have self-confidence. Fortunately, the field of engineering has become a familiar arena for women; women have proven themselves as successful professionals in all engineering disciplines. It has become easier for women to find places in engineering schools and in the job market. Yet we must always remind each other to never forget we are females!

And on that note, I'll conclude with the following important lessons I've learned from my life spent in engineering academia.

- Have confidence, have respect for others, and don't allow

yourself to be provoked by males. If women keep these things in mind, they will never feel suppressed.

- Maintaining a strong personal network and exploiting opportunities are very important for any woman's success.
- The qualities that women in general have—an artistic point of view, sensitivity, attention to detail, and emotional intelligence—can lead to success, especially in STEM. And letting other females know they are doing well, perhaps by thanking her publicly for an achievement or sending a letter of appreciation, will not only give her job satisfaction but will make a big difference towards her future success.
- Gender is not a factor to success. Education, knowledge, and never giving up, even after failure, certainly are.
- Women generally are adaptable, and can adjust their situation to be able to work in any environment. Tradition should not be a factor in stopping their ambitions for success and positive thinking.
- Political experience may strengthen a woman's character and knowledge. However, overwork is unsustainable, so balance is needed before she decides to move into the field of politics.
- Family should always come first—not only for women, but for men as well.
- Continuous learning and training are the keys to sustained

success regardless of age, nationality, working environment, or other factors.

I hope my lifetime of experience highlights to you the challenges female engineers are facing in developing countries, and the ways these challenges can be met so that they not only become leaders in their community, but are recognized regionally and globally. We should work together to share our experiences, which will help pave the way for more women to become a part of the engineering profession.

JOURNEY 22

FROM OUTSIDE-IN: PONDERINGS OF AN EDUCATOR

PRATHIBA NAGABHUSHAN

Educational Psychologist & Sessional Lecturer
Australian Catholic University

AUSTRALIA

I am not an engineer. Other than having been married to a mechanical engineer for nearly three decades, I never dreamed that I would have anything to do with engineering, let alone engineering education! Having been in the field of education and psychology for many years, a spark of zeal was fired only relatively recently. During the Christmas break in 2015, a friend of mine mentioned that the International Conference on Transformations in Engineering Education, organized by the Indo-Universal Consortium of Engineering Educators (IUCEE), was to be held in January 2016, in Pune, India. He urged me to attend the conference as he believed that I could share my knowledge with the participants. As I was already planning to be in India at that time, I decided to attend.

I had no idea what to expect; I felt I was on a path towards The Great Unknown. However, once there, I sensed very deeply the positive vibes that pushed me to plunge into this new field—a field that I knew nothing about and that I had not explored before—with utmost confidence and a great deal of motivation. Ever since, I have not looked back. As an educational psychologist and a classroom practitioner, I have always felt that I have a lot to share with the fraternity of engineering education, and a lot more to learn from the fast-growing (and trending) field of engineering education. This first exposure gave me the impetus to explore the current issues and trends in engineering education, especially in India, and how there is a lot of scope for us to create a unique collegial culture

ABOUT THE AUTHOR

Prathiba Nagabhushan is an educational psychologist who completed her PhD at the Australian National University in Canberra. She has more than three decades of teaching experience in a variety of educational settings and at different levels of the educational system—with diverse students and across a wide range of cultural contexts—in India, Mexico, and Australia. Prathiba's publications include student motivation and engagement in learning, global trends in education, and pre-service teachers' emotional well-being. Her current research interests include self-efficacy in students, ICT in education and educational practices, and research in engineering education. Prathiba is currently teaching Psychology at St. Mary MacKillop College in Canberra, and English Curriculum and Teaching Methods to MTeach students at the Australian Catholic University, also in Canberra. She is engaged in voluntary service as an Educational Consultant to several secondary schools in India and is a core member of the Indo-Universal Consortium of Engineering Educators, based in Boston, US.

of engineering education for the present— and for the future, sustaining a glorious world for the next generation.

Having lived in Australia for more than 20 years, I had very little knowledge about how engineering is being imparted to students in India. All I had known was that it was hard to get admission into an engineering college, and I had heard from my relatives and friends that one needed to either score very high marks in the pre-university course and the entrance exam for engineering courses, or have parents who are rich enough to pay a huge donation to engineering colleges.

I also wasn't aware of the course syllabi and assessment procedures used in the engineering courses, nor of the pedagogy practised in engineering classrooms. The various sessions that I attended at that first engineering education conference were eye-opening. I experienced a spring of ideas popping in my head, ideas that I thought should be tried to boost the standard of engineering education. This was when it dawned on me that my varied and vast experience of teaching and learning all these years could, perhaps, be put to use for the benefit of engineering education.

The National Knowledge Commission (NKC), an Indian think tank, argues that "engineering education is among the key enablers of growth for transforming India's economy." Considering this powerful statement, I also became aware of the institutions and organizations striving very hard to transform the existing ecosystem of engineering education. Any experimentation towards transformation cannot be designed without taking into account the existing context. As we all know, if an educational system is to thrive, it needs to be built on a robust foundation of a strong curriculum, competent faculty, effective pedagogy, and fair assessment of the content taught. While doing so, especially in engineering education, it is pertinent that the knowledge and skills imparted match against the industry requirements.

I have been a part of exploring the status quo of these different dimensions of engineering education in an Indian context. So, I want to address here each of these dimensions as I have understood them through my interactions with engineering students and faculty members, to shed light on the concerns that have plagued the system.

Firstly, examining things from the students' perspective, my conversations with the first year engineering students early this year have brought to light some serious issues that students face on their admission into an engineering college. Students have experienced enormous amount of stress owing to:

- a sudden hike in the standard of education; high expectations of academic standards; and newness of the content;
- adjusting to a new environment (weather, food, and hostel accommodation, and sometimes having to learn a new language) due to all of the different engineering colleges across India;

- the caste reservation system (allocation of seats based on social stratification that has evolved owing to political and economic changes over time), along with high fees and high cut off for general category students;
- an inability to make career-defining decisions due to a lack of exposure to different industry requirements;
- the fact that not every student in an engineering college wants to be an engineer; some are there because of parental pressure;
- a lack of facilities in the college and a lack of engaging and competent lecturers teaching the engineering subjects;
- having to study a branch of engineering different to a student's choice, thus students attending a class where no general information about that branch is given to students (e.g., what the branch is about and what kind of jobs are available after their graduation);
- the disconnect between knowledge acquired and the skill-set required by the industry upon graduation, sometimes leading to frustrating situations of unemployment.

When I was making that list of issues that I was hearing from students, I was in no way thinking about solving them any time in the near future. However, I should confess that the passion of the educator in me made a loud clamor warranting my attention.

Secondly, when exploring the educational system from the perspective of faculty members in the engineering colleges, I was able to relate to their woes very deeply. These faculty members are the teachers who are thrown into the deep-end, with a solid content knowledge but without any training in the teaching and learning process nor the necessary skills to understand students. William Ward wrote about teachers, "The mediocre teacher tells. The good teacher explains. The superior teacher demonstrates. The great teacher inspires." This cannot be achieved without going through systematic training, rigorous practice, or gaining vast experience in the teaching process.

If there are more than 10,000 technical education institutes in India, at least 100,000 faculty members are required who are well educated, qualified, and sound educators with the backing of not just a PhD qualification but also the ability to teach, engage, and inspire students, to keep up with industry demands, and have the ability to motivate innovation and research. It's not a great situation, either for the engineering faculty member starting an academic career or for students who are embarking on their dream profession.

Thirdly, even government regulations can be blamed to a certain extent for its bureaucracy in different sectors of engineering education. There is a lack of scope for free thinking and active international collaboration, and a lack of training, freedom and assistance for faculty members to attend engineering education related conferences, workshops, or seminars. It is time to trigger a dramatic change in this field for better outcomes.

Finally, engineering institutions themselves have expressed their own concerns related to a number of issues, such as not-so-friendly government policies and procedures, a system that is geared towards text-book driven examination, a lack of creativity and innovation, a lack of competent faculty, and their research publications. Many thinkers and education experts have proposed a number of suggestions to improve the overall standard of engineering education in India. Suggestions, to name a few, relate to its connection to knowledge network, industry, society, and national and global networking of professionals. However, very few steps have been taken to transform the current engineering education system to cater to the needs of 21st century learners, communities, societies, and global challenges.

When I view the ecosystem of engineering education in India, I strongly discern the need for change to happen at the grassroots level, that solutions to the global challenges lie in the engineering classrooms, where the crux of the engineering knowledge and skills are imparted, shared, learned, evolved, and inspired. William Yeats wrote, "Education is not the filling of a pail, but the lighting of a fire." It becomes the duty of every individual who is passionate about engineering education to kindle the spark of a burning desire to contribute to society by facilitating better living standards and better solutions to the problems, so as to pass on a better world to future generations.

In addition to an individual's motivation towards and engagement in the teaching and learning process in engineering education, I envisage organizations or associations both at the local and international levels initiating an opening for the sharing of the knowledge and the required skill set for preparing engineering educators across the globe to use a technology-based curriculum. This can be done by creating an exclusive portal for three things: introducing some of the basic educational and psychological understanding of self, students, peers, or colleagues; how to conduct research (and the mechanics of reporting research); and finally, in particular, understanding the community needs.

These introductory modules could be delivered by experienced educators. And, for an in-depth understanding of these topics, the participants could be directed towards specific courses delivered by different experts from around the world based on a systematically developed curriculum on each of the above-mentioned topics; this could lead to training the participants to receive a certificate of attainment. Such an approach would provide engineering educators with a sense of accomplishment and a boost to their self-confidence, in addition to the knowledge and skills related to teaching and research—particularly in the fast-developing area of engineering education.

Here is a brief description of the topic areas that could be addressed in such a global portal:

i. **Know your students.** This topic can highlight the characteristics of different learning styles, readiness, and motivation of students to learn; the unique features of cognitions and behaviors of 21st century students; physiological, psychological, and cognitive aspects of a learning brain; and challenges of addressing various factors that operate on student learning.

ii. **Know yourself as a teacher.** It is unlikely that engineering faculty members would have gone through specific training in becoming successful teachers prior to choosing an academic career. Hence, it is pertinent that new recruits as well as those who are not trained to teach are exposed to the fine art of teaching, which encapsulates the most significant aspect of the 21st century learning model: life-long learning. This includes various aspects of teaching, such as an understanding of different pedagogical, psychological, philosophical, and sociological approaches to teaching a particular unit/course; designing and implementing assessment procedures in different courses; reflecting on one's own strengths and weaknesses as a teacher; engaging in professional development to cater to the needs of students who are consumed by information overload and engulfed in technological and social change; and, finally, identifying the ingredients for becoming an effective teacher.

iii. **Know your peers/colleagues.** Collaboration is the key word in the world of academics, be it for teaching or research in any field—and engineering education is no exception. True to Helen Keller's words, "Alone, we can do so little; together, we can do so much," it becomes essential to have a proactive rapport with peers and colleagues to get the best out of one's own abilities, which may have an impact on their own teaching, and especially on students.

iv. **Know how to know.** "The more we learn the more we realize how little we know" (R. B. Fuller). This urge to know more directs us to reflect on what we know and what more we want to know, which paves the way for research. This warrants a solid understanding of a scientific approach to research and to research reporting in engineering education.

v. **Know your community.** As has been rightly said, the very purpose of education is for improving the lives of others and for leaving our community and world better than we found it. This is especially relevant to engineering education as it aims to prepare engineers to make a difference in the community. This requires a sound knowledge of the community. Budding engineers could engage in addressing these problems and concerns using pragmatic approaches to alleviate the hardships that the community is facing on a day-to-day basis.

Creating such a platform of virtual outreach would enable engineering educators around the world to take an introductory peek into the basic requirements of knowledge and skill for educating the engineers. It would also be an impetus for qualifying to be competent engineering educators through completing further online courses.

Just before concluding, I want to add something about women in engineering. When I began my foray into engineering education in India, my focus was mainly on the educational aspect of the courses. The issue of gender either in the faculty or among students did not emerge until I started visiting various colleges of engineering in India over the past three years. Indeed, I found there were far more men than women in the engineering colleges, be it among the faculty members or the students. Also, my exposure is limited to the Indian context, as is my knowledge and understanding of how the dynamics of gender roles and expectations work in a traditionally male-dominated country. India is a country where women are "socially wired" to bend to the pressures of their in-laws, as the scholar Sohini Jana wrote at Poverty.org, and drop out of the labor force after marriage to give priority to their caregiving duties at home. Therefore, I am really pleased to see that a number of women hold responsible positions alongside men in engineering colleges and in industry. This speaks volumes about how Indian women are soaring to exponentially greater heights. All I can say to Indian women is, keep up the spirit of liberation; *carpe diem*!

I'll finish with this: While I have been making an effort to gain a comprehensive and bigger picture of the state of engineering education in India in general, and to figure out where to take it from here, I have a barrage of ideas. Although I am daunted, and wonder whether I can make any difference to the situation at all, a compelling optimism springs through me like an arrow shot from a bow. After all, as the Chinese proverb says, a journey of a thousand miles must begin with a single step.

JOURNEY 23

DAUGHTER, MOTHER, WIFE: MY LIFE AS AN ENGINEER

ADRIANA CECILIA PÁEZ PINO

Dean
School of Exact Sciences & Engineering
Sergio Arboleda University

COLOMBIA

I hope that telling my story will show the new generation of female students that they can achieve their dream of becoming engineers.

I was born in Bogotá, the capital of Colombia, and I still live here, 52 years later. But my life has been heavily influenced by the cultural aspects of the south of my country, where my mother, Sara, was born. Cali, in the region of Valle del Cauca, is known for "La Salsa," the music that my brother Juan Carlos and I have enjoyed since we were teenagers. Typical cuisine of that region includes green bananas on the table and dishes like "aborrajados," (beans with ripe banana), "patacones" (twice-fried plantain slices), and "lulada" (a traditional Colombian beverage made with the local fruit lulo, lime juice, water, and sugar), among others.

My mother's family moved to the capital when she was 18, but sadly, shortly after that her father died. He had worked on the national railway. From that moment, my mother and my aunt Mariela had to assume responsibility for the family by getting jobs, so they could no longer attend university. My mother went to work for a telecommunications company, which helped support her younger siblings so that they had the opportunity to study.

As for my father, Carlos, he worked as a systems engineer for companies with large computers, including IBM. He is 80 now, but I still remember how wonderful it was to have his encouragement back then: he really sparked my imagination by explaining so many amazing things

ABOUT THE AUTHOR

Adriana Cecilia Páez Pino is Dean of the School of Exact Sciences and Engineering. She graduated as an Electronics Engineer from Santo Tomás University in Bogotá, Colombia, and became a Specialist in Telecommunications Engineering at the Polytechnic University of Valencia in Spain. She has a Master's degree in Economic Sciences from the University of Santo Tomás and earned her Doctorate in Education at the University of La Salle of Costa Rica in San José, Costa Rica. Adriana has experience in formal processes for qualified registrations and accreditation of academic programs, and evaluation of new programs, at both the undergraduate and graduate level. At Santo Tomás University, she served as Director of Laboratories, Vice Dean of Telecommunications Engineering, and Director of the Department of Basic Sciences. Adriana was an academic advisor to the School of Communications of the ESCOM Army, and has the distinction of having received a San Gabriel Military Medal in recognition of and testimony to the efficient services provided to military communications. She also participates in various national and international networks, including as President of REDIE (Network of Electronic Engineering Programs) and President of LACCEI 2018.

to me. When he asked me what I wanted to be when I grew up, I always answered, "plant scientist."

Technology was of great interest in our household, and we had many science-fiction books, including those by Jules Verne. My brother and I also loved our encyclopedia called The World of Children, which was full of games and experiments. We enjoyed its activities; we built cities with Lego-like pieces, and we loved fantasy stories. I wrote poems, but I never really enjoyed playing with dolls. I preferred physical activities like riding my bike, rollerskating, and playing basketball, baseball, and tennis.

I was often the only girl in my group of friends, although my education was at an all-girls school called Siervas de San José, which offered personalized education: we had individual work, and we also worked together to solve problems. I dedicated most of my time to studying mathematics; I loved this subject. As the years passed, I began to informally teach two neighbor girls, Marcela and Alexandra. We'd meet at my house, and I'd explain the topics we were studying at school. I didn't realize it at the time, but now I think that I became their mentor. As for my own mentor, I suppose that my love of mathematics was due to the influence of one of my teachers, Constanza Hernandez; thanks to her realization that I was good at it, mathematics became my passion, and was leading me towards a career in engineering.

I remember when I had to make the decision to choose a path in engineering. I considered many areas, but ultimately chose electronic engineering because I imagined myself building devices that can solve problems. (And I had some crazy dreams of what I could build, including a robot that cleans the house, cooks, and performs all the housework!) Going into engineering was a tough decision, though, because I had such a strong passion for sports, and I seriously considered doing a bachelor's degree in physical education. My parents discouraged me from doing that; my father and I had many arguments about it. And my mother felt that engineering would open more paths for me, and would allow me to take advantage of my love for mathematics.

Studying electronic engineering in Bogotá was not easy for a woman in the 1980s. When I went for my university interview, I felt I was going to be rejected because I was a woman. The interviewers expressed to me that women came to engineering school only to get a husband, not to study, because it's a male-dominated profession. But not enrolling in engineering was not an option for me. I wanted to make my dad proud.

It was so different studying among mostly men compared to my all-girls' school experience. On my first day, I would blush when teachers asked me a question. I wore pink, and was given the nickname "pastelito" (which literally means "pastel pink"). It was a difficult time. One of my teachers asked me what I was doing there; shouldn't I be at home washing the dishes? I felt I was graded toughly on all the exams and projects compared to my classmates. But later in the year I found myself in the same classes as another female, so we presented projects together. Our teachers were hard on us, and the bar was higher for us than it was for the male students. But we kept moving forward.

    As an aside, that situation reminds me of my daughter's. Like me, Maria Andrea is as passionate about sports as she is physics, statistics, and numbers. She got a scholarship four years ago to play golf and study at an American university. She decided to study industrial engineering, and her father and I were very proud, although we knew she would be presented with so many challenges: leaving her country, studying in another language, living alone and assuming household responsibilities, and many others. But I think what affected her most was that her coach asked her to change majors so that she could continue on the golf team, since the demands of lab work and the tough subjects made it difficult for her to travel to tournaments. So she chose something she felt had a similarity to industrial engineering: supply chain management. Today she is an industrial distribution professional, and although it's not quite what she had wanted as a career, fortunately physics is a part of this work. I often think of my daughter's case as being similar to my own in that I had to choose either sports or engineering. We have to change the conventional wisdom that women are not capable of reaching more than one goal, that a woman is not allowed to have two dreams.

    Back to my story. I remember once in a digital course when the teacher gave me extremely difficult questions, and I know it was because

I was a woman. I got a 2.9, so I failed the subject. At times like that, I wanted to abandon these studies and this career choice. But I focused on the good things, including other activities I did such as being a monitor in the university's welfare department.

Then I met my future husband, Carlos, an electronics engineer. When I became pregnant with our son Sebastian, I delayed my graduation and my thesis project (shockingly, the dean at the time told me I couldn't come to the graduation that year because I was pregnant, and "children were not allowed to attend the ceremonies"). The discrimination was also obvious during some job interviews I did at that point. A couple of the interviewers were fixated on my being a woman, and said that if I expected to have more children, I wouldn't have time to work. One even told me that I should focus on being a mother and a wife, and taking care of the house.

I took time off after Sebastian was born, delaying pursuing an engineering career. I focused on a weekend business I had selling desserts and floral arrangements until my son was six months old. I was ready to enter the working world, but my husband wanted me to stay with the baby for longer. This made me feel so guilty; I thought, am I a bad mother for wanting to leave my son? But, the life of a stay-at-home mother was not the life I had worked so hard for. I had overcome so many barriers and had a title that had cost me so much. That's when I remembered that my university's rector had offered me a role. This was a wonderful opportunity that would give me the flexibility to work and have a family. And so began my working life at the university.

My first job as laboratory director started with two difficult circumstances. For one, my co-workers thought that I was too young, and that I would not be able to do the job. Secondly, I was in charge of men, and was replacing an engineer who was about to retire, so they didn't think I had enough experience. I did have weaknesses in the administrative area, so I took a master's degree in administration. I studied every night and some Saturdays. My training in mathematics favored my studies; the structure that engineering gave me was fundamental to my ability to take on challenges through the course of my life.

My due date to have my second child, Maria Andrea, coincided with my final week to complete my master's degree. I have to say, it was really not very easy to be a mother, a student, and a woman with a career in engineering all at the same time. I started my doctorate in telecommunications engineering in Spain but did not finish it as it was too complicated to leave my young children, and we needed my income.

Later, when I did my doctorate in education, I felt discrimination from a woman I had known for years who was in my work group. She was studying philosophy and she simply thought my ideas were not valid since I came from an engineering background.

That was two years ago, but these kinds of things continue to happen. We really don't yet have gender equality in engineering, at least not in Colombia. This is the reality not only in academics but in our daily lives. All the examples of this inappropriate treatment in my working life—of some men who took my ideas and presented them as their own, who did not know my experience, or who simply did not believe I had contributed—have hardened my character. (And I think that at the root of this is these men's envy of me.) Whereas for years I have trusted and believed in people, the mistreatment has eroded that. Sometimes I have felt that my good heart has been used. This saddens me, and to some extent I have even had to change who I am.

But I do take positive aspects from the situation, and always move forward. It challenges me to come up with creative solutions, and it has led to me making some excellent relationships and connections that favor my work. And I get lots of fulfilment in other aspects of life, such as spending time with my family and going with my children to their tournaments. I play tennis, do yoga and Pilates, use the elliptical trainer, and do rumba classes. And trying to find this balance has paid off: I will never forget when my son, who is now 24, graduated from school at age 18 and said to me, "Mother, you don't know how much I appreciate that you have always having been there for me in the moments that I needed you. You were with me all the way, and your presence was so important for me. I don't know how you do it." It filled me with emotion. But I have to thank my own parents for supporting all my studies, because they have been a primary factor in spending time with my children when needed. This has been a blessing.

Women always take on more responsibility in their daily work.

Luckily, we are very disciplined. And to me, team building among men and women is important; I think our contributions and views are different. I participate in voluntary activities and associations. I have formed networks like the REDIE (Network of Deans and Directors of Electronic Engineering) and for a long time was a volunteer with the Latin American and Caribbean Consortium of Engineering Institutions (LACCEI) before becoming president in 2018. One of our initiatives was a book promoting women engineers in Latin America called Matilda and Women in Engineering in Latin America. These types of initiatives fill me with joy when they materialize, just as helping students and building new programs do. Those are the times when you feel your ideas are part of the plans and add value for the university. Yes, sometimes these things are clouded with repression; sometimes your proposals are not accepted because you are a woman. But I always think that a smile is more powerful. I keep in mind that the dreams that we are making into a reality are bigger than the problems we may find along the way.

  Achievements have sometimes empowered me. I believe that our girls, our daughters, cannot be stopped from achieving their dreams. Engineering is a world where women have much to say, create, and contribute to the development of society in this new industrial revolution. We must generate programs where girls feel immersed in projects that contribute to this world. The world requires significant change to address the huge leaps we've made in technology, and if new generations are going to help these changes materialize, schools must strengthen their STEM efforts. Women should know that being an engineer does not limit you from having a family and work. I want to shout this: It is possible! If someone has a taste for science and mathematics, it can't be fulfilled in high school. Girls must be encouraged to follow their dreams. Remind them that many of the best inventions have been made by women. And the inventors and entrepreneurs in different scientific fields are now being recognized with greater vigor. In short, each of us contributes to the development of engineering.

As the years go by, the role of female engineers in society is increasingly recognized. But in my country the percentage of women engineers hasn't increased significantly. So it is important that governments promote engineering, establish programs, give scholarships, and motivate women to study and practice professional engineering. Promoting equal rights and job opportunities for women in the field of engineering will help, as will creating books like this that give visibility to female engineers in the profession. They play a role in their family, in society, and in a profession that has the power to transform the world. That is why our stories transmit experiences, knowledge and values that will guide future engineers in the mission of continuing to make a better world every day.

So many of us are happy and successful. Telling my story has been a beautiful opportunity and I hope it will help influence others to make the world a better place.

JOURNEY 24

MAKING HISTORY, AND LEADING WOMEN INTO THE FUTURE

SARAH A. RAJALA

Dean Emerita
College of Engineering
Iowa State University

UNITED STATES OF AMERICA

Growing up in the 1950s and '60s on our small family farm in Michigan state's upper peninsula provided me the opportunity to freely explore my surroundings and ask questions about the world beyond. This was thanks to a family history with branches extending to places far from my hometown of Dukes. My paternal grandparents had immigrated to the United States from Finland in 1912. They met in a lumber camp in Michigan, where my grandmother was a cook/cleaner and my grandfather a lumberjack. There were many immigrants from northern and eastern Europe in this area, so it was not unusual that my father started elementary school speaking only Finnish. (In fact, as long as my grandparents were alive, Finnish was spoken in our home by family and friends.)

As for my mother's side, my grandmother was originally from Missouri, in the US Midwest, and met my grandfather in the town of Joliet, Illinois. (He had been born and raised there, but had left home at the age of 15 and explored the world for 20 years.) They moved to Dukes, not far from the shores of Lake Superior, after my mother finished high school. My parents met each other there, at the local post office, and married in 1945. Mom was an elementary-school teacher and my father worked for the railroad, loading iron ore boats, and was also an electrician.

I was the eldest of three daughters and as children it was clear that my parents expected each of us to continue our education after high school. My formal education started at the age of 4, when I would accompany my

ABOUT THE AUTHOR

Sarah Rajala became dean of the College of Engineering at Iowa State University in 2013. She retired in 2019 and holds the title of Dean Emerita. Rajala is an internationally known leader who has served on many academic and association boards. She is a past president of ASEE and past chair of GEDC. In 2016 she was awarded the national engineer of the year award by the AAES, and in 2015 received the national Harriett B. Rigas Award, honoring outstanding female faculty, from IEEE's Education Society. Rajala's previous leadership positions were at Mississippi State University as dean of engineering from 2008-2013, and chair of the electrical and computer engineering department prior to being named dean. She also served at North Carolina State University as associate dean for research and graduate programs, and associate dean for academic affairs in the College of Engineering. Rajala has consistently broken new ground for women in engineering and serves as a role model for young women. She is passionate about diversity of thought and culture, especially as it relates to the college environment. Rajala earned her bachelor's degree in electrical engineering from Michigan Technological University and her master's and PhD degrees from Rice University.

mother to school where she served as a substitute teacher. I enjoyed it, and by the following year, I attended kindergarten in the morning and first grade in the afternoon. I loved reading, math, and geography. Outside of primary school, I was active in 4-H, church, music, and traveling with my family throughout Canada and the US, often to visit family. These trips were always by car and included visits to state and provincial capitals, national parks, Washington, DC, and Expo '67 in Montreal.

I have a vivid memory of reading *Endurance: Shackleton's Incredible Voyage* in the fifth grade. My grandfather was an able-bodied seaman on Earnest Shackleton's 1914-1916 expedition to the Antarctic, and although I was aware of this and some of his other adventures when he traveled the world before getting married, seeing my grandfather's name in print inspired me to learn more, as did his curiosity about the world. My career as an electrical engineering professor and administrator would provide me with the opportunity to pursue my interests not only in math, science, and engineering education, but I'd also learn about people and cultures around the world. To date, I have had the privilege of visiting all seven continents, all 50 states in the US and more than 45 countries.

So, what inspired me to study engineering? I attended high school in Marquette, Michigan, since my local country school only went up to eighth grade. Now I could take a wide range of subjects, including advanced math and science, French, music, and creative writing. Although I was never very good at the latter, it did lay a foundation for developing my communication skills. What we didn't get much guidance on in high school was career planning. I really did not know what I wanted to do and the options for women in 1970 seemed very limited: teaching, nursing, or secretarial services. At least that is what my guidance counselors thought. I wasn't very interested in any of these options, but did like mathematics. I chose to attend Michigan Technological University (Michigan Tech) and study mathematics.

I knew nothing about engineering and didn't even realize that most of the students at Michigan Tech studied it! I also was unaware that the ratio of men to women at Michigan Tech was about 25 to 1. I was barely 17 when I started college, naïve, and thrown into an environment that was quite hostile to women. Also, I didn't realize that the conventional wisdom about "girls" who came to the school was that they were only there for their "Mrs." Degree. Although I faced many challenges, my interest in music (marching band, symphonic band, jazz band, and choir) and a music fraternity (yes!) provided me an outlet and a cadre of friends with similar interests.

During my freshman year I decided I wanted to find a way to apply my mathematics. With the encouragement of a couple of caring faculty members, I switched my degree program to electrical engineering. I still did not know much about the discipline but after acing my first circuits course I never looked back, in spite of hearing many times that "girls can't be engineers." Needless to say, there were times that I doubted my ability and questioned whether I was making the right choice. However, I was determined to prove everyone wrong and ended up graduating in four years. In addition to staying active in music, I served as president of the student chapters of Eta Kappa Nu (electrical engineering honor society) and Tau Beta Pi (engineering honor society).

As an undergraduate, I also really enjoyed my biology courses. My interests in medical applications and devices increased during an internship at GE Medical Systems. By the time I graduated in 1974, I was determined to find a way to blend engineering with the biomedical sciences. I had an offer from GE, but I didn't think I knew enough at that time to be successful as a biomedical engineer, so I decided to go to graduate school to learn more. I chose Rice University in Houston, Texas, where I continued my pursuit of electrical engineering with a biomedical option.

Graduate school was life-changing! Although I still doubted my abilities at times, the culture and environment were very different, both inside Rice and in the community. There were other women in my classes, faculty were supportive, and I made many friends among the graduate students. I was able to blend my interests in the biomedical sciences and electrical engineering, and develop expertise in image processing. As graduate students, we were all expected to participate in the educational mission of the department, as well as conduct research. By the time I finished my masters and PhD, I knew I wanted to be a faculty member.

I met my husband, Jim Aanstoos, an electrical engineer, at Rice.

We were married in December 1978 and by the spring of 1979 we were both ready to start our careers. Finding positions for two professionals in the same location was a challenge in 1979, as is often still the case today. We decided to move to the Research Triangle Park in North Carolina, where I accepted a position as an assistant professor at North Carolina State University and Jim accepted a position as a research engineer at the Research Triangle Institute. We were very fortunate to have these opportunities available to us.

Over the years, I broke ground for women in engineering at NC State. I was the first tenure-track woman on the faculty in engineering when I began. Although I had a successful start to my career and a very supportive department chair and dean, some faculty and students were skeptical. However, it was an exciting time at NC State and in the Research Triangle Park, and I was often asked to participate in new initiatives. In my second year, I was co-principal investigator on a National Science Foundation (NSF) award to establish an industry/university research center. I also participated in the development of the Microelectronics Center of North Carolina and launch of the first VLSI design course at NC State. I was successful in obtaining funding for my research and because of the success of our research center, I had numerous opportunities to collaborate with industry. On campus, I served on numerous faculty committees, as well as on the faculty senate.

In retrospect, I took on more responsibility than any junior faculty should. We didn't have mentoring programs for new faculty at that time and I wasn't sure who I should turn to for advice. Learning how to set priorities linked to my long-term goals was something I learned over many years. However, one of the smart things I did as a young faculty member was to become active in my professional society, the Institute of Electrical and Electronics Engineers (IEEE), both at the local and national level. This provided me the opportunity to build networks of professional colleagues outside the university and to begin my world travels. The good news was that in spite of some of the choices I made, I was tenured and promoted to an associate professor in my fifth year.

My husband and I did not plan to have children when we first got married. With two careers, we weren't sure how to make it all work. However, in January 1986 we discovered I was pregnant, and although it was not planned, we were excited about the addition to our family. What wasn't so clear was how the department and college would react to this news. I had tenure, so I wasn't worried about losing my job, but I wasn't sure what impact having a child would have on my career path. Not only was I the first tenure-track woman on the faculty, I was the first woman faculty member in engineering to be having a baby—and at that time, NC State did not offer vacation or sick leave to faculty members on academic appointments.

I needn't have worried; the College of Engineering found a way. The dean decided to treat my pregnancy in the same way he would treat a male faculty member having a heart attack! I co-taught a course in the fall semester, so there was someone to cover the classes after I gave birth. I would continue my research on my schedule. In October 1986, we welcomed our daughter Kristen into our family. I was back on campus about three weeks after her birth, bringing Kristen with me and nursing her in my office. By December, we found someone to be Kristen's caregiver while Jim and I were at work.

Another positive event occurred in 1987: I was awarded an NSF Fellowship for Women. This award provided funding to support me on a professional leave of development, or sabbatical, for one year. I spent the academic year from 1987-88 at Purdue University in Indiana working with colleagues on image processing research. During this year, Jim began working on his PhD in atmospheric sciences.

The timing was great because we had a little more flexibility in our life to enjoy our daughter. In May 1988 we took Kristen on her first international trip, to an IEEE conference in Helsinki, Finland. We returned to North Carolina in the summer and by that fall, I was pregnant with our second daughter. Stephanie was born in July 1989. So now we had to figure out how to juggle my work and allow Jim time to continue his PhD, all with a family of four. Although we had no family living in North Carolina, my mother often came for long visits to help out and even traveled with me to professional meetings to help take care of our children.

In addition to continuing my research and teaching, I also continued to be active in university service. Of importance to me and the growing number of women on campus was the development of a maternity- and family-leave policy and the establishment of child-care facilities. We worked hard to get both accomplished. I was also active in my professional societies, taking on increased leadership roles both locally and nationally.

Although it took more time than I planned or hoped, I was finally promoted to full professor in 1992. This was an important affirmation of my many contributions and my desire to take on a leadership position. Although I had learned a lot from the volunteer leadership positions I held, I wanted to further develop my leadership skills. I was invited to participate in an academic leadership program for women offered by the University of North Carolina General Administration. It was not only an opportunity to learn more about academic leadership positions, but to meet and network with an extraordinary group of women leaders and colleagues throughout the state of North Carolina. It also provided a safe environment to ask questions and learn new skills.

My first opportunity to take on a leadership position was as director of a research center—the industry-university center that I helped establish 15 years earlier. It was a good fit and allowed me to continue working with a group of faculty and staff that I knew well. However, the center was at a turning point: to continue to receive funding from the NSF, we had to expand our operation to include another university. Colleagues at Duke University were potentially interested, but it was my responsibility to build the collaboration among the faculty, identify new industrial partners to support the expansion, and work with Duke's research administration to get the partnership approved.

We were successful, and I served as director of the research center for the next three years. This leadership experience helped me learn to put others first, to listen more than speak, to manage staff—and that true success comes from partnerships. I enjoyed the experience and started to think about other opportunities to serve. However, deciding what to do next was not easy with young children and a two-career family. The logical next step would have been a department chair position, but that option was not available locally and my husband and I did not want to move. Then, in 1996, Nino Masnari—my first department chair and someone I highly respected—became dean of the College of Engineering, and when he asked me to serve as associate dean for academic affairs, I enthusiastically accepted. It was a wonderful opportunity that matched my interests and skill set.

For the next six years, my team and I focused on enhancing the undergraduate education of our engineering students, with a particular focus on the first-year engineering experience; creating a diverse and inclusive culture, including establishing the Women in Engineering and K-12 Outreach Programs in the college; expanding the Minority Engineering Program and co-founding the Women in Science and Engineering Living and Learning Village; and establishing a faculty development program with a focus on new faculty. We also launched a mechatronics engineering program in Asheville, North Carolina, and pre-engineering programs in several other locations in the state. It was during this time that I expanded my research interests in engineering education with a focus on assessment and accreditation. I became a program evaluator for the Accreditation Board for Engineering and Technology (ABET) and more actively engaged in the American Society for Engineering Education (ASEE). To this day, I continue my involvement in accreditation and engineering education through ABET, ASEE, and IEEE.

In 2002, I had the opportunity to move to the position of associate dean for research and graduate programs. By this time in my career, I was interested in considering opportunities to serve as a dean of engineering but felt I had more to learn from Dean Masnari and the scope of responsibilities of a dean. During my four-year tenure, my team successfully grew the college's research portfolio, improved research administrative services, grew and diversified the graduate program, and expanded our distance-education programs. As the senior associate dean, I was also responsible for space management including the building of two major buildings and a number of large renovation projects; managing the Mineral Research Laboratory, Analytical Instrumentation Facility, NC Solar Center and the Precision Machine Shop; and serving on the North Carolina Mining Commission. I never had a shortage of opportunities, including service to the profession as a member of the board of directors of ASEE and service on the Engineering Accreditation Commission of ABET. Although I enjoyed everything I was doing, after 10 years I was ready to consider other opportunities. It was also a good time for our family for me to do so, as our youngest daughter would soon be finishing high school, and my husband was open to considering other opportunities.

One of the challenges I faced as I considered my next step was whether I would be considered for a dean's position without experience as a department chair. It soon became clear that even with my extensive experience as an associate dean, including most of the responsibilities handled by a department chair, not having served as one would limit my options. I decided to take the position of head of the department of electrical and computer engineering at Mississippi State University. The move was also a great opportunity for my husband, as the university had an opening in his area of expertise as a research professor.

I enjoyed serving as department head, especially working with the faculty and students, but it quickly became clear that I had already handled most of the responsibilities. As fate would have it, the dean's position opened up within the first year and I was encouraged to apply. In June 2008, I assumed the role of dean of engineering of the Bagley College of Engineering at Mississippi State University. And in July 2008, I started my service as president of ASEE! It continued to be a busy time in my life. Serving as dean was a rewarding experience as I was able to contribute to the field of engineering education. At the university, I built a strong team and successfully moved the college forward in research, education, and diversity and inclusion. Professionally, I continued my service to ABET, ASEE and IEEE and participated in the development of the Global Engineering Deans Council (GEDC) and the International Federation of Engineering Education Societies (IFEES).

Over the years, I have been approached about other leadership opportunities, including dean, provost, vice-president for research, and president. However, as I considered what my passions are and how I wanted to contribute during the next phase of my career, I decided that I could have the most impact as a dean of engineering. In 2013, after six-and-a-half years at Mississippi State, I accepted my role as the 12th dean of engineering at Iowa State University. Iowa State had the eighth-largest undergraduate engineering program in the US when I started and a total student population in engineering (both undergraduate and graduate) of more than 7,500 students. (By the time I retired six years later, I was responsible for more than 9,500 students, 500 faculty and staff, 12 academic majors, multiple research centers and programs, and 11 buildings that comprise the engineering complex.)

Once again, I focused on building a strong team to lead the college into the future. Together we made great progress by establishing a shared vision and strategic plan, hiring excellent faculty, investing in our research programs and infrastructure, and expanding our fundraising to support our students and faculty. Iowa State has a very supportive alumni network, and it was a pleasure getting to know people and to develop friendships with so many of the college's alumni.

In June 2019, I completed my 40th year as a faculty member, and my husband and I decided to launch our next adventure: retirement. As I enter this next phase of my life, I will continue to contribute to the engineering profession through my volunteer service in my professional societies. My husband and I plan to travel and spend time with our families. I have a long list of sewing and quilting projects that I will now have the time to tackle, and I hope to take golf lessons soon.

As I look back on my career, I hope I have been able to make a difference in the field of engineering education. I believe most of our colleges and universities are more welcoming, and our cultures more inclusive, than they were when I started as a faculty member. But our work is not done.

JOURNEY 25

THINGS ARE NOT ALWAYS AS THEY SEEM

JULIE M. ROSS

Dean
College of Engineering
Virginia Tech

UNITED STATES OF AMERICA

I grew up in a small farming community in central Indiana, US. My father and uncle, who had grown up in a nearby town, were the local dentists and my mother was the high-school guidance counselor. My parents had both gone to college and had graduate degrees, which was quite unusual in our town. I don't remember it ever being a question of *whether* I would go to college. The only questions were where I would go and what I would study.

Because the school in my town was very small, it was difficult to accommodate students who were academically ahead. There weren't very many of us. So, beginning in second grade, I took third-grade classes, and that was the pattern for the rest of my elementary, junior high and high school years. In fourth grade, when I was only nine years old, I took a beginning Spanish class with high school freshmen and sophomores. It was not ideal—socially, it was difficult—but there were no advanced courses, so the school system made do as they could.

Going into my junior year, it was clear I would soon run out of classes to take, but I didn't want to graduate high school early. I was a swimmer and didn't want to miss my senior season. So I went to high school half time and drove 30 minutes each day to Purdue University to take college-level courses. Most of them were remedial preparatory courses

ABOUT THE AUTHOR

Dr. Julia Myers Ross is the Paul and Dorothea Torgersen Dean of Engineering at Virginia Tech and professor of chemical engineering and engineering education. Dr. Ross holds a BS degree from Purdue University and a PhD from Rice University, both in chemical engineering. From 1995 to 2017 she was on the faculty at the University of Maryland, Baltimore County (UMBC), serving as Dean of Engineering and IT from 2014 to 2017 and Chair of Chemical, Biochemical and Environmental Engineering from 2006 to 2013. In 2013 Dr. Ross was selected as Fellow of the American Council on Education, the premiere higher education leadership development program in the United States. Dr. Ross has been awarded nearly $10 million in external grants as Principal Investigator to support her research in cellular engineering and engineering education. She is an elected Fellow of the American Institute for Medical and Biological Engineering and has received the American Society for Engineering Education Sharon Keillor Award, University System of Maryland Regents' Award for Collaboration in Public Service, and the National Science Foundation CAREER Award. Dr. Ross serves on the Executive Committees of the Global Engineering Deans Council and the Engineering Deans Council of the American Society for Engineering Education.

in math and science, but I was also able to take the English course, a French course, and a freshman engineering programming course.

I had no idea what I wanted to study in college, but I was good in math and science, and people told me I should consider engineering. I didn't know what that was, and I didn't know any engineers. I was inspired by the American astronaut and physicist Sally Ride, and thought being an astronaut would be amazing. I was itching to get out of my small town, and lots of astronauts were engineers. So that's what I decided to apply to. Although I really wanted to go out of state to college, maybe to Illinois or Michigan, I enrolled at Purdue; it was hard to justify the out-of-state expense when a world-class engineering school was right in my own backyard.

During my first semester, I learned about the co-op program and it sounded like the ideal way to get out and explore. When I applied, I had to designate what type of engineer I wanted to be. It was still my first semester and I didn't even know what engineering was yet, let alone what the different types of engineers where. There was a list to choose from and I was embarrassed that I didn't know what any of it meant, and I was afraid to ask. So I chose chemical engineering because I liked my chemistry class. Decision made. A couple months later, I found myself interviewing for co-op jobs. I had several offers and decided to accept the one from Eastman Kodak Company, because I had heard of the company and the offer they made to me in biotechnology sounded interesting. And, I was going to work in New York! (I didn't know there was such a thing as "upstate" New York, far from Manhattan; I'd be located in Rochester.)

My co-op experience was, without question, the best experience of my undergraduate career. I was assigned to the Kodak Research Laboratories and learned I really like research. I did five "work blocks" in three years, and I credit that time and experience for keeping me in engineering. My engineering classwork didn't really resonate with me. It was very theoretical and there wasn't much hands-on work or applied learning. I was successful in class, but rather indifferent about what I was learning; I had no passion for school. There was also very little support. Because of that, I figured out how to learn on my own, to be independent and to work with my classmates. But I loved the work on co-op, and each semester it reinforced to me why I was in engineering.

As a junior, I wanted to do undergraduate research, and was fortunate to find a faculty member who welcomed me into his lab. I thought it might give me a distraction from my coursework, and it did. It also reinforced my love of research. For my senior year, I applied for jobs and for graduate school. I knew I had a passion for research, but I was exhausted by school and didn't really have an interest in continuing. I received a number of very good job offers, but in the end, I wasn't really very excited about any of the work. During a chance encounter in a hallway, one of my professors asked me where I was applying to graduate school and what I was interested in. I told him my list and he suggested adding Rice University in Houston, Texas, because it was very good in bioengineering (a still-emerging field at the time). On his recommendation, I applied to Rice and was admitted. When I visited, I knew it was where I wanted it to be. It was the exact opposite of Purdue—very small, private and urban. It was just what I needed.

In my first class at Rice, there were only seven of us and I was the only woman. I distinctly remember feeling very uncomfortable and exposed. I knew that if I wasn't prepared it would be obvious. I would stand out. There was no place to hide. Despite my success as an undergraduate, my confidence level was low. I kept hearing the things my undergraduate professors said in class; for example, "If it's hard, maybe you're not cut out to be an engineer. Maybe you should change majors." I had heard different versions of that so many times and didn't realize how much I had internalized the message. So I worked harder than I ever had, determined to be successful. Although I didn't know it at the time, it was a classic case of "imposter syndrome" (when you are convinced you don't deserve what you have achieved).

When I passed my qualifying exams at the end of the first year, I gladly embraced the opportunity to earn my PhD directly (without doing the MS first). My years at Rice were wonderful. I loved graduate school, particularly once I was past my coursework and could focus on my thesis research. I was in my element. When I saw classmates taking jobs in academia, I began to see myself there, too. Staying on a college campus, doing my research and teaching all sounded great to me. When it was time to interview, I talked to my husband about possible locations we could go. He is an aerospace engineer at NASA and wanted to be able to stay with the space agency, so our options were limited. I had a few interviews and received an offer from the University of Maryland, Baltimore County (UMBC), a school I had never heard of. But it was growing and had a dynamic new president, and Maryland was a location that could work for my husband. I accepted the position quickly, although the startup package was not competitive and I received advice from many that I should target a highly ranked school. In many ways, they were right, but the location worked for my personal life. Decision made.

I defended my thesis a few days before the Christmas holiday, moved from Texas to Maryland and started work as an assistant professor at UMBC in the first week of January. That spring, my husband and I bought our first house, and soon after, I became pregnant. Many people, including colleagues at UMBC and people I knew in the field, told me I was crazy and that it would be the end of my career. Some just shook their heads in disbelief that I had made such a preventable "mistake," and I could tell they no longer fully trusted my judgement. A few people told me so directly. I distinctly remember calling Human Resources to ask about maternity leave benefits at the university. I was asked whether I was faculty or staff and when I said I was faculty, there was a long pause on the other end of the line, and then I was told there were no benefits for faculty and that I would need to talk to my department chair.

Wow. The mid-1990s, and no benefits for pregnancy for faculty. No time off, no reduced workload, no change in my tenure clock. No policy. I was at the mercy of the man who led our department, and I was extremely lucky that he was supportive and let me suggest a plan. Three years later, I had my second daughter, also before tenure and still with no benefits or policy. Those early years are very fuzzy for me now and hard to remember, probably because I was sleep-deprived for a very long time. Somehow, I managed working full time (there was no other option), teaching my courses, learning to write and then secure research grants (including an NSF CAREER Award), writing papers, building collaborations, and graduating PhD students. But as I said, I don't remember very much of it. When I earned tenure, I just kept going, continuing to build my research program and raise my family. Luckily, my department gave me the flexibility I needed to make it all work for many years.

In 2006, I was approached by the provost about being the next chair of my department. I was still an associate professor (although I was preparing my dossier for promotion) and my research was going well. I had NIH and NSF funding and was leading a large research group. For those reasons, I was not interested in the job, but I cared deeply about the department and we had two new young women on our faculty who were facing a challenging departmental culture. After much soul searching, I agreed to serve because I was concerned about the direction of the department and I wanted to support our junior faculty. I was promoted to professor a year later, the first woman in my department to make it through the full promotion and tenure process. I was (and still am) the only woman to serve as a department chair in the College of Engineering and IT at UMBC.

My years as department chair were personally the hardest of my career—and probably led to the most growth. I've heard the position described as one that is "up close and personal" and it certainly was for me. Colleagues viewed me differently than before, and some friendships that had lasted for years dissolved in ways I didn't understand. I was suddenly seen as "other" by some colleagues. My motivations were questioned, and I was treated in ways that were much more adversarial and personal than I had ever experienced. I was forced to learn how to manage people and conflict, something I had actively avoided in the past.

Despite the challenges, I loved the opportunity to support the success of my colleagues and the department. It was fun thinking about the "big picture" and planning for the future. I learned a great deal about how universities operate and how to successfully navigate the system for the benefit of my unit. Most importantly, I learned how to lead, and I came to understand what that really means. It took several years for me to realize it, but I really liked academic administration. Our department was thriving, and I took pride in all that we had accomplished.

After seven years as department chair, I was ready for something new. Things were going well for me and for the department, but I didn't feel like I was learning new things in the role. It was time for something different. I let my dean know that I would be stepping down at the end of the year. My provost and president nominated me for the American Council on Education (ACE) Fellows program and I decided to do that for a year while I thought about what would come next. Because of my family obligations, I spent the year close to home working at the University of Maryland, Baltimore (UMB), in the office of the president. There, I learned all about professional education (medicine, law, pharmacy, dentistry, etc.) and building transdisciplinary inter-institutional research initiatives.

While I was at UMB, the dean position at UMBC opened up and a national search was launched. I was actively discouraged from entering the pool and it was made clear to me that an external candidate was preferred. At the last possible moment, I decided to apply anyway because I thought I had strong credentials and knew what the college needed from the new dean. If nothing else, I thought it would be good practice. But I had zero expectation that I would get the job.

I found it difficult being an internal candidate with a search committee full of colleagues I had known and worked with for years. It felt more personal than professional. I was selected as a finalist and had a full campus interview, but still had low expectations. It felt like they were doing me a courtesy, rather than seriously considering me. When the provost called and asked to speak to me, I thought it would be a conversation about what I would do next. Much to my surprise, he offered me the position! I had the privilege of serving for three years as dean of engineering and information technology at UMBC.

I was not actively looking for another position, but my youngest daughter was entering her senior year of high school and I was starting to think about the next phase of my life and career, and the idea that it wouldn't have to be in Maryland. When the description of the position of dean at one of the largest and best engineering colleges in the United States, Virginia Tech in Blacksburg, Virginia, landed in my inbox, I didn't bother to read it until a friend suggested I take a look. When I finally read the description, I reread it several times. It sounded just like me. They were looking for someone to work on the things I cared deeply about, and they wanted the skill sets I believed I had. Diversity and inclusion experience? Check. Building health sciences? Check. Growing transdisciplinary research? Check. Collaborative leadership style? Check. I decided to submit my material just to see if I was competitive. I didn't apply for any other jobs and wasn't really looking for a move.

I now lead one of the largest engineering colleges in the United

States as Virginia Tech's first female dean. It's something I never could have imagined all those years ago in a small rural town in Indiana, or even when I was an assistant professor trying to learn how to manage my time and achieve some balance in life. But one day at a time, one step at a time, this is where I've landed, and I'm absolutely thrilled to be here. The secret to my success? I actively take on roles and responsibilities that force me to learn new things and to grow, and I try to say "Yes" to opportunities that present themselves. I've stayed curious and open to new things. And perhaps most importantly, I've learned not to let the naysayers define me.

What have I learned from my journey? Not to be afraid, and to stay optimistic. Attitude is a choice, and it matters. I've learned to believe in and rely on myself, and to trust my instincts. There have been people along the way who had a profound impact on my trajectory in both positive and negative ways, and I am eternally grateful to each and every one of them. Each has encouraged or forced me to grow. In the moment, I didn't realize it, but with hindsight it is clear. Now, I try to do the same for others, but always in a positive way.

Things are not always what they seem. When you read my curriculum vitae, the path looks direct, as if all the right pieces fell into place at all the right times according to some grand plan. It looks clear and linear and almost obvious, that all the things I did before brought me to where I am today. Easy. Straightforward. But reality, as I lived it, was so very different. It was messy and hard, full of difficult choices, doubt and fear, disappointment in myself and others, and of course much joy amid all the chaos.

From the perspective I have now, I can see the inequities I couldn't see in the moment. I have witnessed how men are assumed to be competent until they prove they are not, but women do not have the luxury of that assumption. My experience over the years has been one of having to prove myself over and over again, each time I have started in a new role or job; my latest role has been no different. It does not affect me much anymore because I have accepted it as what I need to do. But it is tiring, frustrating and wrong, and I work to change it every day.

What do I want others to learn from my journey? That it's important to hear a person's story, and to learn about their accomplishments and their struggles. A CV only tells you the smallest bit, the highlights. Who am I? At the end of the day, I'm still just a regular kid from a small rural town who thought it would be amazing to be an astronaut someday. I've just learned a lot of other things along the way.

JOURNEY 26

WHAT MOTIVATES A WOMAN TO STUDY ENGINEERING?

MARTHA RUBIANO GRANADA

Dean
Faculty of Engineering
Universidad Libre

COLOMBIA

When I was a schoolgirl in my hometown of Bogotá, Colombia, I wondered what the future would be like for me and my siblings after we finished our studies; what would each of us become? There were four kids in my family, and I was the youngest, with eight years separating me from my next eldest sibling, my sister. My two brothers were older than her.

I didn't know what I wanted to do when I grew up, but by the time I started secondary school in 1981, my eldest brother Rigoberto was entering the National University to study mechanical engineering. I thought this could be a very interesting discipline, and when I saw my brother studying and drawing, it got my attention. Meantime, I was amazed to see images of engineers—and they were always men—wearing helmets and standing in front of buildings that were under construction. To me, engineers seemed like important and intelligent people.

So I started to imagine myself in that position. I liked to imagine that in the future, maybe I could be the person standing there wearing the helmet at the construction site. I set myself the goal of becoming an engineer, and although I wasn't sure yet what discipline to go into, it didn't matter; I was simply inspired by the image of those engineers at work, and the fact that my brother was an engineering student. And I'm so fortunate I had those influences, because without them, I might never have become an engineer. Certainly I had no other references to the profession either in my upbringing or at school.

I studied in a public school and was a good student. My favorite

ABOUT THE AUTHOR

Martha Rubiano Granada is an Industrial Engineer with a master's degree in organizational management. She is a specialist in quality management of products and services with 34 years of professional experience (30 of them in management positions); she spent six years in the field of construction, 24 in education, and four in industry. In the Universidad Libre, she has directed from different academic units, such as: the industrial engineering program; academic secretariat; administration of the Bosque Popular Campus; the national directorate of quality; and, currently, she is the dean of the faculty of engineering. During this time, she has formulated and executed plans for the development and improvement of the infrastructure of the Popular Forest Campus of the Libre University. As Director of Quality, she achieved quality certification under the ISO 9001 standard for the Libre University at the national level, and recently presented the first PhD program for the engineering faculty to the Ministry of National Education.

subjects were diverse: chemistry, English, algebra and calculus. My idea that I could be an engineer became stronger whenever I saw my brother studying for his physics or calculus exams. Because those were subjects I had an affinity for, I came to associate them with engineering. This reinforces my point that it was not from school that I got the idea of being an engineer.

It's a relevant point, because the situation hasn't changed much to this day as young people try to identify their skills and what career possibilities could come of those skills. The rectors of several schools allow universities to promote their programs and explain to students the programs they offer. In a practical sense, it's a marketing plan that universities make in schools, but in this way they also contribute to greater clarity of programs for school students. But I believe we must do a more complete and systematic exercise from the time students are in middle school, to help identify the potential of children and young people. When it comes to girls in particular, this is very important. Never during my schooling was I given any frame of reference for the field of engineering.

Seeing my mother work so hard at home, in addition to attending to household chores, was another reason for why I wanted to study: to be able to choose to be more independent in my life. My father worked as a civilian in the Colombian air force, and I never saw him attend any family activity. In fact, I almost never saw him; he worked during the days and spent his free time with his friends. He was at home very little, and when he was, it was usually to sleep. So of course my mother was always very busy attending to all of the family commitments.

I also saw the sacrifices she made to take care of the home and her children, and it's for this reason that I understand the value in having a sense of responsibility, tenacity, motivation, and the desire to excel. All of this is thanks to the influence of my mother, who encouraged all of her kids to study. She kept alive in me the desire to finish school and go to university to study engineering; many girls of my generation and previous generations simply followed in their mothers' footsteps and did not typically get a post-secondary education, especially not in engineering. And I'm sure that part of the reason I did pursue my education was also because I didn't want to make all the sacrifices that my mother did.

There are other paths women can follow, such as the one my sister took. She got married at age 21 and had one child, and when the child was almost eight years old, she decided to go to university to study accounting. I consider her to be a fortunate woman: to marry and have a family, yet still be able to advance her studies, despite assuming most of the responsibility for taking care of the home and family. But I think engineering is such a demanding discipline that it may not be possible to "have it all." In my case, I became an engineer by age 21 and a mother at age 39.

I joined the industrial engineering program at the Libre University in 1981. In the first semester I was 16 years old and I remember that in my course of 56 students, nine were female; that's 16 percent. The graduation rates of female versus male engineers at Libre University are far less lopsided: in 1985, the year I graduated, just over 27 percent of graduates were women (30 years later, in 2015, that percentage was about 37).

According to data from the Ministry of Education, the past three years has seen a downward trend in applications to study engineering. Of especially low demand among women are metallurgical, mechanical and systems engineering; male students far exceed females in these programs. Environmental engineering programs, on the other hand, are the most attractive for women; the number of female students who enroll is far higher than the number of male students.

It's important that all students get some guidance on what programs might best suit them. I almost went into metallurgical engineering (at the time, the university offered only metallurgical and industrial engineering courses). You see, in the faculty of engineering at the Libre University, I made a good group of friends that included many metallurgical engineering students. In 1982 I started to think that since this discipline had a chemical component, which was one of my favorite subjects, perhaps I should focus on it instead of industrial engineering.

At home one day, I mentioned to my older brother that I was interested in changing programs, and he advised against it. He described that as a metallurgical engineer, I would have to be in plants in front of a blast furnace, breathing fumes and ash, but that with industrial engineering there were opportunities to work in a variety of companies, and that it would provide better opportunities. I trusted that my brother knew what he was talking about, and decided to continue in industrial engineering.

What was it like for a woman in engineering school in Colombia in the early 1980s? There were "jokes" from classmates, things like, "There are nice women, regular women, ugly women—and engineering women." In other words, the stigma was that for a woman to be intelligent enough to study engineering, she must be ugly. Another anecdote I remember is when a male teacher was giving a lesson and, wanting to illustrate his point by giving an example, he said, "For the men, it's a compressor; for the women, it's a pressure cooker." These are only a couple of anecdotes; I could tell many more. But the point is, we learn to adapt, survive, and successfully finish our studies, and to do this, women typically are more disciplined and dedicated.

My first job after finishing my studies in 1986 at the age of 21 was as a warehouse manager in a copper profiles factory on the outskirts of Bogotá, where I worked for a year. I then worked in various sectors, including construction, commercial, and banking. Then I joined the Libre University, where I have worked for 24 years and held positions both in the administrative and academic area. I have been dean of the faculty of engineering since 2016, the first woman to hold this position since the faculty began in 1963. Becoming the dean had been my goal, but I had earlier been passed over for the position, so I decided to look to other horizons, thinking that there were no further possibilities for professional development at the university. I worked in another sector (as an integration professional on a construction project of an oil pipeline and a crude station) before being shortlisted again by the university for the dean's role. This time, I reached my goal.

From my personal experience, I see several reasons why relatively few women enter engineering programs. The first is the influence in their own homes when they are girls, because as I've mentioned, in most homes it is a woman who is the main caretaker of the home and the family. This context doesn't exactly lead to girls becoming engineers! In my last year of secondary school, out of a class of 35, approximately 15 were girls, and as far as I know I was the only girl who went on to study engineering. During my time as dean, I have met at least five other deans of engineering in Colombia who are women; of those, one is single, and four are married. Only two have children. Indeed, it's difficult to be a mother in the engineering profession.

Motherhood is another reason for such small numbers of women in this discipline. From my point of view as dean, I think it's important that I comment on this. Although Colombia has been developing legislation for protecting women's jobs during pregnancy, maternity has long been a barrier to advancement in their chosen discipline. Women employees having children is often seen by organizations as a problem; some companies can only foresee her being absent for maternity leave. One industrial engineering student I knew couldn't find a job to fulfill her business practice obligation because she was pregnant. So I had her work as a practitioner in the faculty so that she did not have to delay her studies. Another example of this challenge for women is when I did the field work as an integration professional on the oil pipeline and crude station. A fellow woman engineer told me of her conflicts with her husband because he wanted to have a child, but her role involved a lot of field work, and she traveled home only on weekends. She couldn't see how it was possible to both work and bring up a child, so she decided to stop working; she hoped she would be able to resume earning an income in her discipline later.

And finally, as mentioned earlier, to get more women interested in engineering programs and the various disciplines, it's definitely necessary that the universities support schools in offering guidance to kids in their younger years—and not only in the last year of school. I think a program based on the STEAM model must be designed for at least the last three years, and should include planning for basic education, so that students leave with a clear idea of which discipline—in particular, which engineering discipline—suits them best.

I believe that we women who have managed to reach leadership positions must take more action to help inspire other women to study engineering. It's not easy, because we can feel like we're drowning in the day-to-day work and responsibilities of the job, and we don't get the time for addressing issues like the need to attract more women to the field of engineering. But we as leaders should be looking into what motivates female engineering students to study, and what motivates female teachers to teach. We should also explore what barriers they have experienced and how they have overcome them. That way, we can design strategies that encourage young people to study engineering. My recent quick data analysis of what areas of engineering women have enrolled in most between 2014 and 2018 showed me how important environmental engineering is to them. Why this program in particular? I feel it's likely that environmental studies—which involve sensitivity and protection—appeal to a woman's nature. This could be another factor to consider in the research.

 In fact, writing this chapter has inspired me to do some research and I'd like to eventually write a book on the theme of women engineers and motherhood. I want to know more about female engineers; this is a good time to think about developing objectives for sustainable gender equity. My perception is that many women feel they must choose either motherhood or engineering. And I simply do not think this is fair.

JOURNEY 27

KNOCKING DOWN STEREOTYPES

KARIN SAAVEDRA

Chile's first aerospace engineer
Assistant Professor
University of Talca

CHILE

I was born in Chiloé, Chile, a magical island at the southern end of the world that has a unique cultural and architectural identity due to its geographical isolation. On Chiloé—more than 1,000 kilometres from Santiago—women are the main bearers of folklore traditions; they stand out for their work and their organizational capabilities. But the same gender pay gap that exists throughout the rest of my country exists there, too. In Chile, the average salary of working women reaches just 70 percent of a man's salary, and the difference is even bigger for women with a higher education. In fact, the education system across Chile is very segregated, although fortunately for me, when I was growing up I was able to attend one of the last public schools in which students from different socio-economic backgrounds coexisted (it's likely that this school was still operating because of Chiloé's lack of connectivity and infrastructure). But even as a girl, I was aware of the disparities in Chilean society.

I am the eldest of three sisters, and my parents are both public officials (my mother is a kinesiologist and my father is a special education teacher). I had an atypical childhood, in which games and creativity were not classified by gender; I felt I was free to choose to build castles, repair artefacts or cook mud pies. But when I was only two years old, I was diagnosed with an immune disease and I was frequently hospitalized for reasons that healthy children are not (a cold, toothache, or headache). To entertain myself, I became a big fan of video games—I remember receiving a Nintendo one Christmas when I was in the hospital—and I taught myself to program an Atari when I was just 10 years old. From then on, nothing

ABOUT THE AUTHOR

Dr. Karin Saavedra was born in 1984 in Castro (Chiloé, Chile). Currently Assistant Professor at the University of Talca, she is Director of the master's program in mechanical engineering and Academic Secretary of the Faculty of Engineering at the same institution. Karin studied at the Inés Muñoz de García primary school (Castro), the Galvarinos Riveros Cárdenas high school (Castro) and the Arriarán Barros high school (Puerto Montt). She became an Aerospace and Aeronautical Engineer after studying at the University of Concepción, and earned a master's degree in advanced methods for designing structures and a doctorate in mechanical engineering at the École Normale Supérieure de Cachan (France). Since 2012, she has been with the engineering faculty at the University of Talca. In 2017, she was a finalist for the InspiraTEC award (from Chile's Ministry of Economics Undersecretariat). In 2018 she was one of "100 distinguished engineering women" who graduated from Universidad de Concepción (2018) and was named a "distinguished woman" by the government of the Maule region in Chile. She and her husband, Jorge, have two children.

interested me more than logic, mathematics, and understanding how things work. And, fortunately, my illness went away on its own during my adolescence.

After I finished high school in 2002, I had to leave my family to move 800 kilometers north to study at the University of Concepción. I was among the country's first aerospace engineering students; up until then, joining Chile's air force was the only possible path to this field of study, and that path was virtually restricted to men. (In fact, it was only 20 years ago that women gained admission to the Chilean air force, and only since 2009 have women been able to reach all levels.) My parents did not hesitate to support me when I told them of my choice, because although I had never before shown a particular interest in aerospace, I was really excited to learn about designing airplanes and rockets.

Looking back now, I realize my academic world was one of men; there were no female professors, and the few female students who there were disappeared in the upper grades. I think that my excellent academic performance was essential to validating me and giving me recognition among my professors and classmates. I loved programming, and mechanical simulations became my favorite subject. In 2007 I graduated as the first female aerospace engineer in Chile. It was around this time that I met my husband, Jorge, a mechanical engineer with whom I share a lot of professional interests.

Because I liked to be constantly learning and teaching, I decided to dedicate myself to a career in academics, but that meant I had to once again study far away from home, since Chile had no graduate programs specializing in aerospace. (In terms of Chile's aeronautical and space industry, it is growing, although it's still not as big as in other Latin American countries—Brazil, for example.) There was a possibility I could get a scholarship in France, and when I did, I jumped at the opportunity, although I knew it would not be easy because of the language. I was very lucky, because my husband was also able to obtain a doctoral scholarship at the same time and at the same institution. We would be together in this adventure.

I attended École Normale Supérieure de Cachan (which is near Paris) for almost five years, earning my master's degree and my doctorate, both in computational mechanics. Just as before, I was one of the few female students, but I don't recall experiencing any episodes of discrimination either as women or as a foreigner. Jorge and I took advantage of being in Europe to travel and visit many other countries. We met wonderful people from different cultures, and I was able to quickly become fluent in French. When we finished our respective doctoral theses, I was seven months pregnant with our first child, and we decided to come back to Chile.

I am currently an assistant professor at the University of Talca in Chile, and one of the few women in my country with a doctorate in mechanical engineering. Generating and transferring knowledge is my great passion. I have specialized in the development of algorithms to perform computer simulations that allow predicting the mechanical behavior of structures; I participate in research and technology transfer projects; and I teach mechanical engineering students and different postgraduate programs. I recently assumed new responsibilities as director of the master's degree in mechanical engineering and as academic secretary of the faculty of engineering.

On many occasions I have been the first or the only woman. Almost 20 years have passed since I entered university and now, as an academic, I am often the only woman in the classroom or in meetings with my peers. Working in a masculinized environment certainly generates additional pressure; assessments of ability are often based on prejudices, and there is a constant need among women, whether internally or externally driven, to validate our skills. Being the mother of two children—Helena, age seven, and Mariano, age four—I have also experienced disadvantages that made motherhood incompatible with competitive scientific productivity.

I find myself in a scenario where women are doubly absent: there is segregation due to the area of knowledge, and segregation due to hierarchical distribution. By understanding these difficulties, it has become clear to me that I am not the one who is in the wrong place and who must adapt. Rather, it is the socio-cultural structures and professional spaces that must adapt in order to include the talent of women or of people who come from isolated areas. It is not easy when education is so segregated. I know, because I have lived it. At the same time, I recognize and thank my academic advisors (all men) who have always trusted my abilities, and the many wise women who have given me selfless support, especially the Network of Women Researchers of Chile.

I am aware that technology moves the world today; it's a field that demands more workers and offers better salaries. Yet women are still a minority in this field. In Chile, one in 10 women study for a career in technology, while half of the men are drawn to this area. A greater presence of women will not only reduce the pay gap, but also enrich solutions when solving complex problems. From my position in a public university, and someone who is trying to keep a career as a researcher, I participate in discussion spaces about vocational decisions; I promote favorable mechanisms of retention of women in STEM (Science, Technology, Engineering, and Mathematics); and I coordinate robotics workshops with gender parity for schoolchildren. I have also helped create an admissions system exclusively for women in order to increase female enrollment in the engineering faculty at the University of Talca.

My daughter, Helena, wants to be a scientist. Without fear of failure, she imagines conducting experiments. In her mind, she gives herself the opportunity to be astonished, to complete her research logbook and—with scorched hair if the experiment fails—to forget worrying about her appearance. I believe we girls and women should all have this opportunity.

JOURNEY 28

FEELING GRATEFUL

ARIELA SOFER

Associate Dean
Administration & Faculty Affairs
Professor
Systems Engineering & Operations Research
George Mason University

UNITED STATES OF AMERICA

I was unaware. Unaware of the stereotype that girls can't do math. Unaware, until I was a doctoral student in the United States. Unaware, until a fellow student told me about the struggles she had with her father, growing up in the south of the US, when she wanted to go into math. I was shocked to learn that such stereotypes of women's abilities existed in a Western country.

Growing up in a secular family in Israel, I had not encountered such stereotypes. Women could do anything men could do. Women could be scientists, doctors, lawyers. Just as men, women in Israel were required to serve in the military. Women could also be leaders: Golda Meir became prime minister way back in 1969. My own mother led several professional societies. I never sensed I was being held back because of my gender. I never encountered the obstacles that so many other women worldwide have confronted and still continue to encounter. I grew up with the expectation that I could do anything and everything.

If there is a true hero of this expectation it is my mother, Sarah. Hers is a true story of grit and determination. It started in Katowice, in southwestern Poland where she grew up, the second of three daughters in a well-to-do family. Life initially was very comfortable. During the school year the girls would take piano, tennis, and horse-back riding lessons; in

ABOUT THE AUTHOR

Professor Ariela Sofer is Associate Dean for Administration and Faculty Affairs of the Volgenau School of Engineering at George Mason University. Prior to that she served almost 16 years (2002-2017) as Chair of the Systems Engineering and Operations Research Department at Mason. Dr. Sofer received her BSc in mathematics and her MSc in Operations Research from the Technion in Israel. She received her Doctorate in Operations Research from The George Washington University in 1984 and joined Mason upon graduation. Her major areas of interest are nonlinear optimization, optimization in medical applications, and systems thinking. She has also been involved in various airport design problems. She is coauthor of the textbook Linear and Nonlinear Optimization (SIAM Books, 2008, and McGraw Hill, 1996). Dr. Sofer is a member of the Board of Directors of the International Council on Systems Engineering (INCOSE). She has also served on the boards of the Institute of Industrial and Systems Engineers (IISE) and the Institute of Operations Research and Management Science (INFORMS), and as chair of the INFORMS Association of Chairs of Operations Research Departments. Dr. Sofer was elected Fellow of INFORMS in 2016 and Fellow of IISE in 2018.

summers the whole family, including the maids, would travel to some resort on a beach or in the mountains. This all changed abruptly on October 27, 1938. Across the border, the Nazis arrested thousands of Jews with Polish citizenship who were living in the Reich and deported them to the Polish border with only the shirts on their backs. Katowice was a first destination for many of the refugees, and the local Jewish community mobilized to help them. My grandfather was a leader in this effort and soon thereafter my grandparents had whole families of refugees living in their house for months, with their three daughters assisting in their care.

Recognizing the ominous threat of Nazi Germany, my grandfather left Katowice in spring of 1939 to establish a new home base for his family in Tel Aviv, in what is now Israel. My grandmother, together with her 12-, 14-, and 15-year-old daughters, set out from Katowice to join my grandfather on August 31, 1939. As bad luck would have it, there was a problem with the spelling of the middle name on my mother's travel pass, and they were delayed. And on September 1, 1939, Hitler invaded Poland, and Katowice immediately fell under German attack. Thus started a six-year unimaginable ordeal. Under heavy bombardments they fled on a five-day train journey eastward to Lvov, which soon thereafter was annexed by the Soviets. They spent the bitter winter of 1939 in hiding and in 1940 were captured by the Soviet NKVD (the law-enforcement agency) and deported in cattle trains to work camps in Siberia.

There, under an extremely cold and harsh climate, my mother and her sisters worked at felling trees. They managed to escape in 1941 but could not leave the Soviet Union. Somehow they made their way to Kazakhstan and ended up in a kolkhoz, a collective farm, where they stayed until 1945. Throughout this period, they endured bombings, starvation, lice, typhus, and other diseases, but overcame. At the end of the war they finally escaped the Soviet Union, making their way through Tehran and Baghdad to Tel Aviv. (My grandfather, an orthodox Jew who had last seen his daughters as three teenage girls, now met three tough, independent-minded women.) My mother and her sisters joined the Haganah, a precursor of the Israel Defense Forces (IDF), and fought in the 1948 War of Independence. In the process, my mother became the second female officer to be trained by the IDF.

And what about their education? After all, the three sisters did not have a single day of school throughout the war. Yet in ways still mysterious to me, they caught up. My mother went on to become an architect who designed many public and private buildings in my home town of Haifa; her younger sister went on to become a leading specialist in internal medicine at, among others, the Mayo Clinic; and the eldest sister became a well-known fashion designer.

With this perspective in mind, I view my own journey as a stroll in the park. I didn't even know about my mother's experiences in the war until I was in my late 20s: like many Israeli youth of my generation I was driven to look to the future and was loath to look back at the past. Nevertheless, from an early age my mother instilled in my sister Naomi and me a "can-do, nothing-is-impossible" mentality. And when I eventually learned of my mother's journey, I realized that I had very high standards to meet. To this day, I feel obligated to meet them.

My father, of course, also had a great influence on who I am today. Born in Hamburg, his family fled Germany in early 1933, shortly after Hitler became Chancellor, and settled in Haifa. My father joined the British Army and, during World War II, served in the Jewish Brigades that fought the Germans in North Africa and Italy. He later joined the Haganah, fought in the 1948 War of Independence and continued his career as a naval officer. From my father we gained a strong sense of duty and honor.

MATH AND BEYOND

I was always good at math and my mother encouraged it. When I was four years old, she introduced me to the multiplication table for the numbers one to four, and I joyfully went on to develop it by myself up to 12. I liked math games and riddles, logic games, and jigsaw puzzles. Still, in my earlier years I really wanted to be a ballerina when I grew up. Or perhaps a trapezist.

Which brings me to the second hero of my story. In high school my age group was split into three cohorts: humanities, biological sciences, and physical sciences. My cohort, physical sciences, comprised 11 girls and

17 boys. Our head teacher, Israel Matzliach, taught us math and physics. Mr. Matzliach was young and energetic, and brought a lot of excitement into the class. On occasion, if the class did really well, he would stand on his head on his desk in the classroom to everyone's utter delight. For homework he often assigned optional challenges: "starred questions." Getting a correct answer to a starred question would merit a notable mention in class. Five of us (myself and four boys) would always compete to solve them. The competition was tough; we were considered "talented" (indeed, each of us ended up with doctorates in STEM fields, as did many others in my cohort), and all of us were very determined. I loved the competition, and I loved the intellectual challenge. I always aced the math questions, and most times aced the physics. My classmates referred to me as a "math genius" and occasionally I even believed that was true. I realized I wanted to do math when I grew up. Mr. Matzliah had inspired me.

Most Israeli high-school graduates are drafted to the IDF immediately upon graduation. I, however, entered an academic reserve program that allowed me to defer the draft and first complete my university studies before joining the IDF in a position that utilizes my professional knowledge. The program required that I do basic training throughout the first summer of college, and officer training throughout the second summer. Thus, I enrolled in the bachelor's program in mathematics at the Technion - Israel Institute of Technology. As someone who had not yet completed military service I was among the youngest in my class.

With the exception of one semester—the one when my father died unexpectedly—I was a very good student at the Technion. But over time I began to discern that perhaps I was not meant for pure math. The first inkling came in my sixth semester, when we started to take classes with students in their senior year and graduate students. There were two young men who were exceptionally bright—head and shoulders above everyone else. It was humbling to realize that while I might be pretty good, I wasn't even close to being a math genius. I also began to recognize that I was not that singular in my passion for math: I had other interests competing for my time, including painting, sculpting, gardening, and of course, pretty clothes and boyfriends.

The final impetus, however, came in my last semester during my third course in complex analysis. The professor had presented the Bieberbach conjecture on the magnitude of the coefficients an of the Taylor series of certain "univalent" functions. The conjecture, I learned, had been made by Bieberbach and proved for the case n=2 in 1916, then proven to be valid by other mathematicians for the cases n=3 in 1923, for n=4 in 1955, and for n=6 in 1969. As the professor was excitedly relating the history of the conjecture my heart sunk lower and lower. If this was what mathematicians were spending years of their life on, I wanted no part of it.

Luckily, a friend opened my eyes to the field of operations research

(OR), the application of mathematical analysis for complex decision making. After my military service, I enrolled in the OR master's program offered by the Faculty of Industrial Engineering at the Technion, and followed that with a doctorate in OR from The George Washington University in Washington, DC. (It was there that I learned of the travails of inequality for some of my fellow female students.) Upon graduation I was fortunate enough to find a position as an assistant professor of operations research at George Mason University (Mason) in nearby Fairfax, Virginia.

Operations research has been a career I have loved ever since. While initially I focused very much on development of algorithms, I have had a chance to apply it to many applications. These include satellite spacing, assessing the reliability of software, protocols for biopsy for prostate cancer, PET image reconstruction, techniques for radiofrequency ablation, satellite imaging, and redesign of the new Hong Kong Airport airfield lighting power distribution. I find every new application to be an exciting new world, and I love it. My coauthored textbook, Linear and Nonlinear Optimization, introduces not only the theory and algorithms of linear and nonlinear optimization but also the many applications, the influence of theory on the interpretation of applied solutions, and the influence of applications on the algorithms.

About 15 years ago I made a foray into the world of systems engineering. At the time, this was driven by necessity rather than by research interest. I had been chair of the Systems Engineering and Operations Research (SEOR) department at Mason for about two years when I began to realize that although the department had outstanding systems engineering faculty (including a member of the National Academy of Engineering), we still needed a driving force who would overhaul our systems engineering academic programs and represent our perspectives in professional societies. I took it upon myself to learn as much as I could about systems engineering. Today I am considered an expert on systems engineering education and serve as academic director of the International Council on Systems Engineering (INCOSE).

LEADERSHIP: THE BEGINNINGS

I don't consider myself a born leader. As a young girl and through most of my teens I was always a team player but never a team leader. Although I was fun loving and friendly, I was basically quiet, shy, and deeply introspective. All this changed abruptly when I was 16, going on 17. I studied the girls in my class who were popular with boys: why, I wondered, were they successful with the boys, while I wasn't being noticed? I came to realize that if I wanted to snag the boys whom I deemed worthy of my attention I needed to be more outgoing. Overnight I transformed myself into a more extroverted version of myself. Lo and behold, that proved to be a successful strategy! To this very day I hover on the boundary between introversion and extroversion, flipping occasionally back and forth—an extroverted introvert, if you like. I believe that straddling this line has helped me tremendously as a leader.

I gained many valuable lessons in leadership through my military service, starting from basic training, through officer training, and capping this with my 20-month compulsory service. For my service, I was assigned to a naval base in Haifa as a math and physics instructor, primarily to naval cadets. Together with my friend Drora, we were the only two female instructors in the Naval Command School, while all the other instructors and the cadets were men. I didn't view that as particularly unusual, and I loved teaching these ambitious young men.

One of the most interesting challenges I faced, however, was teaching a course in physics not to cadets but to future submarine machinists. The 20 young men in my class came from a background that was worlds apart from mine: they mostly came from low-income families of North African descent, and most of them had graduated from a vocational school. They were a rowdy, fearless bunch, far less inclined to listen or study, and more apt to just horse around. Yet I had to admire them for their indomitable spirit and courage in going into a lonely, dangerous service. In fact, four of these young men had lost an older brother when the submarine Dakar mysteriously vanished in the Mediterranean on its maiden voyage to Haifa a few years earlier. Realizing that I could not reach them either by pulling rank or using the stuffy class notes I had originally prepared, I tried to build on their strengths: while they were not academically prepared, they had great mechanical aptitude and problem-solving skills. I also learned to listen, to speak to them in their own jargon, and to appeal to their wacky sense of humor. The class ended up a success, and it was a great experience for me. Listening to and understanding whom I am working with was an important lesson for me not only as a future educator but as a future leader.

By far the most trying and difficult time in my service was the Yom Kippur War. I was called back to the base early on October 6, 1973, due to a state of alert: the Egyptians and Syrians were amassing tanks on the border with Israel. It was Yom Kippur, the holiest day on the Jewish calendar, a day where there were no radio or television broadcasts, and no public transportation. I was ordered to be on call in the faculty office, a lone one-story building located in a remote part of the base, and await further instructions. Apart from a single office room with four desks, the building had a small back room with a cot for the on-call officer, and a tiny kitchenette. I was there alone; my male colleagues were assigned to their ships and Drora to another far-off location. It was eerily quiet, with no one else either in sight or within earshot. Yet I was not worried. The chance that war could break out, we were informed, was considered very low. Little did we realize that in a few hours Israel would be on the brink of destruction.

At 2 p.m. the shriek of air raid sirens broke the silence, a piercing wail that is impossible to forget. Radio transmissions came back on. Egyptian and Syrian forces had jointly attacked Israel and were progressing rapidly. There were no air shelters on the base, and I was told to wait in my quarters until further orders. I spent the afternoon taping the windows and covering them with the best thing I had on hand, brown wrapping paper. As night fell, the news was increasingly worrisome. The Egyptians had penetrated deep into Sinai, the Syrians had captured a great portion of the Golan Heights, and there were many casualties. Sirens repeatedly sounded. More grim news came from close to Haifa: Syrian planes had fired missiles onto the Ramat David Air Base less than 30 kilometres away.

By then it was nighttime and the whole country was in total blackout; it was pitch dark. There were airplanes flying above, but I could not tell whether they were our forces or theirs. I retreated to the back room, which had no windows, so I could safely use a flashlight. But eventually the batteries ran out and I had only one battery left in case of emergency. There was nothing I could do but to try to go to sleep. As I lay there in the small military cot listening to the sounds of war, there was another noise, much closer to home. A scuttling sound. My flashlight hit his glittering eyes and pointy snout straight on: a mouse! So there I lay in total blackness, with the swooping noise of low-flying aircraft overhead, the occasional wailing sirens, and the scuffling mouse. I pulled the sheets over my head and prayed. Prayed that I would be alive the next morning, and that the mouse would not crawl all over me. I woke up early the next morning and discovered to my great relief that I was still alive.

So did a mouse contribute to my leadership skills? No. But the experience was one of a number of trying experiences (some very sad) that I encountered in my young life in Israel that not only made me resilient, but also confident and proud about my resilience. It is this confidence that guides me in much of what I do to this very day.

LEADERSHIP: THE AFTERMATH

There are many different ways that women become engineering leaders. Each woman will have her own very different journey. My own has not been one of leaps and bounds. I did not fantasize about being an engineering leader when I was growing up, or even when I became a faculty member. Rather, every next step seemed to have been a natural succession to the previous one, as I was reflecting on how I could best make an impact for the "overall" good. In that sense, becoming a leader was perhaps inevitable.

I was astute enough not to pursue leadership positions early in my career. My focus was on research publications, research funding, and of course teaching. But with time I gradually assumed leadership roles throughout my career. As a nine-year member of the faculty senate at Mason, I chaired several key committees, most notably one that created a post-tenure review system at the university. In 2001 I was asked to run unopposed for the position of faculty senate chair but ultimately decided against it since I was just about to take on the chairmanship of my department, SEOR. I served close to 16 years as department chair, for a total of four terms.

I am especially proud of all the great and diverse talent that SEOR hired over this time, the great strides we made academically, and that after 16 years the faculty still liked me. I am also proud to have brought our graduate programs, which were previously unranked, up to 27th in the US in the category of industrial, manufacturing, and systems engineering. For the past year, I have served as associate dean for administration and faculty affairs in the Volgenau School of Engineering at Mason. From handling 20 faculty as a chair, I now deal with 220 at the school level. The much larger range of human "variability" has been an interesting revelation for me, and I am still very much in the learning stage.

I have also taken on numerous leadership positions in my professional societies. I have served on the boards of three major professional societies and was a candidate for president of one of those but lost. I have co-chaired a number of conferences and am the general chair of the INFORMS 2020 Annual Conference in Washington, DC, that is expected to attract more than 7,000 participants.

There are many different ways for women to be successful leaders. My approach to leadership starts by setting an example. This includes getting my hands dirty when needed; listening and learning; encouraging teamwork; instilling a team spirit as well as a strong team vision and ethics; and making the hard decisions when it is necessary. Integrity is above all the most important quality of a successful leader, and I work very hard to do what I believe is right, and to maintain honesty and transparency in all my professional actions and relationships.

I attribute all of these elements of leadership to my upbringing and my experiences growing up. But then there are the quirky aspects that are unabashedly me. I have an adventurous streak, which in the past led me to scuba dive with sharks, rock climb—once, I was hanging 2,000 feet above the valley far below—and ice-climb a frozen waterfall. I have always embraced my femininity and I am very proud of it. (You might notice that in how I dress, but I will say no more.) It's the same adventurous streak that led me to pack two suitcases and leave Israel to study in the United States (though I expected I would return as soon as I completed my studies). Yes, I have been on the receiving end of the occasional pass from men, or inappropriate comments, but it didn't happen a lot, and I typically brushed such actions and their perpetrators aside. These things never stopped me from being myself and didn't negatively affect me. In terms of sexism, I have experienced very little compared with what several other authors in this book have suffered. I have been very fortunate. I can only be grateful.

JOURNEY 29

"NATURAL UNUSUALNESS"

ŞIRIN TEKINAY

Chair
Global Engineering Deans Council
Professor
Electrical & Electronics Engineering
Sabanci University

TURKEY

What do you say to yourself when you see the words "Why Be Normal?" or a "Normal Is Boring" on a t-shirt? We all think we know what "normal" is, and we defend our view—our individual, unique view. That's a conflict by definition, isn't it?

I'm sure most readers of this book are not easily confused, but for the benefit of those who may be, please indulge me as I start by defining the obvious. Rare natural occurrences, as unusual as they may be, are, like recessive eye colors, NORMAL. They are every bit as healthy, respectable, and capable as more typical occurrences. Unfortunately, people often confuse "normal" with "usual"; or, they judge the majority to be normal, and vice versa. Therefore, your personal definition of normal depends on how much you've traveled, read, how many people you've taken the time to get to know, how many bridges you've crossed, how many places you've seen, and how many cultures, climates, and cuisines you've experienced. Of course, there are also the prejudices, assumptions, unquestioned beliefs, pre-conditioned reflexes, and comfort zones—everything that you started with, and your willingness to let go of them... to "un-learn," to question, to accept change, to absorb new things, and to grow.

The reason I am hung up on these definitions is that I have heard them about myself: I have been called "unusual," "special," or plain "different" ever since I was born, in 1967. I was naturally strong and athletic, started to

ABOUT THE AUTHOR

Şirin Tekinay is a professor of electrical and electronics engineering at Sabancı University. During her 20-year career in the US, she served the telecom industry (Bell Labs and Nortel), got tenured, and was promoted to Associate Professor of Electrical and Computer Engineering at New Jersey Institute of Technology. From 2005-2009, she served the US National Science Foundation as Program Director. Over the last decade back in her home country of Turkey, Dr. Tekinay held the positions of Dean of Engineering and Natural Sciences, Vice Rector for Research, and Rector. Dr. Tekinay holds a George Mason University PhD, and MS and BS degrees from Bogazici University, all in electrical engineering. Dr. Tekinay holds nine patents. She founded the first FabLab in Turkey, and pioneered new approaches in project-based education and transdisciplinary research. She is an expert reviewer for the European Commission; member of the Open Science Group of the European Universities Association; elected member on the Board of Directors of the European Society for Engineering Education; and Chair of the Global Engineering Deans Council.

read and write at the age of four with virtually no instruction, and, before my school years, displayed an exceptional talent for arithmetic, geometry, and music. I'd chosen my field of electronics engineering possibly because of my fascination with the legendary TV series Star Trek. That was when I was just five, well before I could pronounce my "R"s; I announced I was going to be an "electyonics engineey."

None of this made me feel any different than anyone else; all I felt was the sheer joi de vivre that Mother Nature seems to instill in kids. Remember, everything is new and unusual to children. Children don't judge. But they do absorb the parental or cultural judgements that surround them, seemingly out of thin air. I thought I was my family's pride and joy (I certainly would be if I were a boy, don't you agree?) but I wasn't 100 percent sure. Because there were those added whispers at the end of generous praises, like "in spite of being a girl," or "even though she's a girl," or "like the best of, or even better than, the boys," or worst of all, that terrible "unlike normal girls." I had to bear the awful burden of being an "abnormal girl," so in my mind, my gender role was, "I'm a girl, but...."

Don't get me wrong; I was very fortunate to be born into a family that supported my sister and me towards our unique interests and strengths. My father, may he rest in peace, was a professor of civil law, and he was a particularly fervent spokesman for women's and children's rights. He was especially beside himself with pride about his "extraordinary" daughter.

My mother, on the other hand, was trying hard to hide her resentment of dad's incessant bragging. She had her reasons, and they were cultural: she believed that all this "extraordinary" business could bring on the badness of jealous "evil eyes." Or, I would get a big head, or it would at the very least create a healthy dose of sibling rivalry because my older sister was, as far as she was concerned, better at being normal (today, my sister is a successful, internationally recognized professor of literature).

Beyond all that, though, Mom was also genuinely worried about me, although I never understood why. She made a few fruitless attempts at making me "a normal little girl" by trying to interest me in dolls and other "normal things." For example, when I was three or four, she got me an annoying life-like baby doll that, when squeezed, either randomly screamed bloody murder or giggled happily. I promptly opened it up to examine the circuitry to see if I could train this little demon into being happy all the time. (To this day, I believe engineering is the way to refine human life and make people happier.) That might have been when Mom gave up on me. She had to resign herself to the fact that no doll would match my attachment to my favorite toy: the screwdriver set.

By the time I was 10, it was pretty much imprinted in my head that I was "extraordinary," which brought some pride and a load of anxiety. I was certain I had to perform to some unnatural norm to be accepted as I am. If I were unexceptional, I would be ordinary, boring, and unremarkable.

That's why my contribution to this book is dedicated to my dear friend Prof. Dimitris Ioannou, with gratitude for making me feel that I am an interesting person because I represent a less frequent occurrence in population (or nature), and for making me feel at the same time that I am completely normal.

※ ※ ※

That I was one of two girls in a class of 55 electrical engineering majors, and one of the precious few girls among hundreds of engineering students in mass classes, was not an issue for me at all, because I had expected this. Further, I was surrounded by a small circle of my best friends from high school (I had been printing useless fun electronic circuits with these guys for years). It was only an issue for the other males in my class. It was like I was the Eiffel Tower: Everyone was aware of the pink elephant in the room, but pretended not to notice. What I wore, whom I sat with, what score I got, and where I went for spring break were all topics of conversation among my otherwise soccer-crazed classmates.

In all fairness, Turkish culture has an inherent respect for the status of "sister (bacı)," and so I was immediately elevated to potential colleague. For the benefit of the female engineering students reading this, let me fast-forward to today: I stay in touch with my classmates from engineering school, and we have frequent reunions. They are married and some have daughters. I find that nowadays, I am more into soccer than some of them, and on the flipside, some of them are more into "girly" things than I am. We're all extremely fond of each other. We are equals, but not the same, and I enjoy their chivalrous attentiveness.

Still, during those student days it was not easy to be one of the few girls. I felt the pressure of representing a minority. Not only did I have to be successful in classes but I also had to be perfect in every other way. I starved myself to be thin, I fussed over what to wear, I carefully planned what little social life I had...and it was exhausting. I was mostly quiet in classes but provided homework support or gave my notes away freely to my classmates. I knew that doing so put me on the fringes of the honor code but I confess it felt good to be sought after for my notes or homework solutions, and to be thanked. (I am proud to note that, as an academic, I have maintained a zero-tolerance ethics policy.) It was the girl's lot I had half-begrudgingly assumed because, basically, I was trying hard to not feel lonely.

During my undergrad years, there was no shortage of daily comments from academic and administrative staff about being a female engineering student, especially in the electronics program. I specifically remember a physics professor who asked me why I didn't prefer industrial engineering like most other girls in engineering. And there was a lady in the student affairs department who insisted such a pretty girl was wasting herself in such a hard program instead of getting married. (I didn't think I was pretty, nor did I think the EE program was all that hard; what did she know?) On the other hand, I took to electromagnetics and communications classes like a duck to water; it was as though I had studied all the material in a previous lifetime. It all made sense, it was fun, it was exciting, and best of all, connecting up the world was a good, meaningful thing to work on. In junior year, I chose the communications and system track, and my grades soared even higher than before.

Many years later, when I got hired as assistant professor at the Department of Electrical and Computer Engineering of New Jersey Institute of Technology, I hung up a sign in my office that read, "Why Be Normal?" It stayed up there on my cork board for many years, on proud display among other knick-knacks like my Australian boomerang, Brazilian samba dancer figurine, Singaporean lion, Turkish anti-evil eye, and so on.

You see, I have traveled a lot and I continue to do so. I don't buy souvenirs anymore, as I'm happy to snap photos instead; it helps that cell phones became wonderful cameras. (I say that with pride as I specialize in wireless communications, but I digress....) The point is, I have let go of wanting to show off how well-traveled I am. You see, somewhere along the way, I began to think it's—you've guessed it—normal.

It must be the rich souls I am privileged to have met along the way, people who have hearts filled with experiences and people that allowed me to grow, and transform my previous mentality of, "I'm a girl, but..." into "I am a woman, and...."

I am grateful not only for the support of my family but for the privilege of the great education I got. I was accepted into the top-ranking middle and high school, the American Robert Lycee, and then the top-ranking electrical and electronics engineering program at the prestigious Boğaziçi University in Istanbul. In 1990, I went on to do my graduate work in the US, at George Mason University in Fairfax, Virginia (at my beloved Alma Mater, the avant-garde, young, dynamic, daring GMU that had spun off of the University of Virginia in the 1970s with a "can-do" spirit).

I was euphoric to be accepted with a graduate assistantship to do research in communications networks. One day, I saw a sign in the mailroom that offered scholarships for "minorities, women, and individuals with disabilities." I had to see that in bold letters for it to dawn on me: I still, and perhaps always will, have additional responsibilities of representing an underrepresented group.

My gratitude came with anxiety.

※ ※ ※

I've learned that representing a minority as an engineer, an engineering professor, an engineering dean, a vice rector for research and development, or a rector means you have to be top-ranking in what you do; you are not helping yourself or the group you represent by delivering anything less than top-notch. Otherwise, you will be assumed to be "not a very good one." Having added to my CV tens of graduate students, many patents, lots of research funds, hundreds of publications and the highest offices of academic administration, I feel I have done a decent job. I also have a high blood pressure problem. The doctor that diagnosed my hypertension during my tenure-track years said it was "normal." I think this hypertension comes with not having a safety net, not having a "plan B."

The safety net is an awful place that affirms low expectations. You have to be stubborn and keep climbing. You may rest briefly to recharge your batteries, though not for long, because you feel guilty for any wasted second. You have to be resilient, because you're fighting with less support than your competition. You are normal, natural, and unusual, but that's not good enough: now you have to be abnormal, supernatural, and extra-unusual.

I got tenured and promoted to associate professorship at New Jersey Institute of Technology, which at the time was a 75-percent male campus. The war tales of condescension and underestimation are endless, as are the stories of being bombarded with discriminatory messages, some sent and received at the subconscious level. However, it was also at NJIT that I was groomed to become associate provost for research, for which I was sent to the Higher Education Resource Services (HERS) summer program. HERS is a boot camp of sorts to raise academic administrators, from deans and directors to provosts and presidents. It was a wonderful experience to be surrounded by the class of HERS 2007, a group of more than 70 smart, successful, ambitious, fun female leaders. I never became the associate provost at NJIT, because I got recruited as the founding VP for research and technology at Ozyegin University in Istanbul.

I am proud to be just a regular member of diverse groups of extraordinary colleagues, no matter how you slice it: Global Engineering Deans Council; IEEE and its technical societies and women's branches; European Society for Engineering Education (SEFI); and so on. My sense of "normal" has been straightened out; these days, I feel natural, and authentic. But I'm not yet at peace. The constant burden of proving myself is always weighing on my shoulders. Men seem to get ahead based on their ambition, and women have to build on proven track records.

To help address that, last year we, the board of directors of SEFI (European Society for Engineering Education), rolled up our sleeves to work on our position paper titled "Diversity, Equality and Inclusiveness in Engineering Education." This work helped finally to fill a void in my understanding of my own and others' professional identity. It was thanks to the work of the SEFI working group on gender and diversity (especially the work of our dear colleague, Prof. Susanne Ihsen, who passed away too soon) that the missing component of identity fell into place for me.

Professional identity has three components. The first, of course, is what the profession entails; the associated responsibilities, tasks, and required competence. The second is the individual identity—the one with which the individual identifies herself (here's a respectful nod at the #ilooklikeanengineer movement spurred on by the Global Engineering Deans Council). The third is the social identity, one that the society, colleagues, and others identify the individual with. Without the third, no matter how competent and self-confident, the underrepresented individual—the unusual, the unaccepted—will not be able to claim the whole professional identity they so rightly deserve.

I am afraid we are teaching our students only the first component. On the second one, they are on their own; this is where women often suffer from the imposter syndrome that cripples anyone in minority, and the undeserving (often, the men) feel boosted by unfounded confidence. The third one simply has to be taught as part of the curriculum so that the second will, in turn, get healthy.

Last semester I taught Gender in Science and Technology, a new inter-faculty course that two other professors at Sabanci University and I developed together. It was well received and we will continue to teach it. We are getting requests from students to include the material in freshmen curriculum. I am delighted to report that the trial run of the class attracted 40 students, a pretty good mixture of male and female, some graduate, and not only engineering majors.

I have faith that the next generation will have a much wider scope of professional identity in every sense. Diversity will be accepted as a value, as a virtue, and as an objective. We, the authors of this book, and others who made it as leaders in our respective countries, areas and institutions, have to pay it forward. When I was approached with an offer for the position of rector, I was a happy dean, looking forward to another three-year term with my faculty of engineering and natural sciences. We had started Turkey's firsts: a FabLab, an industry-sponsored Center of Excellence for Urban Engineering, with an associated master's degree program in urban engineering. I didn't think anything could pull me away. However, the offer letter meant I was single-handedly deciding whether there would be plus or minus 10 percent of female rectors in my country. I decided I could not look my female students in the eye if I opted out. I will continue to do my part as long as I am able.

JOURNEY 30

FROM COMMITMENT TO IMPACT

CRISTINA TROIS

Former Dean
School of Engineering
University of Kwazulu-Natal

SOUTH AFRICA

"Fortune favors the brave." This motto has accompanied me throughout my life and best represents my professional and academic journey. There is a fundamental dichotomy between being fortunate and being brave. Being fortunate may imply that you leave your life to fate (and faith!), and professionally speaking you may adopt a passive attitude towards your career. On the contrary, being brave implies that you take chances and seize opportunities, but also that you courageously shape your own destiny and, most importantly, that you are audacious, innovative, disruptive, and creative enough to make bold decisions.

I believe that throughout my academic life I have been both: from being an engineering student to becoming the first full professor and the first woman dean of the faculty of engineering in my university. I am fortunate to do the "best job in the world" and I must thank my father, also an accomplished university professor in mining engineering. He helped me realize from an early age while I was growing up in Cagliari in Sardinia, Italy, that I had a passion and vocation for science, engineering, and technology, which led me to pursue an academic career in environmental engineering.

However, growing up with a professor as a father is not necessarily an advantage; indeed, it was the opposite in the Italian academic environment of the late 1990s. I remember I wanted to become an architect, but because there was no faculty of architecture in Cagliari, my father suggested that I

ABOUT THE AUTHOR

Professor Cristina Trois is the former Dean of the School of Engineering at the University of KwaZulu-Natal in Durban, South Africa. A Full Professor in Environmental Engineering, she is currently the South African Research Chair in Waste and Climate Change (SARCHI). Prof. Trois moved to South Africa from the beautiful island of Sardinia in Italy in 1998 and has been working at UKZN since 1999. She holds an MScEng (summa cum laude) and a PhD in Environmental Engineering from the Department of Geo-Engineering and Environmental Technology of Cagliari University (Italy). She is a Professional Engineer (Italy) and a fellow of the SA Academy of Engineers and of the Global Engineering Deans' Council. Prof. Trois is coauthor of more than 100 peer-reviewed publications. Her fields of expertise include waste and climate change in sustainable cities, and alternative building materials. She developed and coordinates the first Master Programme in Waste and Resources Management in South Africa. Prof. Trois has been principal investigator as well as project coordinator of many multimillion-dollar projects in South Africa and Africa. During her tenure as Dean, she initiated international programs such as "Engineering is a Girl Thing" and "Hub for the African City of the Future."

register for a civil engineering degree instead. Those were the years when a new "hybrid" degree was available in Italian universities, which were following the example of more progressive northern European institutions. Traditional civil/chemical/industrial engineering departments were "recycling" themselves into new environmental engineering courses. At that time, it was not very clear what environmental engineering really was, and if it would be there to stay or only briefly in fashion. So, as naïve and rebellious as I was (and still am), and because I was also motivated by the idea of joining something multidisciplinary and interesting, I signed up for this brand new and exciting environmental engineering degree. Its roots were in mining and geo-engineering, its branches in civil and infrastructure engineering, and its heart in chemical and industrial engineering. DIGITA at the University of Cagliari was a rich coalition where expertise, backgrounds, and academic cultures collided in this new degree that contributed to (and still does) shaping the Italian and international scientific landscape in a fascinating engineering discipline.

In more than 20 years in engineering education, I still find it amazing that engineering students, no matter their origins, always have a strong sense of their status in society and their role in shaping infrastructure development in their countries. They are generally very motivated, competitive, focused on their studies, and basically convinced that they will change the world with their ingenuity. However, on top of it all, if you happen to be the daughter of a faculty member, you constantly feel the responsibility to excel and to prove that you are passing the exams with good marks because of your hard work, and not because of your surname. Those were important years of study and self-realization for me, shaping the future direction of my career and leading me to graduate *summa cum laude*.

In my early career days, I was fortunate to have had three important guides, even mentors, who not only inspired the focus of my research, but were also my first exposure to what it means to be an academic. There was my father, of course, but then I was fortunate to be supervised by Professor Raffaello Cossu for my master's dissertation. He is considered one of the fathers of environmental sanitary engineering in Italy, Europe, and, arguably, the world. A visionary, his example taught me to lead and be innovative in research, to always be a step ahead of others, and to anticipate the need for solutions, innovation, policies, and behaviors. He taught me the art of being entrepreneurial.

And then came my third mentor. The poet Robert Frost wrote: "Two roads diverged in a wood, and I—I took the one less traveled by, And that has made all the difference." After my master's, I could have continued studying within Professor Cossu's research group. But I decided to open my horizons by diverting the focus from municipal solid waste management to mining engineering, and signed up for a PhD with Professor Giovanni Rossi, another world leader and pioneer of BioHydro-Metallurgy. A scholar of incredible intellect and a fine experimentalist, Professor Rossi taught me reactor and experimental design, the importance of breaking silos, and the importance of taking a multidisciplinary approach in research by harnessing the expertise of many different disciplines. These concepts may seem obvious in modern-day research centres, but mixing engineers with biologists, scientists, and even humanists in the same research group was pioneering, to say the least, in a small-town university in 1996.

Professor Rossi and my father, despite having high international scientific profiles with an "h-index" equitable to modern international standards, were always regarded as outsiders in their own department, and often spoke of the nemo propheta in patria ("no man is a prophet in his own land") syndrome. Only years later, after experiencing a similar sense of detachment from the academic environment of my alma mater, did I realize that their disillusion with the nepotistic and insular academic system in Italy at that time subliminally contributed to my decision to leave Italy for an academic career abroad.

Again, I took the road less traveled. I had the choice of the prestigious University of British Columbia in Vancouver, Canada, or the little-known University of Natal in Durban, South Africa. I chose the University of Natal (which later became the University of KwaZulu-Natal, or UKZN). It was 1997, three years after the first free post-apartheid elections. South Africa, "the beloved country," was a land in transition and in search of a new identity. As a young female lecturer in a very traditional civil engineering department, I soon became aware of how male-dominated engineering was. I also noticed that ethnic groups tended to stick together in the classrooms.

However, in comparison to the rest of the country, where the tension post-apartheid was tangible and the various ethnic groups still segregated, by choice or by design, the university campus felt like an oasis of freedom and collegiality amid the madness of a complex society.

My university has always been very progressive and has prioritized transformation. Over the past five to 10 years the female engineering student population has increased to 40 percent thanks to a concerted effort by senior management, and the "Engineering is a Girl Thing" campaign I initiated when I became dean. Nonetheless, in the South African academic environment there is still resistance to advancing women to positions of senior leadership, as our professional, scientific, and academic credibility is always challenged by a male-dominated professoriate.

I only became fully aware of my role as a woman leader in a male-dominated environment later in my career, when I assumed positions of leadership and worked with fellow female leaders by getting involved in international platforms such as the GEDC, IFEES, and the South African Academy of Engineering. I presume one reason for this apparent myopia is because studying engineering in Italy is widely accessible; engineering is not perceived as a male-only profession. With respect to role-definition and career-awareness and preparedness, perhaps women in Italy were generally more "emancipated" than their counterparts in South Africa. Perhaps my myopia and my natural boldness was a strength rather than a weakness: I didn't feel I had to prove anything to anybody, and the progress I made in my career was not driven by any sense of rivalry towards my fellow professors who were male.

If I could offer a few words of wisdom to young female academics on how best to proceed in their careers, I would certainly start with the importance of understanding their profession, their career choice, and the so-called "rules of the game" of an academic job. I notice that very often young graduate PhD students become postdocs and then researchers and then lecturers, without proper training as engineering educators and fully-fledged academics—just as professors become deans, provosts, or vice-chancellors/presidents without proper leadership training. For us engineers, things are even more complicated as we live a constant "identity crisis" between being professional engineers and professional engineering educators. We have to serve two masters— academia and the engineering profession—and this dichotomy can be very disruptive at times.

Becoming an academic is a specific career choice, with fundamental rules and expectations. Understanding these clearly at the onset would avoid unnecessary delays and ensure a successful and fulfilling career. The four pillars of any academic job are: teaching and learning; research and scholarship; university service; and community engagement. It is also critical that the emerging academic understands the specific academic context and landscape in which he or she operates, and develops the four areas harmoniously without neglecting one in favor of another. This is essential for women leaders in particular, as we often have to lead a male professoriate that may be academically more established and older.

This was certainly my experience. In becoming the first woman dean of engineering in the history of my university, just a few years after entering as a professor, I had suddenly become an Imbokodo (which means "strong woman" in IsiZulu) and catapulted into a role model for the many young female students and emerging academics. But I also had yet to acquire credibility and gain the respect of the older and more established professoriate. I felt very unequipped. It is thanks to a strong sense of self, the caring support of my family and my postgraduate students, and the commitment of my department heads and the management team that I overcame my initial fears of failure.

I've been fortunate to be involved in pioneering environmental engineering in South Africa and creating a strong research base. I believe in research-led teaching and learning, in transformative curriculum development that is context-specific, and in applied research that is innovative and solution driven. The research field of environmental engineering has always been neglected in the civil engineering program at my university in favor of more conventional civil engineering topics. Immediately after joining the faculty of engineering in 1999, I initiated a new research area in environmental engineering focusing primarily on waste management and water/wastewater management and treatment. I established an analytical laboratory for environmental engineering research that is fully equipped with state-of-the-art testing equipment. I have strengthened scientific collaborations nationally and internationally in the same line of research in order to encourage continuous knowledge and skills transfer.

Over the years, I have been actively involved in research activities, scholarship, research exchange programs and collaborations, and bridging young engineers into environmental engineering practice and research. Working in a highly specialized niche like waste science and environmental engineering enabled me to strengthen research collaborations with local industry partners and leading national and international research institutions. The successful development of a dynamic research group in environmental engineering, the establishment of scholarship programs, the creation of a center of excellence, and the ongoing opportunities to scientifically collaborate at national and international levels with experts of great caliber are a clear reflection of the ability to stimulate, initiate, and supervise research. But they are also a testimony to determination, focus, and a clear vision in research and scholarship, which are fundamental attributes of any academic leader.

"Making transformation our everyday business" was the slogan of the five new "young" deans of UKZN's College of Agriculture, Engineering and Science who started their mandate in 2012. This came after a painful restructuring exercise in 2011 and an even more painful merger of the founding universities of UKZN in 2004 (Natal University, traditionally "white," and the University of Durban-Westville, traditionally "black").

In a country where the term "transformation" has many connotations, depending on your gender, background, ethnic group, and qualification, promising transformation as modus operandi can be regarded not only as difficult, but also as very ambitious. At that time, I had been a professor for only a few years and was still building my own research profile. How could I promise transformation if I, too, was transforming?

Developing a five-year strategic plan for the faculty of engineering became an opportunity for robust engagement with and reflection on the effectiveness of the teaching-research nexus in facilitating and supporting student learning, and in embracing the concept of (and need for) a truly research-led university. As dean, I was responsible for the accreditation processes of all nine professional degrees offered in our school. This has resulted in a very strong engagement with the Outcome Based Education (OBE) context in South Africa and the need for intense curriculum reform. Those were the years of a movement here in 2014 and 2015 called "#TheFeesMustFall," when students across the country were demanding free university education and the "decolonialization and transformation" of our curricula.

That resulted in a stronger engagement with many things: higher education, the need to develop strategies to achieve effective academic support for underprepared students, curriculum development, the need for achieving accreditation of all our degrees, the strategic focus on supporting and driving the teaching and learning policy and agenda at UKZN, the need to maintain high quality standards and relevance of our curricula in an African context, the need to effectively mentor junior staff by sharing teaching experience and best practices, and the need in engineering to simply create a conducive environment for enhancing teaching and research performance of both students and staff. With respect to teaching and learning, the main consequence of being in a position of leadership was that teaching and scholarship had now become more focused on impact rather than commitment.

I believe in engineers as vehicles of social cohesion. My goals in teaching are to shape engineers who think critically, always see the global picture, and are never afraid to question their own positions. I want to create professionals who are driven by a natural sense of discovery and who can interact with others with confidence and competence. However, as a modern engineering educator I am faced with the constant dichotomy between my mission of forming independent and critical thinkers and the need to build capacity and impart skills in graduates who are "employable" in industry from day one after graduation, and who are competent enough to sustain the unprecedented infrastructure development of our country—while still being marketable in the global arena.

I often need to negotiate my beliefs between the need to foster transformative learning and to form future citizens who are socially conscious and the responsibility of imparting skills and preparing competent engineers for the ever-changing complexity of the workplace—which, paradoxically, could be achieved more easily by favoring a more traditional assimilative learning process.

The requirements from the Engineering Council of South Africa and Department of Education in terms of outcome-based education (OBE) have become the basis of development of my courses and my teaching methods. However, I have always found it limiting that the engineering curriculum remains extremely structured, has limited lateral fluidity, is content-based, does not easily encourage a multidisciplinary approach, and allows for very few non-engineering elective modules—negating their purpose of exposing students to disciplines outside of the sciences in the attempt to "open their minds."

The OBE requirements provide a solid platform on which the engineering educator operates. However, training our students in specific skills alone will not enhance their independent thinking, focused enquiry, and problem-solving, nor will it develop the knowledge and confidence they need to access information, which are essential in modern engineering. The challenge is to accommodate other higher education goals and values such as developing self-sufficient and independent learners and nurturing future citizens that are vehicles, in and out of the classroom, of social transformation. This can help ensure that higher education is a diverse, dynamic, and sustainable system that responds to transformational, social, and economic development needs.

I would describe my teaching philosophy as completely student-centered and focused on a fundamentals-learning, problem-solving and multidisciplinary approach. The modern engineer must have both technical and managerial qualities and must be open to dialogue in a multidisciplinary arena. My main teaching goal is to nurture a culture of exploration and discovery, motivating the students to grow as scientists and as engineers, thus enabling them to make active contributions to transdisciplinary projects.

However, since I became dean, I have been particularly preoccupied with issues of how my students' diversity influences access, throughput, dropout, and exclusion. It is easy to blame the South African secondary schooling system for the underpreparedness of our students that superficially seems to affect throughput, dropout, and exclusion, but the reality is different.

Our engineering student population is diverse demographically (40 percent are of Indian descent, 35 percent are African, 15 percent are white, and the rest are colored; and in terms of gender, females now make up 40 percent). It's also diverse socio-economically. More than 40 percent of our students come from disadvantaged schools and/or communities, are studying in their second language, and might not have been exposed to advanced teaching and learning methods and aids.

The change in the student population in the past 20 years and particularly since the merger of our institution in 2004 is remarkable and has profoundly affected the shaping of my teaching beliefs and strategies. As access to tertiary education opened more widely to all South Africans, it became evident that our teaching had to accommodate a diversity that went beyond differences in how students learn; it had to negotiate issues such as why students learn differently and how their culture, social background, and schooling influenced their present predisposition to learning.

Coming from a European academic context, my first challenge was to modify the classical European teaching philosophy, which favors a formal teacher-learner approach where the learner is generally seen as a "subordinate" receiver of information and is not always in a position to critically address the material taught. I felt that it's important to have an approach that suits the unique and diverse requirements and needs of my students, while remaining always conscious that our curricula must be rooted in African scholarship and contribute to the development of our students as researchers.

In this landscape, it is essential to have an environment of equality, encouragement, interaction, and incentive both in and out of the classroom. My approach is to create a learning environment where all possible differences are cancelled; I aim to instill a sense of equality in my class so that every student feels they are a part of a common team and see themselves as "vehicles of social cohesion." I encourage continuous interaction and I always try to share my own passion for engineering and for teaching. I have the great opportunity to lecture on subjects that coincide with my research interests; it is, therefore, very easy for me to transmit my passion to my own students. In order to make the exchange vivid and useful, I enhance the spirit of equality in the class by empowering my students with what

I consider the most precious gifts: self-confidence and critical thinking.

I firmly believe that teaching is a relationship of trust: the students trust the teacher's knowledge and competence, and believe, in good faith, that the teacher has only their best interests in mind. As a receiver of this trust, I feel the great responsibility of forming new engineers and giving them the essential tools to proceed in their future careers. But teaching (and learning) is also a constant exchange. It's a dialogue that should always occur in the same language (figuratively speaking). In order to find a "common language" that can be easily understood and appreciated by the students, I always make a great effort to understand their background, to learn about their present needs, and to picture their future development in a constantly changing working environment.

To meet the knowledge and skills outcomes specified in each course, I developed the "toolbox" technique.

Learning any type of practice is like carrying a toolbox made of different descending compartments. You must fill the top compartment with the most useful tools—the ones that are always needed—and fill the other compartments with specific tools that may vary with the nature of your project. In our case, I fill my students' top compartment with the theoretical fundamentals. The second compartment is filled with experiential methods (practical techniques, laboratory testing, in situ investigation) that allow students to enhance the efficiency of the fundamental tools. The third compartment is for the highly specialized tools, the ones that are suitable only for specific problems and applicable in prevailing conditions, but that are often necessary to complete the job. The bottom compartment is the "lunch-compartment" that students (or engineers) should reserve for their natural sense of discovery, common sense, imagination, and critical and lateral thinking.

Most importantly, be prepared: the journey of the "servant leader" can be a challenging and lonely one. I had to deal with many curveballs and re-adjust many of my beliefs during my tenure as dean. Professional accomplishment came with personal sacrifice. But I also gained a lot of new friends and rejoiced at the many young graduate engineers/scientists that have chosen environmental engineering as their profession. During this journey I often reflected on the impact that academia and our research has on society, on the communities that we serve. I often felt the need to break boundaries and experiment with new "voices" that go beyond the scientific publications or the big "door-stopper" theses on the bookshelf. I truly believe that we as engineers must be vehicles of social cohesion by using our science and our research to bridge the inequalities between the rich and the poor, between the global north and the global south.

I would like to dedicate this chapter to my son and to all the amazing women—students, collaborators, friends, and sisters—who walk this journey with me, keeping me inspired and on my toes. To them, I say this: I wanted to change the world, but I didn't; I changed many worlds.

JOURNEY 31

A CAREER OF INCLUSION

RENETTA TULL

Vice Chancellor
Diversity, Equity, & Inclusion
University of California, Davis

UNITED STATES OF AMERICA

My name is Renetta. Renetta Garrison Tull. I am from the United States, and I am an engineer who is now serving as a university vice chancellor. Some might say that engineers are born, that math and science skills are innate, and that one enters the field of engineering after years of cultivating, and talent that existed at birth. I would like to submit that my entrée into engineering is a story of actualized diversity, inclusion, and perhaps most importantly, exposure. This chapter consists of a series of short essays that describe my engineering journey to leadership.

My story starts in New Jersey, a small state on the east coast of the United States, and this chapter will end with an experience in Mexico.

More importantly, it may reveal that each person's journey is important, and that experiences—no matter how disjointed or disparate—can be looked upon as oddly shaped pieces that fit together to create a life for a unique purpose. One's triumphs should be celebrated, but the challenges and seemingly off-beaten paths should not be dismissed as errors. While parts of my story will be told on these pages, my hope is that readers will reflect upon their own stories and appreciate their value.

ABOUT THE AUTHOR

Dr. Renetta Garrison Tull is Vice Chancellor for Diversity, Equity, & Inclusion at the University of California, Davis. She previously served as Associate Vice Provost for Strategic Initiatives at the University of Maryland, Baltimore County (UMBC), Professor of the Practice in UMBC's College of Engineering and Information Technology, and worked with the University System of Maryland (USM), co-leading several NSF-funded initiatives, e.g., PROMISE AGEP, PROMISE Engineering Institute, PROMISE Academy, and USM's Louis Stokes Alliance for Minority Participation. Tull earned engineering and science degrees from Howard University and Northwestern University, was an Anna Julia Cooper Postdoctoral Fellow at the University of Wisconsin-Madison, and has held faculty positions at the UW-Madison and the University of Maryland College Park. Externally, Tull has been involved with projects for Puerto Rico's ADVANCE Hispanic Women in STEM, the Latin and Caribbean Consortium of Engineering Institutions, the National Academies of Science, Engineering, and Medicine, and UNESCO. Recognitions include: Global Engineering Deans Council/Airbus Diversity Award Finalist, ABET Claire L. Felbinger Award, and the Student Platform for Engineering Education Development Global Mentoring Award. Tull, a Tau Beta Pi "Eminent Engineer," lives in California with her husband of 26 years, Dr. Damon L. Tull. She engages on Twitter @Renetta_Tull. This chapter includes excerpts from Dr. Tull's blog, "Renetta Garrison Tull: Living Life Online."

THE INFLUENCE OF PARENTS, AND OF SCHOOL PROGRAMS

On June 16, 2017, to celebrate Father's Day in the US, I reflected on the influence of my father in a post on my blog titled, "My Daddy Taught Me Calculus." This section is adapted from that essay.

> My father was an engineer. George Carter Garrison Jr., born in New Jersey, was a tall guy (6 ft., 1 in.), who ran track, played piano and trumpet, and loved math. He went to Howard University in Washington, DC, in the 1960s to study electrical engineering, and his first job as an engineer came during the Vietnam War, where he worked on "special projects" at Philco, a company formerly known for its work in batteries and radios. I am the only girl in my family of three brothers, and my father believed that I should be exposed to as much math as possible. My identity as an engineer was shaped by my father. I remember him telling me that girls could be doctors, and that math was an objective measure. (He also taught me about being proud of my brown skin color and that "all hair is good hair. There is no such thing as 'bad hair.'" My mother had long straight hair, so this was a much-needed affirmation in the life of a little Black girl who was born with thick, tightly curled hair.) Having dealt with racial discrimination as a young African-American man, he believed that cultivating mathematical skills was a way to

combat unequal treatment. As a child, he used to tell me that people can argue with your opinions about all kinds of topics, but math is an objective measure, so if you are right... you are right! As I was learning about discrimination, he encouraged me to enjoy math. He strongly believed that if you were good at math, you wouldn't be subject to people telling you that you were wrong about knowledge, because the math would stand on its own. He would say, "1+1 will equal 2, and when 'x' is the unknown, solve for 'x'."

I am a child of the public school system in Plainfield, New Jersey. The public school system in the US does not require payment, and is funded according to residents' and citizens' taxes. As a result of my parents' decision to keep me connected to mathematics, my father and mother started to bring me math workbooks to complete during school breaks. They enrolled me in a Project SEED algebra after-school program in fifth grade, which later led to all kinds of engineering and science summer programs. In seventh grade, I participated in an Introduction to Engineering summer program at Union County College, one of the local New Jersey two-year community colleges. At the end of 8th grade, I went to an Introduction to Engineering summer program at the University of Massachusetts, Amherst, and at the end of ninth grade, I participated in a chemistry summer program at California Institute of Technology (Cal Tech). Participation in these summer programs definitely facilitated a level of college readiness, because I enjoyed "pretending" that I was a college student while spending time on those campuses as a young adolescent. I have been a professor, and am a college administrator today, so those early days of spending a lot of time at universities built a level of comfort with college and campus life.

THE EMPOWERMENT OF ORGANIZATION—AND THE JOY OF RESEARCH

Keeping up with family tradition, I was accepted to the electrical engineering program at Howard University in Washington, DC, in 1986, following in my father's footsteps, and continuing the legacy that he and my mother, Patricia Medley Garrison, started when they met on campus as teenagers. My parents were in college during the time of the legal end of racial segregation, chronicled by the Civil Rights Act of 1964 and the Voting Rights Act of 1965, and during the last years of Martin Luther King's activism and life. Many of my classmates at Howard had parents who were part of combinations of revolutionary racial protests as students, with up-and-coming access to middle class economic opportunities as young adults. As children of parents who lived through the death of Dr. King, and various forms of discrimination, my classmates and I were determined to be worthy of a Howard education. For us, this meant that we needed to be both focused on academic excellence, and committed to serving our communities. Pursuing excellence amidst the rigors of an engineering curriculum doesn't typically accommodate attention to activism, but by joining the university's chapter of the National Society of Black Engineers (NSBE), I found a home that merged both ideals.

My engineering journey through Howard University was not easy. I loved the university's atmosphere, and attention to African-American history and cultural experiences, but I found the curriculum to be quite difficult. I had been used to doing very well in math and science, one of the top students in my class in high school as rankings go. I had taken calculus in high school, and had been involved in introduction to engineering and science programs at Union County College, the University of Massachusetts at Amherst, and Caltech. I thought that I was ready! I was not prepared for the struggle, and I struggled miserably. There were several ups and downs during my college years. I'd struggle in math classes, in physics, and in my own major, electrical engineering.

Despite a loveless relationship with electronics and electromagnetic theory, I found that I was becoming increasingly adept at certain topics. I was very good at differential equations, so much so that I became a tutor to my classmates. My love for research and my interest in innovative applications grew as I learned more about image processing and satellite technology (following internships at GE Military & Data Systems, which later became Lockheed Martin). Plus, I became a fan of the television show Star Trek. My senior paper dealt with the concept of using 3-D holographic imaging for communications. At the time, I was interested in applying the technology to connect military families, and to facilitate global communication. My interest in building connections across the miles continues today.

That love of discovery led to admission to the MS-PhD program in electrical engineering at Northwestern University in Evanston, Illinois. There, my struggle with engineering courses continued. However, my dismay turned to excitement with the support of three professors. One sat me down during office hours and asked me to solve a network theory problem in front of him. As I went through the derivation, he noted that my way of thinking was a bit more "circular" than "linear." This was an important revelation. It resonated because it also spoke to the way that I approached research problems: it was not sequential for me; rather, it was big-picture, spherical, circular.

My digital speech processing professor encouraged me to take a class in phonetics, the science of speech production, in the department of Communications Sciences and Disorders, and that opened a completely new world for me. My interests were coming together because my phonetics class was taught by a speech scientist with an engineering background, and we learned about automatic speech recognition systems as a confluence of engineering, phonetics, and vocal physiology. I was hooked, and my professors recognized that following conferral of my master's degree, I was a better fit for the PhD program in speech science at Northwestern, which was comprised of engineers who conducted research focused on the vocal mechanism.

This new set of courses in physiology, neurology, linguistics, and acoustic phonetics set my brain on fire. I was hooked! I was able to add more speaker recognition technology research through an internship at a Rutgers University lab where former Bell Labs engineers were conducting research on speech recognition, and informal mentorship from legendary speech processing engineer James Flanagan. Further speaker recognition technology that focused on frequencies of speaker differences and dialects came through an informal mentorship from Dr. Sadaoki Furui from the Tokyo Institute of Technology in Japan, whom I met at a joint meeting of the Acoustical Society of America and the Acoustical Society of Japan. Dr. Furui was extremely generous with his time. He answered my emails prior to the conference, met with me in Hawaii during the conference, and remained a resource for me throughout my dissertation process. I was a graduate student during this time, and this was a lesson in mentoring, and reaching out to others to ask for assistance. Further, it was a lesson in not being afraid to talk to famous people! Those discussions with Dr. Furui were key to building my confidence in working to apply science and engineering principles to speech recognition, disabilities, and deafness.

A CAREER THAT EMPHASIZES INCLUSION

Following graduate school at Northwestern University, I had a postdoctoral position in vocal physiology at the University of Wisconsin-Madison, and a faculty position with connections to industrial engineering. This experience and others led to a career in administration. The following section is adapted from the ATHENA40.org segment that I was invited to share about women faculty who become multipliers and catalysts for diversity. The segment is titled, "I am a multiplier who motivates thousands of women in STEM."

I became a professor at the University of Wisconsin-Madison following my postdoc in vocal physiology, concentrating on speaker recognition for users with vocal pathologies. I was excited about conducting research connected to accessibility and contributing to technologies for people with disabilities. Although I enjoyed this work as a faculty member, I left university life behind for a while to venture into entrepreneurship, working with my husband's emerging tech company. My work with the company involved preparing pitches for venture capitalists, preparing for trade shows, writing proposals, and representing the company in small-business forums. This experience was rich and rewarding, but I missed life at the university, and the satisfaction of working with students. My newly honed entrepreneurial experience was a good fit for a National

Science Foundation-funded position at the University of Maryland, Baltimore County (UMBC). I became a university administrator, creating professional development programs and influencing policy to prepare diverse students to excel in their degree programs and in the STEM workforce. Serving as a university administrator, assistant dean and, later, associate vice provost, I directed several multi-campus programs, such as the PROMISE: Maryland's Alliance for Graduate Education and the Professoriate (AGEP) and the University System of Maryland's Louis Stokes Alliance for Minority Participation (LSAMP), both sponsored by the National Science Foundation (NSF) in the US. These programs increased the number of women from underrepresented groups who received PhDs in STEM fields from universities in Maryland. As director of these programs, I have enjoyed being a mentor to many of the women, and have watched them graduate and advance in their careers, becoming STEM professionals and mentors, each in her own right.

In the moments of celebration, there are also moments of sadness as I remember the ones we lost. We lost a brilliant math scholar to breast cancer, and a talented chemical engineer to murder. My life, mission, and trajectory changed after that. I was never the same, and I was determined to make sure that my work focused on holistic approaches to professional development that could advance women, and save lives.

THE EFFECT OF WOMEN ENGINEERING MENTORS

The experiences that I have had allow me to appreciate my own mentors all the more, and I am particularly appreciative of women in engineering who have mentored me over the years. Among them are Drs. Janet Rutledge, Julia Ross, Christine Grant, Stephanie Adams, Maria Larrondo-Petrie, and so many others.

To highlight the importance of mentoring, and being open to mentoring at every level, I share the following adaptation from a blog post that I wrote in 2017 after the World Engineering Education Forum (WEEF) in Kuala Lampur, Malaysia. It shares a life-changing professional mentoring exchange that has contributed to my advancement.

> My favorite meal of the day is breakfast, so it is ironic (or rather, a blessing) that women from around the world have encouraged me and my work over breakfast. Today, I reflect on a day in 2015 when I was preparing for a session in Italy. I was having breakfast and was at a table with one of the few open seats in the room. A woman came over and asked to sit, and this set a match that lit a path for a journey. A journey to empower people around the world to use their talents to serve humanity. That woman was Dr. Şirin Tekinay, vice rector of research and development

at Sabanci University, in Istanbul, Turkey. Professor Tekinay is an engineer, and prior to her current position, she was the rector at Işik University and dean of engineering and natural sciences at Kadir Has University. As we had breakfast, and I discussed my work, she told me how important it was, and then proceeded to encourage me to continue to be a voice for women and underrepresentation in engineering. During that conference in Italy, I learned that I was going to be invited to Australia to present before a panel on diversity and inclusion in engineering. Dr. Tekinay told me that I was a leader...and I believed her. I remember marveling and later asking God in my prayers, "Who was that woman? She just came in out of the blue and put this leader vision into my head." We've always learned that God works in mysterious ways, and this was certainly one of those mysterious experiences.

The panel in Australia went well and that led to an invitation to be on a keynote panel in India on women in engineering. That's where I met Prof. Dr. Khairiyah Mohd-Yusof. Dr. Mohd-Yusof is the director of the Centre for Engineering Education at Universiti Teknologi in Malaysia, and I'd seen her for the first time on stage when I was in Dubai in 2014, but she was a distant icon. It had been my first trip to the East, and it was the first time that my American views on women in engineering were challenged. I met women from Asia, India, the UAE, and other countries, and they were strong forces... fountains of knowledge. I was in awe of Dr. Mohd-Yusof and others in Dubai. When I went to India, I will never forget the moment over breakfast in Pune, when Dr. Mohd-Yusof told me that she liked my work, and that I should come to Malaysia. She knew my name. She liked my work. She wanted me to come to her country. I was able to go to the World Engineering Education Forum in Kuala Lumpur in November 2017, and the three of us took a photo together.

There is an interesting element to this post, and that is the connection to international graduate students. I'd met students from various countries in Africa and the Caribbean as an undergraduate at Howard University, but my first experience with students from parts of the world who looked different from me came as a graduate student at Northwestern when my electrical engineering study group included students from the US, Germany, India, and China. We jokingly referred to ourselves as "the United Nations," but I viewed it as an honor, and I'm sure that it has helped to shape my current perspectives on global diplomacy. As an educator who has specialized in areas of graduate education for many years, I am attentive to the needs of students who come from other countries to study in the US. I've met brilliant students and have no doubt that I have been in the presence of future world leaders. I recently learned that both Dr. Tekinay and Dr. Mohd-Yusof received their PhDs in engineering in the US, and that both were very familiar with issues of inclusion and diversity in America. This means that they could have been your graduate students, or your friends in graduate school. This means that others like them could be in classes with you now, and that they will go on to sow good seeds in the future. They have mentored me. It just goes to show that mentoring can come from unexpected places.

GET RID OF THE "US" AND "THEM" MENTALITY

There have been situations in undergraduate and graduate programs when American students and international students have been given the invisible message that there is an "us" and "them" separation. The situation can be worse for students who are from underrepresented minority groups, who can find themselves separated from both majority students from the US and the international students. Engineering programs often have large numbers of students from India and China, and the invisible walls that seem to encourage separation get higher and higher when there is little communication, or when others unfairly cement blocks within the walls that exaggerate the differences. We have the opportunity to change that mentality. If you are a professor, you can encourage more inclusion within your classrooms, and within your labs. If you are a student, you can make an effort to make connections. This charge is for people from all groups. So often, students from minoritized groups feel the extra pressure of trying to make the connections, but this process would be so much easier if people from all groups would consider the basics of congeniality.

So, can we say "hello?" If not a smile, then a nod to acknowledge one's humanity can work wonders.

You never know who you can empower. Yes, we are different, but the differences should be celebrated. They don't have to separate us. Whether we are seeing differences across groups in the US or between groups from around the world, we should appreciate the differences and wealth that they bring. Within the STEM fields, the differences between groups of students do not have be viewed as a problem. I have been to India, and I have been to China. I have been invited, and accepted opportunities, to mentor students in both places.

I've shared time with students (and trained faculty) in classrooms in these countries, as well as in Latin America. I know that joy and disappointment, laughter and tears, occur across ethnic groups, so we don't have to wonder whether people have feelings or not; they do. People from all groups get lonely, love deeply, and have hopes and dreams. We can feel the weight of so many barriers, so please consider the importance of encouraging one another. Empowerment and encouragement can come in many forms. Even the little comments that are filled with caring and compassion can make a day brighter. Words such as "I appreciate your work," "Good luck," and "You'll do well" can go a long way.

LET'S EMPOWER ONE ANOTHER

Şirin and Khairiyah have continued to encourage me to speak up and speak out, and to develop pathways for broadening participation in engineering and in STEM in general. Interestingly, we have not yet been together on US soil, but whether we have been in South Korea or another country, they have always shared "empowerments" with me, and this hasn't always been expressed words. The hugs make a difference. The waves across the room that say, "Come over and sit here" make a difference. The way that they introduce me to others makes a difference. Little things make a difference, like knowing that I try to fit too many things into a minute, so they say, "Stop, take a minute, come and have a cup of coffee," or "Go get some sleep, we'll see you in the morning." They compliment me whether I wear heels or flats, a dress or pants (which can be "a thing" that plagues women in STEM). They tell me what they liked about my talks, and it helps me to evaluate the strengths.

I think that one of the greatest ways in which they, and other women and mentors in general, have encouraged me is accepting me for who I am and encouraging me in my own "Renetta-ness," while being subtle in how they give cues for ways that I can grow. This has come with acceptance and acknowledgements of my imperfections, but with little pieces of advice that will lead to continuous improvement. With that understanding, I've learned that I have to be observant, and that I have to listen. I have to listen to what is being said, and to what isn't being said. Mentors have also given me a chance to make good when a second chance is needed. I appreciate this more and more these days because as hard as I work, I can't make everything perfect, so sometimes I fall and have to get up again.

Using Şirin and Khairiyah as examples, I would like to think that as scientists and engineers, we can determine to work together, empower one another, and unite to solve mutual problems. We really don't have time to keep people out of the conversation because of race or gender or nationality. There are too many problems to solve to waste time arguing about who should and shouldn't be included in opportunities to address challenges. Let's accept one another's talents and flaws, because we all have them. Let's move forward to make a difference. We have a world to serve. Let's do it, together.

THE FOCUS ON HUMANITY

Connections I've made at conferences of the Latin American and Caribbean Consortium of Engineering Institutions (LACCEI) and WEEF have allowed me to be impacted by the opportunity to focus on humanitarian issues, particularly connected to the National Academy of Engineering's 14 Grand Challenges and the 17 Sustainable Development Goals put forth by the United Nations. I learned about the Grand Challenges at WEEF in Cartagena, Colombia, in 2013, where I was warmly welcomed by engineering professor Claudia Patricia Mendieta Cardona, whom I'd met in Panama at the 2013 LACCEI conference. At the time, Claudia was on the faculty at Universidad de San Buenaventura in Cali, Colombia, and her exuberant, "Bienvenida! Welcome to my country!" and the many welcomes that followed, particularly from other women in Colombia, was one of the catalysts that reignited my love for my profession, and the people within it. When discrimination runs rampant in fields like science and engineering, or when the spaces where engineering is practiced or even discussed seem to strip you of your personality, it is truly heartwarming to walk into spaces where you are greeted by other engineers with kisses and hugs. The National Society of Black Engineers (NSBE) and the Society of Hispanic Professional Engineers (SHPE) provided these kinds of spaces for me in the US, while LACCEI and WEEF provided them for me abroad.

A synergistic connection between the people and the causes began to develop. As I worked more closely with LACCEI, the international student organization Student Platform for Engineering Education Development (SPEED), IFEES, and WEEF, I became even more determined to bring other scholars, particularly women and people from groups that are underrepresented in engineering (primarily from ethnic groups in the minority), into the fold and into a knowledge of this growing initiative in "humanitarian engineering." LACCEI provided the first opportunity, as executive director Maria Larrondo Petrie invited me to share an NSF ADVANCE initiative on advancing STEM women faculty within a "Forum on Women" in Mexico. My colleagues Drs. Beatriz Zayas and Carlos Padín of the Universidad Ana G. Méndez, Recinto de Cupey (formerly Universidad Metropolitana), shared results from our conference in Puerto Rico that focused on issues such as career/life balance, negotiating time and salaries, campus climate, professional respect for family roles as parents and caregivers, and showcasing women's achievements. The LACCEI conference also held a discussion session that highlighted these issues.

The conference in Cartagena shared these findings with a wider audience and briefly introduced the general concept to IFEES during their board meeting. These results led to a new grant from the National Science Foundation's program on Broadening Participation in Engineering, which allowed me to take women STEM faculty and underrepresented graduate students and postdocs to the 2014 LACCEI conference in Ecuador. Results from surveys and conversations discussing strategies for collaborative global professional travel, family care and connection while away, and resources for financing the trip while managing time away, were published by the

American Society for Engineering Education's 2015 Proceedings, under the title, "Factoring Family Considerations into Female Faculty Choices for International Engagement in Engineering, IT, and Computer Science." The study revealed that we should develop opportunities to include people from underrepresented groups in global collaborations by inviting them to participate in projects, coordinating group conference travel, considering compact schedules to reduce time away from family, and creating travel awards to assist with costs. I have been able to contribute to this type of endeavor as either a principal investigator (PI) or co-PI on grants from the National Science Foundation's (NSF) Division of Human Resource Development and its Division of Engineering.

NOTES FROM XALAPA

In closing, I have been strongly influenced by faculty and students from around the world who meet me and say that they have never met an engineer who looks like me or has my brown skin tone. In 2018, I had an opportunity to give a plenary talk for the Institute of Electrical and Electronic Engineers (IEEE) Summer School on Women in Technology in the city of Xalapa in Veracruz, Mexico. I spoke about the UN's Sustainable Development Goals and led the audience through an exercise that helped them to build stronger connections to the goals. Many of the participants in the audience said that they had not met many, or even any, women from underrepresented minority backgrounds who had advanced degrees in science or engineering. As I thought about their comments on the way to the airport, leaving Xalapa to return to the US, I wrote a poem as a reflection of the experience. "Notes from Xalapa, Veracruz," was posted recently on Medium.com. Since then, I've been reading this poem to audiences at the end of various keynote talks and presentations. I share it here to close this chapter.

> *I am the Black woman,*
> *Science and engineering scholar.*
> *I am the vision that you never knew existed.*
> *I am the "out-of-the-box" scholar who loves and hugs and doesn't keep her distance.*
> *I show the future to your sons and daughters,*
> *And am the friend that you never knew you had,*
> *Until you met me.*
>
> *I am the voice that you never knew you needed to hear,*
> *Until you listened.*
>
> *Whether I speak your language or not,*
> *My eyes and smile convey that I see you,*

And value you,

And you tell me that you carry that with you,

And so I am happy to have made your acquaintance.

I learn from you,

You learn from me,

And together,

We are better.

So now that you know me,

Come. Take my hand.

Join me in the struggle to lift others up,

To cast light into dark places,

And to hold truth as dear.

My "I" turns to "we,"

And now, my friends,

We work...

Together.

And we advance.

"Adelante" my dear friends,

"Adelante."

JOURNEY 32

TAKING HEED: MY JOURNEY IN HUMANITARIAN ENGINEERING EXPERIENCES AND DESIGN

CHRISTINA WHITE

Director of Programs
3 Day Startup
Curriculum Developer
Boston Museum of Science

UNITED STATES OF AMERICA

My mentor, the educational philosopher Maxine Greene, helps us to realize that "it is the imagination that releases us, that discloses alternative possibilities." Emily Dickinson also wrote about what it means to "dwell in possibility." Just as Maxine Greene and Emily Dickinson did, I too, dwell in possibility about new ways to make a significant positive impact as an engineering educator. I've taken those words to heart: there are ways our lives can be significantly improved through innovative engineering education and design.

The United States National Academy of Engineering (NAE) reminds us that engineering is about discovery, designing, using our imagination, innovation, and contributing to society, and that engineering turns our imagination and ideas into reality. This means that when we imagine a better world, we can use design thinking to create engineering solutions to make those ideas a reality.

Throughout my career as an engineering educator, I have imagined possibilities for social justice and will share some of my experiences within that context in this chapter. I agree with Maxine Greene, as we are both concerned "with possibility, with opening windows or alternative realities, with moving through doorways into spaces some of us have never seen before. We are interested in breakthroughs and new beginnings, the kind

ABOUT THE AUTHOR

Dr. Christina White recently completed her postdoctoral engineering education research with Singapore-MIT Alliance for Research and Technology, where she explored ways to develop global competencies in undergraduate engineering programs. She completed her doctoral degree from Teachers College, Columbia University, where she studied curriculum and teaching with a focus on engineering education. Upon graduation, Dr. White became the founding director of the National Academy of Engineering Grand Challenges Scholars & K12 Partners Program at The University of Texas (UT) at Austin. Because of her work with UT, she was invited to become a member of the National Academy of Engineering Grand Challenges Steering Committee for undergraduate programs and on the Steering Committee for the new Master's Certification. She is also the Grand Challenges representative for the International Federation of Engineering Education Societies. She consults globally with universities for interdisciplinary program development. Dr. White is a curriculum developer for the Museum of Science in Boston to design the second edition of Engineering is Elementary curriculum. She is the Director of Programs for 3 Day Startup and leads initiatives to activate entrepreneurial potential in students through experiential education and a global entrepreneurship ecosystem. Her current research includes global competencies, entrepreneurship education, design-based pedagogy, humanitarian engineering, and ways to attract and retain traditionally underrepresented groups in engineering.

of wide-awakeness that allows for wonder and unease and questioning and the pursuit of what is not yet." I love exploring these possibilities in my work with humanitarian engineering experiences and design (HEED). I call this, my greatest passion, Taking HEED.

Taking HEED combines aspects of educational and engineering movements to improve societies through humanitarian initiatives that include social justice education and universal human rights. This seems particularly apt, since one of my goals as an engineering educator is to be an agent of change, thus to take heed. I include "experience" because experience, for John Dewey, an American philosopher and educational reformer, is the dynamic transaction or interaction between human beings and their environment. This directly relates back to what we do with user-centered design and social constructivist learning. Two main goals that humanitarian engineering promotes are (a) preventative humanitarian action and (b) humanitarian development. In the past, engineers may have asked, "How do I generate electricity most efficiently?" The humanitarian engineer asks, "How can I help to address healthcare and shelter, support educational opportunities, and reduce poverty by generating electrical power efficiently?" The answer to this question may include generating electricity, but more importantly, humanitarian engineers will facilitate design teams that collaboratively work with citizens of the community in need, and with the local resources. They will attempt to create balances between engineering and technical skills, economic feasibility, ethical considerations, and cultural sensitivity. HEED offers possibilities for educators, designers, engineers, and other stakeholders to discuss, exchange, and construct ideas for sustainable design solutions in critical problem domains such as health, education, energy, environment, community, global action, and sustainable living.

One of the ways that I've chosen to be an agent of positive change is to share my lived experiences and choices to pursue humanitarian work and engineering education by writing this chapter as part of a collaborative group of women in engineering. As women learning and practicing engineering experiences, sharing our stories helps to represent meaning in our lives and offers the possibility for convergences between our lived experiences. Often, women in engineering do not have an opportunity to represent ways in which research, practice, and their lived experiences influence ways of knowing, learning, and practicing engineering. As I consider ways that I can make positive changes in the world, I know that I can start within communities—such as a community of women whose lives intersect with engineering education.

Throughout the last 15 years, I have aimed to be an agent of change by providing spaces for freedom and social justice in my teaching, curriculum development, design projects, entrepreneurial experiences, and outreach programs. I believe that engineering education is an avenue for social justice because the inherent nature of design is to create possibilities for access and equity. The overarching aim of social justice teaching is to equip learners with the skills and experiences necessary to promote social change and equality among individuals. There is significant overlap between social justice teaching and design thinking in engineering education. The interdisciplinary connections, critical thinking, open-mindedness, and appreciation of diverse perspectives are paramount in both.

To make significant positive impacts on society, there must be real-world solutions. Since engineering education and design allow imagination to turn into reality, people are able to create real-world solutions towards social change and freedom. Freedom, as Dewey viewed it, is the power to act, and it can be achieved through reflective choosing. Design provides the power to act and creates opportunities for learners to develop their reflective thinking skills in the process. I join Dewey in adhering to the notion that in striving for freedom, one must have obligation and responsibility. Engineering education and design thinking provides students with real-world scenarios to understand and reflect upon issues of consequences, sustainability, obligation, and responsibility. I experienced this firsthand when I was a graduate student participating in my initial engineering project.

I always knew that I wanted to be a teacher; I never would have imagined that I would become an engineering educator. My journey into engineering actually started as I was earning my master's degree in special education at The University of Texas (UT) at Austin. As an attempt to better understand assistive technology for people labeled with a range of mental and physical dis/abilities, I chose to take graduate mechanical engineering courses in product design. I was intimidated to be an education student with no engineering background in a graduate course at one of the top engineering colleges in the nation. But I was also curious to find out more about working and learning with peers and professors from a new college.

I began feeling apprehension as I walked into the building at the opposite end of our huge campus; the physical distance was an easy metaphor for my perceived opposing atmospheres of the two fields of study. But I was pleasantly surprised to be welcomed by two co-teaching professors who strongly emphasized and valued creativity and interdisciplinarity. Ultimately, our team invented an automated assistive guitar for students with a range of dis/abilities and manual dexterity. This helped to direct my path into a deep interest in engineering education because of the embedded aspects of imagination and design thinking. The experience was salient in other ways, too. It provided me the opportunity to become lead inventor for our awarded patent (US 7,285,709) for this invention, and it is now on exhibit in the Houston Children's Museum. More importantly, I saw how design could create an equitable way for people with varying dis/abilities to engage with the environment. This inspired me to keep exploring designs that could create a more equitable world and also to deeply integrate the arts and aesthetic experiences into engineering as a way to make a more profound, unexpected impact. After all, some bodies can do some things, and others can do others.

I thrive in projects where art, music, and engineering provide new possibilities for making meaning in people's lives. I saw Luke Jerram's "Play Me, I'm Yours" pianos on the city streets of New York City in 2010, and I became curious as to whether others would be interested in bringing player pianos to the sidewalks and parks of Austin, Texas. I worked with the Texas School for the Deaf and UT engineering students to reverse-engineer antique player pianos to become a new part of the Jerram exhibit in Austin. We replaced the wood with transparent Plexiglas to provide opportunities to see the automated or manual playing of the piano. We included bike-powered or solar-powered LED flashing lights that corresponded with key compressions to better connect to the music being played, especially for those who are hard of hearing or Deaf. The lights reflected on the mirrored Plexiglas backing the keyboard. The sounds lit up the days and nights throughout downtown, available for all to play. Perhaps people will become inspired about some aspects of these player piano designs and be prompted to talk about, think about, and learn about product design, engineering concepts, and alternative energy differently and more critically than before.

Social justice and critical theories about curriculum and teaching in engineering became a deep interest of mine because of my first design project, but then grew into a foundational tenet in my work throughout my doctoral program at Teachers College, Columbia University. I had never before felt a sense of being an outsider, being "Othered" in school, until I was one of two women in an engineering classroom of men. That feeling was exacerbated when I was Othered as an educator in an engineering field. The imbalance was a transformational learning experience for me to start to understand issues around power structures, diversity and inclusivity, and social justice.

To explore those issues more during our doctoral program, we were prompted to identify some of the effects of privilege in our daily lives. I was inspired by Peggy McIntosh's research on White privilege and unpacking the invisible knapsack, and by Paulo Freire's work on the pedagogy of the oppressed. From my positionality as a private-school educated, White American citizen, I understand that these are factors that intricately intertwine in the conditions in which I navigate this world. With privileges (including those that are socially constructed) come great responsibility. I believe it is my responsibility to advocate for social justice and equity by using my skills, resources, and research. My doctoral dissertation research was a case study of women (including myself) who chose to pursue and persist in engineering. It made audible and visible the diverse ways in which each participant's identity was negotiated and the manner in which it was affected by fairness, equity, opportunities for free expression, and by the (non)existence of democracy as she chose to pursue humanitarian engineering. It is meaningful to me to extend my dissertation work, now eight years later, into this book chapter.

It is ironic that the engineering fields, which design and build bridges, are the areas where we have one of the weakest bridges in closing the accessibility, achievement, and equity gaps between genders in the United States and many other countries. In 1950, the US Congress established the National Science Foundation with the mission to initiate and support engineering and science education programs at all levels; yet, more than half a century later, problems of access, achievement, and equity for females in these fields remain, resulting in a lack of diversity in engineering. An understanding of women's roles in engineering education, such as through this collaborative book, will provide a foundation for increasing diversity in engineering, problematizing the field of engineering, and, thus, possibilities of creating positive contributions to the global community with engineering education.

Many of my favorite design projects have taken place over the several years I directed both undergraduate and K12 programs at UT Austin. I am thankful to have had the chance to lead the Design, Technology and Engineering for All Children (DTEACh) program simultaneously with the undergraduate Grand Challenges Scholars Program & K12 Partners Program (GCSP). Our DTEACh curriculum design was set within the context of the Grand Challenges. It was exciting to weave the Grand Challenges into after-school clubs, community innovation station Saturdays, and summer camps, and to see the significant impact it had on middle-school students. We were able to increase students' interest in STEM courses, improve their goals to go to college, increase their abilities to do design thinking, and improve teachers' confidence in project-based and design-based pedagogy. I still continue this effort to attract, engage, and retain traditionally underrepresented students in K12 in my recent work with the Boston Museum of Science through my curriculum development. I hope to have far-reaching impact in fostering STEM literacy and design thinking by connecting with science museums and K12 schools worldwide.

I led the design of and directed our GCSP & K12 Partners Program at UT Austin, which was the first university-wide GCSP certificate program in the United States. It took two years of ideation, collaboration, strategic development, and curricular analysis to create a certificate program that met the UT Systems' standards for higher education and the goals of the NAE. Our GCSP and incubator were vehicles for curriculum innovation and student-based start-ups. The GCSP provided a unique framework in which diverse students could contextualize their studies within multi-semester projects of intense interest to them and of great importance to society. Research shows that design projects that are relevant to society and humanitarian in nature, such as the GC, have great potential for attracting and retaining this generation's top scholars to technical and entrepreneurial careers.

I work with a wide range of students and educators and have seen the positive impact that engineering education with a social justice emphasis has made on diverse communities. The real-world design projects—such as our assistive device for playing guitars, the solar-powered light-up "Play Me, I'm Yours" pianos, our clean-water sachet social entrepreneurship business in Ghana, and water purification systems in Tibet—show the students that they can be agents of positive change and promote social justice through engineering. I anticipate more social justice engineering design-meets-art exhibits in my future work with Impossible Projects LLC. I plan to co-design community outreach programs and interactive art exhibits with Impossible Projects founder Sara Fenske Bahat and teams of recalcitrant women unaccepting of the status quo in education, economic development, our environment, and policy.

In the years of writing my dissertation, I often said the doctoral experience was a hybrid of amazing and awful. I surprised myself when I jumped at doing a post-doctorate, but could not pass up the chance to do research with Daniel Hastings and Lori Breslow at the Singapore-MIT Alliance for Research and Technology Innovation Centre. We explored ways that undergraduate programs develop globally competent engineers. Living in Singapore, one of the innovation hubs of the world, also inspired me to improve my own cross-cultural communication skills and pedagogy so that I can better support innovation.

During my time in Singapore, I also worked on a goal to foster stronger relationships between universities around the world, with the hope that they would actively engage in international, interdisciplinary educational experiences framed within Grand Challenges. One of the avenues for that was to propose (and have accepted) a formal membership within the IFEES community. To have a broad impact in engineering education and on facing Grand Challenges, I aim to continue enriching these relationships and supporting universities in creating and implementing GCSP that are tailored to their unique learning environments. As a member of the NAE steering committees for both the undergraduate and master's programs, and as a consultant, I enjoy working on curriculum development, teaching, design projects, creating incubators, and in research. Some highlights for me have been presenting at the White House, the NAE, and for the Indian National Academy of Engineering in both Washington, DC, and New Delhi, India. It is motivating to walk shoulder to shoulder with scholars who are committed to and capable of making significant shifts in the paradigm of how engineering programs prepare our future leaders.

One of the most profound experiences for me thus far has been as a Future Leader, named by the NAE, when I went to Osaka, Japan, to present to and collaborate with numerous Nobel Laureates. During two consecutive years, informally known as the Laureates' Week, I worked closely with these award-winning thought leaders on cutting edge research but more so on STEM diplomacy for universal human rights. I learned in great detail about the philosophies and experiences of several of the laureates who are prominent advocates for universal human rights through STEM diplomacy. For example, Dr. Peter Agre, former Chair of the US National Academy of Sciences Committee on Human Rights, said he and four other Nobel laureates traveled to North Korea to improve diplomatic relations. They also told of helping get political prisoners, who had been sentenced to death in Libya, safely released thanks to their actions as laureates and thanks to the human rights committee. STEM diplomacy is founded on the notion that STEM research and projects can be community builders across nations, because we need cooperation to work on problems across borders and without boundaries—cooperation made possible by the international language and methodology of the sciences. These Nobel Laureates are my heroes, and I hope to make even a fraction of the positive impact that they have made on the world and on human rights.

One of the ways I build upon what I learned from the laureates about STEM diplomacy is through entrepreneurship in engineering education. I believe that teaching people to understand economic contexts and financial literacy in relation to engineering design is a critical component in helping them develop innovation skillsets and mind-sets. I have been invited to many countries around the world for entrepreneurship education in undergraduate programs. Being a leader and female in some of these communities that have cultural beliefs about gender roles and rights that vary from my own became wonderful opportunities for us both to learn more about our commonalities and shared visions instead of our differences. I engaged in STEM diplomacy in the context of Grand Challenges projects and entrepreneurship, and perhaps broadened perspectives in relation to gender roles and rights. This is how I choose to work from the inside and as an "Other" to make changes. I continue this effort: I recently joined 3 Day Startup as its director of programs to support entrepreneurship education throughout the trajectory of startups in countries around the world, and will strive for STEM diplomacy as a way to promote peace and equal rights.

Educator and first African American Congresswoman Shirley Chisholm is known for saying, "If they don't give you a seat at the table, bring a folding chair." Thankfully, my mentors and advocates have included Daniel Hastings, Lori Breslow, Rick Miller, the late Maxine Greene, and the IFFES community, all of whom made space at the table early in my career until there were spaces set for me. I commit to doing the same for those who need the support and space as they find their own voice and place. I am thankful to be part of engineering education initiatives in developing global competencies that enrich cross-cultural community development, environmental improvement, entrepreneurship, and strategies for sustainability and resilience.

I look forward to the coming year to see how we, as engineering educators, have contributed to meeting the goals of the Engineer 2020—and how we can move far beyond those goals by taking HEED.

AFTERWORD

HANS JÜRGEN HOYER

In my role as secretariat of GEDC and IFEES, a critical issue—and opportunity—over the decade since these organizations have been in place has been to identify and more deeply understand the role of women leaders and deans globally. Many of our colleagues, regardless of what position they occupy in the engineering profession and regardless of their cultural background, have faced challenges. This book is one big step towards achieving a broader understanding of those challenges.

Years ago, I had the opportunity to visit Sudan while I was working in East Africa. I traveled extensively throughout the region despite some of the political—even war-related—challenges faced in numerous countries, and was so pleased that Tagwa Musa, the only female engineering dean in that complex society, decided to join our GEDC. I recently reached out to her to ask if she would share with our global community some of her reflections about the challenges she has faced as a leader in this little-understood African country. I was delighted when she responded positively to my request to write a thoughtful article, which we published in our IFEES/GEDC GlobalEngineer bulletin. When I read her article, I felt inspired by her vision, commitment and capacity to deal with a variety of obstacles, and felt that more people should have a window on the experience of women in engineering education around the world.

So I decided to reach out to many of my close colleagues and friends to ask them if they would also be willing to share their personal journey as a female engineering leader in their respective societies. The responses were overwhelmingly positive, and more than 30 leaders from every continent agreed to share their personal and professional experiences by writing a chapter for this book. I feel inspired, humbled and grateful for the thoughtfulness demonstrated by each and every contributor, and hope that readers will appreciate the fact that these engineering leaders are so openly sharing with the world their sometimes-difficult journeys.

The goal of this book is that a new generation of female engineering leaders will be inspired by their peers. Equally important is that many of our male colleagues are sure to be positively impacted as they reflect on the experiences so honestly shared within these pages. My hope is that this book will trigger men in the profession and in engineering education to seriously reflect on how they can be more effective, engaged, and sensitive in terms of supporting women in their leadership roles—regardless of what culture they are in.

Hopefully, there will be more opportunities for all of our colleagues, women and men, to talk openly and frankly about their own journeys, despite their very different backgrounds. After all, the many commonalities shared by deeply committed leaders are a powerful way to make a real difference in this complex global environment.

It is important to acknowledge the individual financial support generously provided by most of the authors to help cover the editing costs of our book. Their contributions are deeply appreciated.

Thanks to Bonnie Munday, who worked with each author to help craft their stories. Based in Toronto, Canada, Bonnie has had extensive experience editing and writing for various magazines around the world, including Reader's Digest, as well as for book publishers. She has worked as a ghostwriter of memoirs, and has edited books on a variety of subjects.

And a special thank you to the invaluable Kayla Hellal, who played the key role of managing and designing this collaborative project. Kayla has been the International Communications and Web Manager with IFEES and the GEDC for the past four years, and recently completed an MS in Nonprofit Management and Leadership.

※ ※ ※

Dr. Hans Jürgen Hoyer is Secretary General of the International Federation of Engineering Education Societies (IFEES) and Executive Secretary of the Global Engineering Deans Council (GEDC). He is a Resident Scholar in Global Engineering at George Mason University and was also Dean of the School for International Training in the United States. He is an Honorary Professor at education institutes in Hungary, India, Kazakhstan, and Peru; an Advisor to SUSTech in Shenzhen, China; and an Ambassador to Monterrey Tech, Mexico. He is a governing board member for the International Center for Engineering Education (a UNESCO organization) at Tsinghua University in Beijing, China, is on the Board of Trustees of Tishk International University in Erbil, Kurdistan (Iraq), and is an advisory board member and co-founder of the Indo-Universal Collaboration for Engineering Education.

Lightning Source UK Ltd.
Milton Keynes UK
UKHW012029270922
409538UK00001B/54